PRAISE FOR CHRISTOPHER ANDERSEN'S *NEW YORK TIMES* BESTSELLING BIOGRAPHIES

"Poignant, intimate. Andersen's insights are as sharp as his details."

—*Newsweek*

"Compulsively readable."

—*Chicago Sun-Times*

"[I]s the most worth reading—comes closest to making Jackie sparkle."

—*The New York Times*

"A detail-packed tear-jerker."

—Associated Press

"Filled with breathless new details."

—*The Washington Post*

"Jam-packed with juiciness."

—*Entertainment Weekly*

"Riveting."

—*People*

"Amazing tidbits are offered on every page."

—*USA Today*

"Fascinating and insightful."

—*The Christian Science Monitor*

"One of the most graphic, searing things I've ever read."

—Liz Smith

"Fasten your seat belts, everybody."

—*Chicago Tribune*

"Vivid . . . illuminating . . . irresistible."

—*Philadelphia Inquirer*

ALSO BY CHRISTOPHER ANDERSEN

The Good Son

These Few Precious Days: The Final Year of Jack with Jackie

Mick: The Wild Life and Mad Genius of Jagger

William and Kate: A Royal Love Story

Barack and Michelle: Portrait of an American Marriage

Somewhere in Heaven: The Remarkable Love Story of Dana and Christopher Reeve

After Diana: William, Harry, Charles, and the Royal House of Windsor

Barbra: The Way She Is

American Evita: Hillary Clinton's Path to Power

Sweet Caroline: Last Child of Camelot

George and Laura: Portrait of an American Marriage

Diana's Boys: William and Harry and the Mother They Loved

The Day John Died

Bill and Hillary: The Marriage

The Day Diana Died

Jackie After Jack: Portrait of the Lady

An Affair to Remember

Jack and Jackie: Portrait of an American Marriage

Young Kate

The Best of Everything

The Serpent's Tooth

The Book of People

Father

The Name Game

GAME of CROWNS

Elizabeth, Camilla, Kate, and the Throne

CHRISTOPHER ANDERSEN

G

GALLERY BOOKS

New York London Toronto Sydney New Delhi

G
Gallery Books
An Imprint of Simon & Schuster, Inc.
1230 Avenue of the Americas
New York, NY 10020

First Gallery Books trade paperback edition November 2016

GALLERY BOOKS and colophon are registered
trademarks of Simon & Schuster, Inc.

For information about special discounts for bulk purchases,
please contact Simon & Schuster Special Sales at
1-866-506-1949 or business@simonandschuster.com.

The Simon & Schuster Speakers Bureau can bring authors to your live event. For more information or to book an event, contact the Simon & Schuster Speakers Bureau at 1-866-248-3049 or visit our website at www.simonspeakers.com.

Interior design by Jaime Putorti

PHOTO CREDITS:
Alpha/Globe: 6, 8, 16, 17, 18, 19, 20, 21, 30
Rex USA: 1, 2, 3, 4, 5, 7, 9, 10, 11, 12, 13, 14, 15, 22, 23, 24, 25, 26, 27, 28, 29, 31, 32, 33, 34, 35, 36, 37, 38, 39, 40, 41, 42, 43, 44, 45, 46, 47, 48, 49, 50, 51, 52, 53, 54

Manufactured in the United States of America

1 3 5 7 9 10 8 6 4 2

Library of Congress Cataloging-in-Publication Data

Names: Andersen, Christopher P., author.
Title: Game of crowns : Elizabeth, Camilla, Kate, and the throne /
Christopher Andersen.
Description: First Gallery Books hardcover edition. |
New York : Gallery Books, 2016.
Identifiers: LCCN 2015050619
Subjects: LCSH: Elizabeth II, Queen of Great Britain, 1926– | Elizabeth II, Queen of Great Britain, 1926—Family. | Camilla, Duchess of Cornwall, 1947– | Catherine, Duchess of Cambridge, 1982– | Windsor, House of.
Classification: LCC DA591.A1 A53 2016 | DDC 941.085092/2—dc23
LC record available at http://lccn.loc.gov/2015050619

ISBN 978-1-4767-4395-0
ISBN 978-1-4767-4396-7 (pbk)
ISBN 978-1-4767-4397-4 (ebook)

To my own Royal Family,
especially Queen Valerie

CONTENTS

GAME of CROWNS

It is not a cozy relationship and never has been.
The family is not set up to be cozy.

—MARGARET RHODES, ELIZABETH II'S COUSIN,
ON THE RELATIONSHIP BETWEEN CHARLES AND THE QUEEN

....

There's a first time for everything.

—CAMILLA, AFTER AN ANGRY MOB SHOUTING
"OFF WITH THEIR HEADS!" ATTACKED THE CAR IN
WHICH SHE WAS RIDING WITH PRINCE CHARLES

Preface

BLACK QUEEN, WHITE QUEEN

They are all straight out of a storybook: the beloved queen trying to hold her family and her realm together; the brooding, philandering, driven heir impatient for the throne; the beautiful, doomed wife; the scheming mistress with ambitions of her own; the upstanding younger prince, and his enchanting young wife and children. These and hundreds of other colorful characters spread out over the centuries have made Britain's Royal Family the world's most riveting, glamorous, critically acclaimed, and longest-running reality show.

Presiding over it all is a woman whose full title is "Elizabeth II, by the Grace of God of the United Kingdom of Great Britain and Northern Ireland and of Her Other Realms and Territories Queen, Head of the Commonwealth, Defender of the Faith." Even this grand appellation does not fully describe the spell she casts on her subjects; recent studies show that at least one-third of all Britons regularly dream about the Queen. In many of these dreams, Her Majesty has dropped by for a cup of tea, and merely wants to chat with a "normal person" about how difficult it is to raise a family as egregiously problematic as hers.

Now, as she celebrates her ninetieth birthday, the woman who is both the oldest and longest-reigning of all British monarchs quietly plans her exit. In his hit play *King Charles III*, Mike Bartlett imagines a future King Charles refusing to give royal assent to a bill restricting press freedom (difficult to imagine given Charles's storied contempt for journalists) and then abruptly dissolving Parliament. A constitutional crisis ensues, there are protests in the streets, and the Duchess of Cambridge hatches a plan that will eventually lead to Charles's forced abdication.

While the plot may have seemed far-fetched at first, as the result of a lawsuit to release previously sealed documents, Britons were shocked to learn in 2013 that both the Queen and Prince Charles's powers were far from merely ceremonial, as had long been believed. While the Queen has never technically withheld Royal Assent—a stamp of approval to legislation that was assumed to be automatically given—on dozens of occasions Elizabeth II and her heir have employed their little-known "Queen's Consent" and "Prince's Consent" powers to veto any bill curtailing their authority even before it is debated in Parliament. Pointing out that the British people had always been led to believe that these powers were "quaint and sweet," legal scholar John Kirhope said it was clear that the Queen and her son wielded "real influence and real power, albeit unaccountable."

Her Majesty, true to form, remained above the fray until the initial furor over the extent of her true power—and more important, that of her decidedly less popular heir—subsided. In times like these the Queen, more than anyone on the planet, embodied the British motto "Keep Calm and Carry On."

In the game of chess, no piece is more useful than the queen. It can move vertically, horizontally, and diagonally, and—like all the pieces on the board—its sole purpose is to protect the king.

And, in some cases, the *future* king.

....

NO ONE UNDERSTOOD THIS BETTER than Diana, the rebel Princess of Wales, although she knew she would never be queen. Instead, as the self-proclaimed "Queen of Hearts" she sought to protect the person she wanted to be Britain's next king—her son William. In the process, Diana first gave new luster to the monarchy, and then brought it to its knees. Once the dust had settled, it became clear that, by forcing the Windsors to connect with their people in ways they never had before, she had breathed new life into one of the world's oldest institutions.

Now, as the era of Elizabeth II draws to a close, there are two queens in waiting—each poised to protect her king. Camilla, the quintessential Black Queen, hid in the shadows for decades, condemned as a scheming adulteress, denounced by the reigning monarch as "that wicked, wicked woman," and blamed for the death of her rival, one of the most beloved and admired figures in the world. Biding her time and tending carefully to her image, she gradually salvaged enough of her reputation to secure a place at her prince's side—and her future as the next queen.

Young, gracious, smart, and stunning, the White Queen, known familiarly as just plain Kate, captured the world's imagination even before she could officially lay claim to her royal lover's heart. Although she lacked both the pedigree and the experience of the Black Queen, she also proved to be inordinately patient—and a cunning survivor of royal dramas and court intrigue. By marrying her Prince Charming and bearing two heirs, the White Queen cast the fate of the monarchy far into the future—perhaps as far as the next century. Elizabeth II could rest assured that, after a tumultuous four decades that nearly saw the collapse of the royal House of Windsor, the future was assured.

Or was it?

Beneath the surface, tensions mounted as the two queens-in-waiting protected the interests of their kings—the lackluster, benighted Prince of Wales and his wildly popular son—and their competing courts vied for the love of the people and the power that comes with it. Elizabeth II herself was keenly aware of this delicate and potentially dangerous situation. While allowing the public to believe that she would never retire, the Queen spent months with her most trusted advisors sorting out the constitutional implications of abdication. "Nobody knows whether the Queen intends to abdicate," wrote British journalist Neal Ascherson in the *New York Times*. "More accurately, she and a tiny palace circle almost certainly *do* know, and have no intention of sharing their knowledge."

Yet details of the Queen's secret abdication plan have in fact emerged. This meticulously crafted blueprint for transition hinges on one thing: Since Charles has no intention of renouncing his claim to the throne so that William can become the next monarch—the Queen has never even considered this option, according to Palace insiders—the Prince of Wales would have to accept what amounts to a self-imposed term limit on his reign. This would enable William, who along with his wife and children is seen as offering the monarchy's best chance for survival into the twenty-second century, to assume the throne before he, too, becomes tired and gray.

The proposed time limit on Charles's reign has varied little. In exchange for the Queen agreeing to abdicate either after turning ninety or, more likely, upon the passing of her husband (Prince Philip turns ninety-five on June 10, 2016), Charles has tentatively agreed to stay on the throne for no more than fifteen years—a reign that would, if it began tomorrow, end when Charles was well into his eighties. William could then be crowned king at a comparatively youthful fifty.

The Queen has not waited until she becomes a widow to share real power with her son. Over the past few years, Elizabeth II has shifted more and more of the monarch's burden to the Prince of Wales, and has made it clear that, in the event that she becomes physically or mentally incapacitated, she wants Charles to wield all the authority of the sovereign as Regent. In the meantime, the Black Queen and the White Queen will continue to be the most dynamic pieces on the royal chess board. Whatever the outcome of this contest, the next Queen of England will be a commoner—the first since Anne Hyde married the future James II in 1659. But in Camilla's case, that is merely a technicality. Although she had no title, the Duchess of Cornwall was always a bona fide aristocrat—a direct descendant of William the Conqueror and the granddaughter of a baron.

Kate, however, could someday lay claim to being England's first true commoner queen, in the modern sense of the word. A descendant of coal miners and the daughter of a former flight attendant, the Duchess of Cambridge is in truth destined to become the first working-class queen. Ironically, she will also be the first college-educated queen.

The House of Windsor is, as Winston Churchill famously described Russia, a riddle wrapped in a mystery inside an enigma. And if the past is any indication, scandal, joy, drama, tragedy, history, triumph, and betrayal will all play their part—as they have for more than a millennium—in the Game of Crowns.

Be who God meant you to be, and you will set the world on fire!

—THE BISHOP OF LONDON, TO WILLIAM AND KATE IN HIS WEDDING SERMON

....

We'll see, won't we?

—PRINCE CHARLES, WHEN ASKED IF CAMILLA WILL BE CROWNED QUEEN

....

You never know.

—CAMILLA, WHEN ASKED BY AN ELEMENTARY SCHOOL STUDENT IF SHE WOULD EVER BECOME QUEEN

....

Charles may love her, but I cannot bear the thought of "Queen Camilla."

—ELIZABETH

1

"THE QUEEN IS DEAD. LONG LIVE THE KING!"

We think we know what will happen—as earth-shaking events go, this is one of history's most well rehearsed. But when the inevitable scenario is finally played out, it will still have the power to mesmerize, and even to shock.

BUCKINGHAM PALACE

These are the familiar sounds of life here—hurried footfalls on plush red carpeting, whispered conversations magnified as they echo through high-ceilinged hallways adorned with the world's masterworks. It is not unusual for chamberlains and chambermaids, ushers and footmen and ministers of state alike to scurry when summoned to attend to their sovereign.

Not Paul Whybrew—the man Her Majesty simply calls "Big Paul." In all his many years as Page of the Backstairs and Sergeant-at-Arms to the Queen, the preternaturally calm Whybrew—at six feet four inches he towers over his five-foot-three-inch boss—has never appeared rushed or flustered, even in times of crisis. No one appreciates Big Paul's typically British stiff-upper-lip attitude more than Elizabeth II, who has made Whybrew one of her closest friends and confidants. So comfortable is their personal relationship that Whybrew and the Queen often spend cozy evenings watching television together in Her Majesty's sitting room.

It isn't difficult to see why the Queen might gravitate to someone like Big Paul. With his high forehead, close-set eyes, thinning hair, aquiline nose, and haughty aristocratic bearing, Whybrew could be Prince Philip's younger brother. In the famous 2012 London Summer Olympics video, it is Big Paul who introduces James Bond actor Daniel Craig to the Queen before they are depicted parachuting into the opening ceremonies together.

As he approaches the Queen's bedroom on this particular morning, the only other person who can claim to be equally close to Her Majesty stands in the doorway, ashen-faced and trembling. Starting more than a quarter-century ago as Her Majesty's personal dresser, Angela Kelly worked her way up to the vaunted station of "Personal Assistant, Advisor, and Curator to the Queen." In the process, the thrice-divorced Kelly, whose decidedly lowbrow Liverpool accent betrays her upbringing as a dock worker's daughter, has so endeared herself to the monarch that she is consulted about everything from affairs of state to baby clothes. (Among other assignments, Kelly supervised the team of British and Italian seamstresses who made the baptismal gowns for the Queen's great-grandchildren Prince George and Princess Charlotte.) During long weekends at Windsor, where Whybrew and Kelly have been given "grace-and-favor" apartments of their own on castle grounds, the Queen invariably indulges her passion for backstairs gossip over tea with the woman she simply calls "Angela."

Kelly, eyes welling with tears, shakes her head as Big Paul approaches. He takes his first tentative steps into the room. Fittingly, the plaintive wail of a bagpipe wafts up from the courtyard below. Each morning at nine the Queen's Piper, David Rodgers of the Irish Guards, stands outside the palace in full Royal Stewart tartan regalia and plays from a list of the monarch's favorite tunes. Wearing the two feathers in his cap that distinguish him from all other pipers in the realm, Rodgers is the fourteenth soldier (and first Irishman) to hold the post since Queen Victoria decreed that every monarch should start each day to the sound of Scottish bagpipes. Wherever she is in residence—be it at Windsor, Sandringham, Balmoral, or Buckingham Palace—this is how the Queen begins each day.

But not *this* day. The heavy red velvet curtains that surround the royal bed have been drawn back to reveal a small, still figure. The Queen's personal physician rushes into the room, and within moments the shadowy figure of Sir Christopher Geidt materializes in the doorway. Burly, bald, suave, shrewd, and more than a little mysterious, Her Majesty's private secretary usually conceals his emotions behind a fixed, deceptively benign smile. Sir Christopher never tips his hand—a skill honed during years spent with British intelligence before being tapped to serve as an aide to the Queen.

At this moment, however, Geidt's defenses are down. Like those around him, he is wide-eyed with shock and—despite the fact that this event had been anticipated and planned for decades—utter disbelief. The first call he must make is to Clive

Alderton, his counterpart at Clarence House, official residence of the Prince of Wales. Blond, boyish-faced Alderton, private secretary to the Duke and Duchess of Cornwall, cannot conceal the emotion in his voice when he is told the news. Alderton must now maintain his composure as he prepares to make the single most important phone call of his life.

"What is it, Charles?" Camilla pulls back the draperies that encircle her husband's massive, ornately carved Georgian canopy bed. Like her mother-in-law, the Duchess of Cornwall has always preferred to sleep in a velvet and damask cocoon, closed off from the outside world. Unlike the Queen, who hadn't shared a bedroom with her late husband, Prince Philip, for more than a half-century—in part because of Philip's habit of sleeping with the windows wide open no matter the weather—Camilla and Charles make it uncomfortably clear to members of their inner circle that they still enjoy an active, even adventurous, sex life.

"It's Mummy . . ."

He does not have to go on. Camilla recognizes the look immediately. She has seen the dazed expression cross Charles's face only three times in all the years she has known him. The first time was in 1979, when the small fishing boat belonging to Charles's great uncle and surrogate father, Louis Mountbatten, was blown up by IRA assassins, killing Mountbatten and three others. Camilla saw that expression of boundless grief again when, in 2002, the Queen Mother died in her sleep at age 101. Charles had been on a ski holiday with William and Harry at Klosters in Switzerland when it happened, but when he flew back to London Camilla would recall that "the look of great sadness was still there."

And then there was August 31, 1997—the day Princess Diana

was killed in a Paris car crash. Charles was vacationing with the rest of the Royal Family at Balmoral Castle at the time, and Camilla was the first person he called with the terrible news. She could hear the anguish in the Prince's voice as he, along with everyone else on the planet, tried to process what had happened.

Yet this moment—as fraught with historical importance as it is with deep shock, confusion, and grief—transcends all the others. It is the moment Charles has been both dreading and eagerly anticipating all his life—the moment when he loses the most important person in his life and, at the same time, at long last steps out of the shadows and into the part he was born to play.

At Anmer Hall in Norfolk, the Duchess of Cambridge is walking the family's black English cocker spaniel Lupo when the housekeeper, Sadie Rice, strides briskly toward her with a cellphone in her hand. "It's Prince William," the housekeeper tells Kate, handing the phone to the Princess with one hand as she takes Lupo's leash with the other.

The Duke of Cambridge is still in the middle of his shift piloting an Airbus H145 search-and-rescue helicopter for the East Anglian Air Ambulance, and Kate knows instantly that something must be terribly wrong; William has never interrupted his work to call her before. Moments earlier, the Prince was in the skies over Bedfordshire, transporting the victim of a motorcycle accident to Addenbrooke's Hospital when his private secretary, Miguel Head, was patched through to the cockpit. Once Head told William his beloved "Granny" had passed away in her sleep, he continued piloting his helicopter to the hospital without saying a word to his fellow crew members.

Now William is flying back to his air ambulance home base

at Cambridge Airport, and sharing the terrible news with Kate. There is silence on the other end—all Kate can hear is the pulse of helicopter blades as William struggles to compose himself.

"It's Granny," he manages to say. "She's gone."

At Buckingham Palace, Geidt and the other "Men in Gray," as Diana called them—the shadowy, behind-the-scenes figures who have always actually run the monarchy—have been carefully preparing for this inevitable event for decades. Only a handful of palace officials, along with their government counterparts at Whitehall, have been given access to details of the secret succession plan code-named "London Bridge." More frequently referred to in palace corridors as simply "The Bridge," this ostensibly referred to the funeral itself—but also to the momentous yet precarious transition from one monarch to another.

Once a year every year since the late 1970s, practice funeral processions for senior members of the Royal Family, such as Prince Philip, Prince Charles, and the Queen, have taken place in the streets of London under cover of darkness. Prince Philip, whose funeral plans were code-named "Forth Bridge" after the span over the Firth of Forth in Scotland, wanted only a private, military-style service at St. George's Chapel in Windsor Castle. Had Prince Charles predeceased his mother, his funeral plan, code-named "Menai Bridge" after the bridge that connects the island of Anglesey to the Welsh mainland, would have had all the pageantry of a royal funeral. But it would not have been a state funeral, for state funerals are reserved for the monarch. For her part, the Queen planned her own funeral down to the most minute detail—from the guest list, flowers, readings, and musical selections to which regimental units would participate and the color of their uniforms.

The media have long been preparing for this, as well. Every six months, they also practice announcing the death of the Queen. BBC anchors, remembering how newscaster Peter Sissons was upbraided for announcing the Queen Mother's death wearing a light gray suit and a red tie, now are careful to keep a dark change of clothes at the ready, just in case.

Over the past two hours, the Palace has notified the Queen's children and grandchildren. Geidt also places a call to 10 Downing Street, where an ashen-faced Prime Minister, whose weekly tête-à-tête with the Queen had taken place less than twenty-three hours earlier, immediately summons his ministers for an emergency cabinet meeting.

It is the cabinet's job to convene an Accession Council—an assembly that includes privy council members, lords of the realm, high commissioners of Commonwealth countries and the Lord Mayor of the City of London—to formally proclaim the new monarch. The formality is just that, since the new sovereign takes over the moment the old one has died. The Accession Council will also formalize the new monarch's name. As Charles Philip Arthur George, the Prince of Wales weighs several options, including being known as George VII or even King Arthur I. He has waited too long to make his own mark; as expected, he will go down in history as Charles III.

"Queen Elizabeth II is dead." Although the Palace has made use of social media to promote the image of the monarchy, it uses a more traditional medium—television—to break the news to the British public. Despite all the speculation, the planning and preparation—or perhaps because of it—this new reality is hard to accept. After all, fully 98 percent of the earth's population has only known a world with Queen Elizabeth in it.

The London Stock Exchange suspends trading. Flags around the world are lowered to half-staff. British television launches round-the-clock coverage, with all stations halting their regular programming to carry BBC-1's live news feed. The BBC will not resume its normal broadcast schedule for days—the network has already announced that all comedy programs will be barred from its airwaves until after the state funeral. In their place will be several prerecorded packages on the life and times of the woman whose life spanned more than eighteen prime ministers, eight popes, and sixteen U.S. presidents.

For three days before her funeral, the Queen lies in state at the Houses of Parliament in Westminster Hall. The magnificent Imperial State Crown sits atop the coffin, which is draped with the blue, red, and gold harp and lions of the Royal Standard. An arrangement of carnations, the Queen's favorite flower, also rests on the coffin, bearing a note with a single hand-lettered word: *Mama.*

Hundreds of thousands of mourners, many of them openly weeping, file past as Charles, his brothers Prince Andrew and Prince Edward (who assumed the title of Duke of Edinburgh on Philip's death), and William and Harry all take turns standing guard by the Queen's coffin in full dress uniform—what has come to be known as the Vigil of the Princes.

The day of the funeral is declared a national day of mourning, and an estimated 2 million people flood the streets of London to witness it. Never in recorded history have so many world leaders appeared in one place to pay their respects to a head of state. They fill the front pews of Westminster Abbey—where Elizabeth II is the first monarch to have a funeral since George II in 1760—solemnly listening to the service being led by the Archbishop of Canterbury.

After the service, the gun carriage on which the sovereign's casket rests is pulled not by horses, as would be the case for anything less than a state funeral, but by sailors of the Royal Navy—a tradition that began when, during Queen Victoria's funeral, the horses bolted and sailors stepped in to pull the coffin along the processional route. Now, with the Queen's equerries flanking the casket and members of the Royal Family walking behind, sailors pull the caisson carrying Her Majesty's coffin from Westminster Abbey to Paddington Station for the trip aboard the Royal Train to Windsor Castle.

Once at Windsor, Great Britain's longest-reigning monarch is interred at St. George's Chapel alongside her husband, Philip, her father, George VI, the Queen Mother, her sister Margaret, and nine other sovereigns, including Henry VIII, Charles I, George III, and the last king to bear her grandson's name—William IV.

Around the globe, an estimated 3.5 billion people are glued to hours of live coverage on television and the internet—a record-smashing figure that far surpasses the 2.5 billion viewers of Diana's funeral in 1997 and the 3 billion people who watched William and Kate's historic royal wedding in 2011. As was the case with Diana, the mood this time is one of deeply felt grief mixed with shock and disbelief. It is as if the entire planet is suddenly awakening to the fact that modern history's most enduringly famous figure—a player on the world's stage for five generations—has vanished.

There will be other, inevitably jarring changes to mark the

dawn of a new era. At sporting events, British subjects will now sing "God Save the King." The Royal Mint and the Bank of England, as well as the Royal Mail, gear up to place Charles III's likeness on all coins, paper currency, and stamps. Wherever the Queen's likenesses have been displayed throughout the Commonwealth—from government offices and embassies to pubs, department stores, and souvenir shops—there will hang a photograph of the new king.

For Charles and Camilla, Elizabeth's death also means a change of address. After several weeks, they move out of Clarence House to take up permanent residence in Buckingham Palace. William and Kate remain in Kensington Palace, leaving Clarence House to Prince Harry and his future wife and family. For those who have served the Queen at Buckingham Palace, in some cases for generations, it is not just her absence that weighs heavily. Something else is missing: Her Majesty's corgis. She owned more than thirty during her lifetime, all descended from Susan, a Pembroke given to Princess Elizabeth on her eighteenth birthday. Over the years, several of the Queen's corgis mated with Princess Margaret's dachshund Pipkin to produce "Dorgis."

The noisy, notoriously willful animals were always underfoot; at the Queen's direction, they slept in wicker baskets just outside her bedroom door (occasionally they slept at the foot of her bed) and moved freely about the palace whether or not they were completely housebroken (footmen always carried blotting paper with them to do a quick cleanup in case one of the corgis had an accident).

The Queen went so far as to mix the dogs' food herself whenever she could (they ate only when she gave the royal command) and carefully prepared Christmas stockings for them every year.

Ever mindful of the potential hazards to her pets, the Queen even carried a small magnet in her purse so she could pick up any stray pins or needles that might have been left on the floor after a dress fitting. Before any toys were given to the corgis, they first had to be personally inspected by the sovereign, who was known to pry a bell from a rubber ball or a noisemaker from a squeaky toy on the grounds that it presented a choking hazard.

To practically everyone but their owner, the Queen's canine friends were the hazard. Paul Burrell, a footman who later became Diana's butler and confidant, was knocked unconscious when nine leashed corgis tripped him up on the steps at Sandringham. "They're yappy, snappy, and we bloody well hate them," another footman declared. Diana, who made no secret of her dislike for this particular breed, called Her Majesty's ubiquitous pets "the moving carpet."

Now only four of the Queen's dogs remain: corgis Willow and Holly, and dorgis Vulcan and Candy. Philip and Charles always despised the "yapping dogs," and William made no secret of his distaste for their "constant noise. They're barking all the time. They drive me mad." In fact, none of the male Windsors are fans of the Queen's corgis—a feeling that was apparently also shared by Princess Anne. In the end, members of the household staff who had cared for the dogs volunteer to adopt them, and within a week the Queen's beloved corgis and dorgis are gone from the palace.

All of this is simply prelude to the coronation ceremony at Westminster Abbey. Viewed by a global audience that obliterates the record set only months before by the Queen's funeral, the crowning of the new king takes place amidst the pomp, pageantry, grandeur, and splendor that only the thousand-year-old institution of the monarchy can provide.

Clad in their own royal regalia, William and Kate—the new Prince and Princess of Wales—look on as the Archbishop of Canterbury begins the elaborate ceremony. Seated on a chair slightly below Charles and to his left is Camilla, Duchess of Cornwall.

After the Archbishop of Canterbury leads the communion service and prayers are said, the Lord Great Chamberlain removes Charles's crimson robe, and the new monarch is seated in King Edward's Chair. Every anointed sovereign since 1308 has been seated in St. Edward's Chair, encasing the legendary Stone of Scone, at the moment of coronation. "Sirs," the Archbishop of Canterbury declares to the assembled throng before anointing the monarch, "I here present unto you King Charles, your undoubted King, wherefore all of you who are come this day to do your homage and service, are you willing to do the same?" Their answer thunders through the abbey: "God save King Charles!"

Charles is then invested with two coronation robes—one white and the "great golden mantle," the Imperial Robe—while the Lord Great Chamberlain touches the king's heels with St. George's Golden Spurs (no longer actually buckled onto the monarch's ankles since the coronation of Queen Anne in 1702 because Anne's ankles were too thick to fit them). Then he is handed two swords by the assembled bishops and archbishops—the Great Sword of State and the Jeweled Sword of Offering—which he passes to a cleric who lays them on the altar.

The Archbishop then hands Charles a "Golden Orb" encrusted with diamonds, sapphires, emeralds, and rubies symbolizing "the world under Christ's dominion" before slipping the coronation ring onto the fourth finger of the new king's right hand. This ruby and sapphire ring represents the sovereign's "marriage" to the nation.

Still seated in St. Edward's chair, Charles hands the Golden Orb to the Bishop of London, and is then presented with two more symbols of royal power. The Royal Scepter, symbol of regal power and justice, is placed in the sovereign's right hand. It is mounted with the largest cut diamond in the world, the 530-carat Star of Africa. In his left hand, King Charles now grasps the dove-topped "Rod of Equity and Mercy."

It is at this point that a memory from Charles's childhood surfaces—the moment when, as a very bored-looking boy of three, he stood in the gallery between the Queen Mother and his aunt, Princess Margaret, to watch his mother become queen. The night before her coronation, Elizabeth, then just twenty-five, had practiced walking with the heavy crown on her head in front of Charles and his sister Anne, dissolving in giggles as she struggled to keep her balance. This would be one of his fondest memories of a mother who, from that point on, had little time to dote on her lonely, emotionally isolated eldest son.

Now, at last, it is Charles's turn—the moment in history that has defined his entire life, his raison d'être. His eyes widen perceptibly as St. Edward's Crown is brought to the Archbishop of Canterbury on a red cushion. It is especially fitting that this, the traditional coronation crown, was actually made for the crowning of the last King Charles—Charles II—in 1661.

The Archbishop carries the crown slightly above his own head as he walks toward St. Edward's Chair. Once he reaches it, the Archbishop raises the crown high and pauses for a moment before bringing it down and placing it firmly on Charles's head. His eyes are vacant; he is utterly expressionless. It is the classic out-of-body experience. At precisely this moment, the male peers of the realm in attendance place their coronets on their own heads in unison—the only time this is ever done.

"God save the King!" Kate, William, and Camilla shout loudly with everyone in the Abbey. "God save the King! God save the King!" There is a fanfare of trumpets, and the Archbishop raises his right hand to speak. "God crown you," he intones, "with a crown of glory and righteousness." While the orchestra and choir launch into William Walton's soul-stirring "Coronation Te Deum," church bells ring across the kingdom and guns thunder in the royal parks—from Hyde Park to the Tower of London.

In full regalia, the crown very literally weighing heavy on his head, Charles rises from St. Edward's Chair and moves to another royal throne closer to Camilla. While the choir sings, William kneels before his father and pays homage to the King, followed by the other "Dukes of the Blood Royal"—Prince Harry, the King's brothers Andrew and Edward—and then a long procession of "Lords Temporal": lesser dukes, marquesses, earls, viscounts, and barons.

Kate is smiling—not the unfettered, natural smile she willingly bestows on the flower-bearing children and awe-struck housewives who flock to catch a glimpse of her at ribbon cuttings and walkabouts, but the slightly pursed grin designed to keep reporters and the all-powerful Men in Gray guessing. The new Princess of Wales, bearer of the title that once belonged to her late mother-in-law, Diana, knows that all eyes will be on her for some faint glimmer of disapproval, or even anger.

Once the parade of peers kneeling in homage to their king

is completed, Camilla rises from her seat and kneels in prayer before the altar. Then she rises and moves several steps to the "Faldstool"—an ancient ceremonial prayer lectern—and again kneels in prayer, this time beneath a canopy held by four duchesses representing the four corners of the kingdom.

As he did with her husband, the Archbishop of Canterbury anoints Camilla, and then slips the queen's coronation ring on the fourth finger of her right hand. Once again, one of the most treasured of the Crown Jewels is brought to the Archbishop on a red velvet cushion. This crown is a national treasure in its own right, as laden with memories and sentiment as any single object in the realm can possibly be. It is the Queen Mother's Crown, made especially for the coronation of Charles's grandmother as queen in 1937. The first royal crown to be made of platinum, it is set with twenty-eight hundred diamonds, including the heart-stopping 105-carat Koh-i-Noor (Mountain of Light).

The Queen Mother's crown was placed on her coffin following her death in 2002, and has been displayed with the other Crown Jewels in the Tower of London ever since. Now the Archbishop raises the crown and gently settles it atop Camilla's head. All the peeresses—the viscountesses, the baronesses, the duchesses—simultaneously follow suit, crowning themselves with the glittering coronets that denote their rank in Britain's aristocracy.

Now "God save the Queen" reverberates through the archways of Westminster Abbey, and Queen Camilla is handed her own two royal scepters. She then takes her place on a throne of her own next to her husband's—a smaller throne, but a throne nonetheless.

It is the scene that Charles, in his effort years earlier to sell

Camilla to the public as a suitable replacement for the adored Diana, repeatedly vowed would never take place. By tradition and by law, Camilla has been for all intents and purposes Princess of Wales—among all women in the realm second only to the Queen in rank. But Charles's wife settled for a lesser title that had also been held by Diana—Duchess of Cornwall—ostensibly as a "wedding present" from the Queen.

The Palace went to considerable lengths to downplay Camilla's status in the royal hierarchy, but the instant Camilla married Charles she became Her Royal Highness The Princess Charles Philip Arthur George, Princess of Wales, Duchess of Cornwall, Duchess of Rothesay, Countess of Chester, Countess of Carrick, Baroness of Renfrew, Lady of the Isles, Princess of Scotland, Dame Grand Cross of the Royal Victorian Order. This panoply of titles aside, Charles had repeatedly vowed that, upon his ascension to the throne, Camilla would become princess consort—never queen. He would not press to have her crowned—and, he insisted to a wary public, Camilla herself had absolutely no interest in rising above her station as duchess.

In truth, Camilla automatically became queen on the sovereign's death. Only a "morganatic" marriage would have prevented this—a strict legal arrangement in which Camilla would have been expressly forbidden from acquiring any of her husband's many titles and privileges. That far Charles was unwilling to go.

There are those who feel this was never Charles's decision to make. But preventing Camilla from becoming queen would take an act of Parliament, followed by the passage of identical laws in the other fifteen Commonwealth countries (out of fifty-three) where the British monarch is head of state—an unwieldy process at best.

Nevertheless, there is no doubting that resentment toward Camilla is deeply ingrained in the British psyche. The reason: For decades the notorious Mrs. Parker Bowles carried on a torrid affair with Charles that sent his naive young bride into an emotional tailspin that ended in scandal, divorce, and death. In the immediate aftermath of the Paris car crash that killed Diana, Camilla became England's—and arguably the world's—most despised woman. "Mrs. PB," as she was known by palace operatives, rightly believed she would never earn the public's acceptance, much less its affection.

In the weeks leading up to Camilla's 2005 wedding to Charles, Diana's friend Vivienne Parry declared "there is only one Princess of Wales in people's minds. And only when Prince William gets married, perhaps many years from now, will it be time for another one." Another Diana ally, Joan Berry, publicly called on the Queen to call off their wedding "even at this late date."

Berry and Parry had public opinion solidly behind them. A poll in the *Daily Telegraph* showed a majority of Britons were convinced marriage to Camilla would cripple the monarchy, and that fully 69 percent of British subjects wanted William, not Charles, as their next king. The *Sunday Times* did its own poll one week before the wedding. Similarly, it revealed that 58 percent of the public wanted William to succeed Elizabeth on the throne, and that 73 percent emphatically opposed having Camilla as their next queen.

Nor did it help matters that, in order for Charles and Camilla to wed, the Church of England—of which the monarch is titular head—had to hastily rescind its centuries-old ban on second marriages for divorced couples. Back then, the Queen refused to attend the awkward civil ceremony at Windsor Guildhall, but she did show up at the forty-five-minute-long Service of Prayer and Dedication that followed at Windsor Castle. At the time, the then Archbishop of Canterbury, Rowan Williams, was so distressed at having to conduct the service that he insisted that an act of contrition be part of the wedding ceremony—that they expressly confess their "manifold sins and wickedness" and offer a public apology for their rampantly adulterous behavior.

Now, more than a decade after her 2005 wedding to Charles, public opinion seems to have changed little. Some 58 percent of Britons still remain adamantly opposed to Charles as their next monarch, with a staggering two-thirds of those aged eighteen to thirty-four wanting Charles and Camilla to step aside for William and Kate.

In the few months since Elizabeth's passing, Buckingham Palace has slowly fed the press and public details of the coronation ceremony. Yet it has only been a matter of days since palace officials confirmed that Camilla would indeed be crowned queen alongside her husband. There has been the expected initial public outcry, but Charles's courtiers assure him that this will quickly subside as the country is caught up in the excitement of the coronation.

To be sure, few things can be counted on to stir the souls of the British people as much as a royal procession through central London. On April 29, 2011, for example, more than a million people lined the route from Westminster Abbey to Buckingham Palace to cheer Prince William and his beguiling and popular bride.

Now Charles and Camilla will take the same five-mile route, giving the public its first glimpse of the new king and queen. Before they leave the Abbey, Charles exchanges St. Edward's Crown for the Imperial State Crown. With its 2,868 diamonds, including the 317-carat Cullinan II, the 104-carat Stuart Sapphire, and the legendary Black Prince's Ruby (not to mention four other major rubies and eleven emeralds), the Imperial State Crown symbolizes the sovereignty of the monarch. The last time Charles saw it, the crown was sitting atop his mother's coffin.

Riding to the palace in the extravagantly ornate, twenty-four-foot-long Gold State Coach pulled by eight white horses, the royal couple waves and smiles, but the reaction of the crowd is oddly muted. Nor can Charles and Camilla fail to hear the odd catcall, or to spot the occasional placard echoing the same sentiments expressed years earlier at their wedding: ILLEGAL, IMMORAL, AND SHAMEFUL.

Still, the people have come for spectacle and pageantry, and on that score the Royal Family never fails to deliver. The procession includes more than twenty thousand troops from around His Majesty's Commonwealth, marching to the strains of "Rule, Britannia," "The British Grenadiers," and of course Sir Edward Elgar's "Pomp and Circumstance" as they make their way past Whitehall, Trafalgar Square, Pall Mall, Hyde Park Corner, Marble Arch, Oxford Circus, and Regent Street before heading down The Mall.

Finally reaching Buckingham Palace, King Charles III climbs out of the carriage, still wearing the Imperial State Crown and somehow managing to juggle the golden orb and scepters. Camilla, the Queen Mother's crown firmly in place on her head, trails a respectful few steps behind.

More than a million people are jamming the mall in front of the palace and the adjacent streets—a sea of humanity stretching across St. James's and Green Parks to Whitehall and beyond.

Some are perched on the heroic bronze statues representing justice, agriculture, progress, and industry that ring the eighty-two-foot-tall Victoria Memorial in front of the palace, and three teenagers have managed to find a purchase atop Victoria herself. Dozens more, camera phones in hand, splash in the memorial's fountains.

Yet crowds in the past have been even larger—notably for the wedding of Prince William to Kate Middleton in 2011 and Queen Elizabeth's Diamond Jubilee the following year. Still, as he watches the tumultuous scene on a television monitor inside the palace with the rest of the Royal Family, Charles cannot help but be moved by the size of the throng and his subjects' obvious enthusiasm.

"Isn't it incredible?" he says, shaking his head as if it has come as a major surprise. True to form, he gazes at the image on the TV screen, not bothering to turn around and look out the window at actual people. "Just marvelous." Camilla's trademark toothy grin disguises whatever doubts she may harbor.

England's new queen—the first queen consort since Charles's beloved grandmother—has never been particularly fond of this room just inside the huge glass doors leading to the palace's famous balcony. This space, known as the "Centre Room," is one of the most intriguing spaces in the palace—an exotic oriental hodgepodge of dragons, Chinese murals, gargantuan cloisonné vases, lotus-shaped chandeliers, and other examples of priceless chinoiserie brought to the palace from the Royal Pavilion in Brighton.

Camilla has always considered the Centre Room as too closely resembling an upscale Chinese restaurant—an opinion shared by Princess Diana, among others. As a practical matter, it serves as the garishly appointed anteroom in which the family gathers before facing the music—both literally and figuratively—on the Royal Balcony. In the role of supporting player, Camilla has always been uncomfortable at moments like these. Today, cast in the female lead, she is plainly terrified.

Palace footmen throw open the twelve-foot-high glass doors, and the muffled roar of the throng outside now becomes clear. "We want the King!" the multitudes cry. "We want the King." Clive Alderton gestures toward the balcony. "Your Majesty," he says, "I believe the people wish to see their King."

Charles, still wearing the Imperial State Crown and his handwoven silk velvet coronation robes trimmed in Canadian ermine, takes a deep breath and walks toward the door. Outside in the palace courtyard, the musical director of the King's Guard band has been gazing up at the balcony draped with gold and red velvet bunting, waiting for the cue to come over his headset. Now it does, and the trumpets burst into a royal fanfare.

As King Charles III suddenly comes into view on the balcony, the crowd cheers wildly. He is, for the first time in his long life, finally stepping out from his mother's shadow. No one understands this better than Charles's Queen, who hangs back, allowing the love of her life to savor this moment that has eluded him for seven decades.

Charles waves to the sea of humanity, letting their adulation wash over him. But within thirty seconds, he turns to beckon his wife outside. To the cameras recording from a distance, it is not evident that Camilla, who at times of stress frequently suffers from what she calls "the shakes," trembles visibly as she joins her husband on the balcony. Then it happens: William and Kate and their adorable children, Prince George and Princess Charlotte, step into view. In an ear-splitting instant, the decibel level doubles as the crowd ramps up from joy to hysteria. The band quickly segues into "Rule Britannia," and as Prince Harry and the rest of the Royal Family drift in behind William and Kate, the din continues unabated.

Just as it appears the noise has finally reached its apex, there is a roar overhead. All heads tilt skyward to see the traditional flypast of RAF aircraft overhead. Still wearing their crowns, the King and Queen shield their eyes to look up as squadrons of Red Arrows, Hawks, and Tornado GR4s scream past.

While the Royal Family files back through balcony doors, Kate, smiling broadly as she holds Charlotte in her arms, turns to give a final wave to the multitude. One last, deafening roar goes up from the crowd. William, who has never sought to eclipse his father in any way, looks mortified; he gently takes Kate by the elbow and steers her inside.

....

IN THE WEEKS THAT FOLLOW the coronation of King Charles III, the British tabloids question whether "The Bridge" from one monarch to the next stands strong or will buckle under the weight of public sentiment. New postcoronation polls indicate that the public, feeling betrayed that Camilla has been crowned Queen despite Charles's repeated pledge that this would never happen, now more than ever want William as their sovereign.

The effects are felt more quickly abroad, where Charles's ascension to the throne is causing a rupture in the Commonwealth. Fifteen of the fifty-three former British colonies and dependencies that make up the Commonwealth had held on to the British monarch as their queen even after winning their independence—an arrangement that survived over the decades almost entirely because of the personal affection the people in those countries felt for Elizabeth. Without her, Australia and Canada now quickly vote to oust Charles as their head of state, opting instead for republicanism. Other Commonwealth member nations soon follow.

Charles and Camilla are also unpopular in Scotland, and the death of Elizabeth removes any impediment to independence. There are calls for a new referendum; within a few months, experts say, Scotland will probably become a republican state and join the European Union.

In Great Britain itself, where in the aftermath of Diana's death Camilla had been called a whore by passers-by in the street ("They've got to blame someone," Camilla said then), the new Queen is costing the monarchy dearly. Poll after poll shows that, while the public has fallen increasingly in love with Prince William's young family, the average Briton chafes at the idea that Camilla has replaced Elizabeth as their Queen.

King Charles does nothing to mollify his critics. In fact, he privately lectures the Prime Minister on a wide range of policy issues—something his politically savvy mother would never have done—and publicly pushes for sweeping urban and environmental reforms.

Having successfully alienated even the monarchy's staunchest allies in the government, Charles endures one humiliating setback after another. Parliament votes to slash the budget of the royal household dramatically. Certain properties from which the crown derives hundreds of millions of dollars in annual income are confiscated. Antimonarchist republicans, whose efforts have been kept in check by the people's love for Elizabeth, make huge gains in the polls.

There is one bright spot for the monarchy: Britons remain as smitten as ever with the Prince of Wales and his young family, although given the Windsors' storied longevity, William will be well into his sixties before Charles's death puts him on the throne. The Prime Minister suggests to the king that he might stave off the inevitable by bowing to public pressure and abdicating in favor of William, but he refuses. William himself, King Charles points out, has vowed he will never be party to such an unprecedented "scheme."

In a breathtakingly short time, the love and respect the British people harbored for their sovereign all but vanishes. It becomes glaringly obvious there may be no future King William V, no King George VII. The monarchy is crumbling under the weight of the King's intransigence. Charles could well be the last to wear the crown.

AS SCENARIOS GO, THE FALL of the House of Windsor is scarcely far-fetched. "As her reign nears its end," observed Scottish journalist and historian Neal Ascherson in the *New York Times*, "the emphasis on person, not Crown, becomes ominous. The British increasingly fear that Charles may be a weak, unpredictable king. If they are right, will the 1,000-year splendor of the Crown outweigh people's impatience with an elderly, melancholy man?" More to the point, will they lose patience with an elderly, melancholy King who broke a solemn promise to his subjects *not* to make his controversial wife their Queen?

Camilla has told friends that, despite her famously easygoing and self-deprecating nature, she has spent countless sleepless nights pondering all the variables. "Don't make the mistake of thinking Camilla is dumb," said the comedian Joan Rivers, who, surprisingly, was a longtime friend of both the Prince of Wales and the Duchess of Cornwall. "She is a very smart lady. She knows exactly what she's doing, what people think of her, and what can happen if she makes one wrong move."

Doubts about the impact she may have on her husband's standing in the eyes of his subjects clearly gnaw at Camilla. "She has always been so in love with Charles," said a former lady-in-waiting to the Queen Mother, "and at the same time she has always been absolutely determined not to come between Charles and his people. Of course, in reality, Camilla has done just that on many occasions."

For members of the Royal Family both old and new, few occasions are more inherently stressful than the monarch's official birthday celebration—and the one marking the Queen's ninetieth birthday in 2016 will be no exception. On the morning of the big event, Camilla does not wake up next to her husband in their giant canopied four-poster at Clarence House. Charles has already been up for more than an hour, and is in his dressing room being attended to by his valet.

Normally, Camilla would not be spending a summer weekend at Clarence House at all. She would be happily ensconced at Ray Mill House, the gray stone mansion in Wiltshire that she purchased for $1.3 million after finally divorcing her spouse of twenty-two years, Andrew Parker Bowles, in 1995. It is no accident that Ray Mill House is conveniently situated just sixteen miles from Highgrove, Charles's lavish country estate west of London.

As the Duchess of Cornwall and the wife of the heir to the throne, Camilla has at least three official residences of her own—Highgrove, Clarence House, and Birkhall, the fourteen-bedroom residence at Balmoral that had once belonged to the Queen Mother. Yet her undisputed favorite is Ray Mill House, a comparatively cozy sanctuary from the pressures of royal life. It is also the one place where she can spend time with her rambunctious tribe of grandchildren and away from the increasingly curmudgeonly Charles.

Critics point out that security measures at Ray Mill House alone cost British taxpayers upward of $3 million a year, but it is worth it to this royal couple for yet another reason. After decades spent chasing stolen moments of passion in country getaways or the homes of mutual friends, Charles and Camilla have concluded that cohabitation is anathema to their relationship. They cannot keep their love alive without the excitement that comes from the carefully planned illicit rendezvous, the furtive liaison at their favorite trysting place.

By 2016, Charles and Camilla are no longer living together in the traditional sense. Instead, he divides his time primarily between Clarence House and Highgrove, while she spends as much time as possible with family and friends at Ray Mill House, waiting for her prince to show up at any time of the day or night—all just as it was during his marriage to Diana.

"You have to understand that Camilla loved being a royal mistress and all the intrigue that went along with it," a Wiltshire neighbor said. "Without all the sneaking around, it just wasn't as much fun as it used to be. So they just set the clocks back and pretend they're still secret lovers. I'm not really sure they'd know how to do it any other way."

Yet on this Saturday morning in June, sex may well be the farthest thing from Camilla's mind. Instead, as the wife of a future monarch and the daughter-in-law of the current one, she will be called upon once again to play an important part in one of her nation's most colorful spectacles. Today the annual Trooping the Colour will take place on Horse Guards Parade by St. James's Park—the ceremony that has marked the sovereign's official birthday since 1748. Full of pomp and pageantry, this is always one of the most important and colorful public dates on the royal calendar. Edward VII, who was born on November 9, 1841, permanently moved the Trooping the Colour ceremony to its current date because June seemed like a more temperate month for a parade celebrating his birthday.

During sixty-four years on the throne, Elizabeth II has missed Trooping the Colour only once—in 1955, when a rail strike caused the cancellation of the event altogether. For thirty-six of those years, this occasion also offered the Queen, an ardent equestrienne, the opportunity to ride sidesaddle from Buckingham Palace down The Mall, resplendent in the medal-bedecked red uniform of her royal regiments. In 1981, a young man in the crowd fired blank rounds from a pistol and startled her horse, nearly pitching the Queen to the pavement. Undaunted, Elizabeth continued to attend on horseback for another five years before finally opting to make the journey in a royal carriage. No longer wearing the uniform, she nevertheless always wears the Brigade of Guards badge, a large jewel representing the regiments that participate—the Coldstream Guards, the Welsh Guards, the Irish Guards, the Scots Guards, and the Grenadier Guards.

This year, Trooping the Colour is even more fraught with historical significance than usual. Although the Queen actually turned ninety on April 21, this Saturday in June is the day that her grateful subjects will mark the occasion with yet another carefully choreographed, but still genuine, mass outpouring of affection.

It is also one of the two days each year when the Queen releases her annual Honors List. This list, submitted by the Prime Minister but always subject to the approval of the sovereign (with added guidance from the Men in Gray), bestows MBEs (Members of the Most Excellent Order of the British Empire), OBEs (Officers of the Most Excellent Order of the British Empire), CBEs (Commanders of the Most Excellent Order of the British Empire), and knighthoods on a thousand or more artists, academics, civil servants, scientists, diplomats, politicians, business leaders, and humanitarians. By 2016, the Queen had conferred on her subjects more than four hundred thousand honors and awards.

No less for members of the Royal Family, Trooping the Colour affords the opportunity to gauge where one stands in the eyes of the monarch—and in the royal pecking order. During the Golden Jubilee celebrations in 2002 celebrating the Queen's fiftieth year on the throne, Her Majesty allowed Camilla to be seen publicly with the Royal Family for the first time—with some important restrictions. At the classical and pop concerts held at Buckingham Palace that year, Camilla could be viewed on the giant Jumbotron, nervously playing with her hair and trying to spy on what Charles and the Queen—Her Majesty's bright yellow earplugs firmly in place—were up to from two rows behind.

....

THINGS WERE VERY DIFFERENT DURING the Queen's Diamond Jubilee a decade later. Eyebrows raised when Prince Philip was hospitalized with a bladder infection and, rather than going solo as she usually did under such circumstances, the Queen chose Camilla to take his place next to her in the royal carriage. "She was sending a very strong message," observed longtime royal commentator Robert Jobson, "that the Duchess of Cornwall deserved to be there." Camilla, more stunned than anyone at that turn of events, could scarcely contain her glee.

Camilla's good fortune—"pride of place next to the queen," the *Times* of London called it—was no accident. For years now, Charles had pleaded with his mother to make a more public show of her acceptance of Camilla, however grudging it might have been. When his father fell ill, he wasted no time in pressuring the Queen to invite Camilla to sit next to her in the 1902 State Landau. Even more important than his personal entreaties to the Queen herself was the deft lobbying with senior Buckingham Palace officials undertaken by Charles's staff on Camilla's behalf. In matters of protocol, the Queen almost always acquiesced, albeit sometimes reluctantly, to the Men in Gray.

The situation regarding Philip was back to normal in 2013, when the ninety-four-year-old Duke of Edinburgh not only rode next to his wife in the royal carriage, but did it wearing the full uniform and unwieldy bearskin hat of the Grenadier Guards. This was particularly impressive given the fact that Philip now officially ranked as the oldest living male member of the British Royal Family—ever. Camilla and Kate actually rode side by side in a separate carriage with Prince Harry, unsmiling and clearly ill at ease as they waved stiffly to crowds lining the streets.

Whether the Queen is again convinced to publicly sidle up to her daughter-in-law as she did during the Diamond Jubilee or decides to give another Royal the nod, Camilla must look as polished and presentable as humanly possible for the occasion. To say she had undergone a Galatea-like transformation in recent years would be a gross understatement. For decades, Camilla's fashion sense was akin to her taste in furniture—decidedly English shabby. She favored torn riding pants or dirt-stained jeans, boxy sweaters, scuffed, mud-caked boots, frayed scarves, and frumpy tweeds. Her fingernails were dirty and jagged, her crooked and chipped teeth stained by decades of smoking. Her hair was a brittle tangle of straw, from which one might at any given moment pull out an actual piece of straw.

That began to change dramatically in late 2002, when, at Charles's urging, Camilla subjected herself to a complete makeover. Despite their shared love of gritty country pursuits like gardening and riding, Charles was also a man of refined tastes who spent well over $100,000 annually on his own bespoke wardrobe. His unwavering conviction about how even the smallest things should be done had servants scrambling. They were instructed that lunch must be served on plates marked with the Prince of Wales crest *precisely* at twelve o'clock. A cup and saucer were to be placed to the right with a silver spoon pointing outward at a twenty-five-degree angle. The royal toast was always served on a silver rack—never on a plate—with three balls of butter (no more, no less) chilled in a small dish.

Even if His Highness merely asked for a cold drink, staffers knew they were in trouble if he looked into his glass and scowled at what he saw. "He preferred round pieces of ice," a former valet said, "because he thought the angles made regular cubes 'too noisy.' We heard that quite a lot."

Prince Charles's valet, Michael Fawcett, was all too painfully familiar with his boss's idiosyncrasies—and his insistence on being catered to in every conceivable way. Fawcett's duties included squeezing the toothpaste from a silver dispenser bearing the Prince of Wales crest onto the Prince's toothbrush, lathering his shaving brush, slipping on and tying the Prince's shoes, zipping up the royal fly, and even holding the specimen bottle while the Prince of Wales gave a urine sample during regular check-ups.

Things were no different on the road. Charles traveled with his own hand towels, cushioned toilet seat, and toilet paper embroidered with the Prince of Wales crest. There were even written instructions to be passed on to hotel chefs stipulating the "dimensions and texture" of royal sandwiches. Prince Charles's childhood teddy bear, which always resided in a place of honor amidst the pillows on his canopied four-poster, was also packed up for every trip and then taken out to be tucked under the covers of His Royal Highness's bed wherever he happened to be. For more than six decades, the only person allowed to mend Prince Charles's ancient, unraveling teddy was his beloved nanny, Mabel Anderson.

Pampered and demanding—at his own dinner parties he often ate a different meal from his guests, on Prince of Wales plates and using Prince of Wales utensils—Charles grew up being told that, as far as the Royal Family was concerned, appearances were everything. The Prince knew Camilla would have to streamline her look and adopt an entirely new style if she wanted to be a worthy front woman for what members of the Royal Family wryly called "The Firm." With Charles's then deputy private secretary and resident media Svengali Mark Bolland overseeing the entire process, Camilla submitted herself to a handpicked team of dietitians, fitness experts, plastic surgeons, dentists, and cosmetologists.

Over a six-month period, Camilla underwent a series of face and neck peels, Botox injections, and laser treatments to erase the wrinkles and lines in her face and neck. She also had her teeth whitened and capped, and even hired a full-time hairdresser, Hugh Green of Belgravia's swank Hugh and Stephen salon, to tend to her champagne-colored tresses.

Shrinking from a size twelve to a size ten, Camilla also began wearing sleek gowns and chic suits by British designers like Anna Valentine, Antony Price, Bruce Oldfield, and Vivienne Westwood. Each morning, royal dresser Jackie Meakin laid out the day's wardrobe for Camilla. And each day, Meakin and the Duchess considered how she would look in photographs standing next to the most stylish woman on the planet: the former Kate Middleton.

....

IN APARTMENT 1A OF NEARBY Kensington Palace, Kate sits cross-legged on the nursery floor, feeding a bottle to Princess Charlotte while her big brother plays noisily with a toy dump truck. If anyone needed proof that even the adored Duchess of Cambridge is not entirely immune to criticism, it is embodied in this Beatrix Potter–inspired room with its cheerful periwinkle-blue walls decorated with drawings of Peter Rabbit. After more than $7 million was spent to refurbish the nursery along with the Cambridges' royal apartment—more accurately, twenty rooms spread out over a four-story wing of the palace—the couple ran afoul of the press when it was announced they would actually be spending most of their time at Anmer Hall, their mansion on the grounds of Sandringham in Norfolk. Sandringham and its twenty thousand acres, along with Balmoral Castle (another fifty thousand acres), are the only two royal residences privately owned by the Queen and technically not held in trust for future sovereigns.

Still, whenever the Cambridges' presence is required in the city—as it always is during Trooping the Colour ceremonies—they make Kensington Palace their base of operations. Soon, Kate hands off both Charlotte and George to their Spanish nanny, Maria Teresa Borrallo. She, too, must now be tended to by her full-time hairdresser, Amanda Cook Tucker, and go over wardrobe choices with her personal assistant-turned-stylist, Natasha "Tash" Archer. Although Kate Middleton's innate sense of style rivaled that of Diana from the very beginning, it was Tash Archer who urged the young wife of the future king to add more polish to her look by wearing Jenny Packham, Alexander McQueen, Emilia Wickstead, and Erdem.

Not surprisingly, what she is going to wear today is of far less concern to Kate than it is to Camilla. Camilla has come along light-years in terms of her appearance and public image, but she cannot compete with a supremely poised natural beauty who also happens to be thirty-five years her junior.

Nor could anyone, for that matter, hope to compete with the newest stars in the Windsor firmament. At the end of last year's Trooping the Colour ceremonies, when the Royal Family gathered on the balcony of Buckingham Palace, the loudest cheers rose up from the throng when William stepped onto the balcony carrying George. It was a rare official outing for the twenty-two-month-old prince, who wore the same powder-blue outfit that William wore when he made his balcony debut in 1984. George waved at the crowd and played with the gold braid on his father's uniform, easily upstaging everyone—including the Queen.

George's appearance was, in fact, historic. It marked the

first time that four generations of present and current British monarchs—the Queen, Charles, William, and George—were seen together on the royal balcony.

"ALL EYES ON GORGEOUS GEORGE!" trumpeted the next morning's *Daily Mail*—although his mother got more than her fair share of kudos. Words like "amazing," "slim," and "radiant" were used in the press to describe how Kate looked as she stood on the balcony, just six weeks after giving birth to Charlotte.

The Little Princess stayed home then, but Kate and William fully intend to have her join them on the balcony this year. Charles will be especially thrilled. A doting grandpa to George, the Prince of Wales is, according to William, "positively obsessed" with Charlotte. At a gathering of RAF pilots who flew during World War II, he boasted that his granddaughter was not only adorable but "already sleeps through the night, and is much easier on Mum than Prince George."

Although Camilla had grandchildren of her own and fully appreciated Charles's affection for George and Charlotte, she also realized that the little Cambridges were the newest pawns in an ancient and very public game. "It can be subtle or it can be very obvious," Harold Brooks-Baker, the longtime publishing director of *Burke's Peerage*, once observed. "But everyone on that balcony is to one extent or another jockeying for position. Being seen up front, and close to the monarch, is everything."

Certainly, each Royal's team of handlers took care to examine the video and the stills, analyzing every position, motion, and gesture. Last year, unable to do anything about the commotion being caused by George's debut, Camilla made an effort to be seen up front in her oversized cream-colored hat and celadon-green silk suit. Kate, dazzling in an ice-blue-and-ivory silk Catherine Walker coat dress and one of the white fascinators for which she had become famous, became so engrossed in keeping an eye on George that for much of the event she was completely out of sight. While Camilla stood up front next to Charles, William, and George, her chief rival for the public's affection—Kate—was hidden behind the sovereign. The Prince of Wales, who still complained bitterly over perceived slights to his wife, laughed at the next day's photographs. They showed all the Royals smiling and waving, but in Kate's case only her fascinator was visible, sailing above the Queen's head.

....

WHILE TWO QUEENS-IN-WAITING FRET ABOUT their futures, the current one stirs awake on the morning of her special day. It is seven-thirty, and a chambermaid is gently rapping at her door. Elizabeth, like her daughter-in-law Camilla, has always been sensitive to light and wears eye shades even though her bed is also encircled by heavy curtains. She sleeps more or less bolt upright, propped up on a pile of down pillows with custom-designed Porthault linens bearing the royal insignia. It takes only a minute or two for the Queen to pull back the curtains and arrange herself in bed. She then beckons the chambermaid in with the words she uses every morning without variation. "Yes, yes, come in!" she chirps. "I'm ready for you!"

The maid enters a room that, save for its occupant, seems wholly unremarkable. Neither Kate nor Camilla have ever been in the Queen's bedroom, and it is certainly nothing like Camilla imagines it; there is not the slightest resemblance to the regal boudoir she has conjured in her dreams.

True, the Queen's bedroom is located in the east wing not far from the Throne Room, where tourists can pay to see the high-backed velvet chairs bearing the initials E.R. II and P (for Philip) and the seat cushions bearing the imprint of the royal derrieres. For those who know where to find the secret latch hidden in the oak-paneled wall, there is actually direct access from the Throne Room into the Queen's private chambers. On other floors of the east wing, guest rooms have the name of the occupant posted on the door: Prince Charles, Prince Harry, Princess Anne, and so on. There is no such name tag on the Queen's bedroom door.

Although the ceilings are twelve feet high, it is roughly the size of a bedroom in any suburban American home—about sixteen by fourteen feet. The furnishings can only be described as spartan. Instead of a king-sized bed or even the more obviously appropriate queen-sized bed, Elizabeth has always preferred to sleep alone in a double bed—granted, a bed surrounded on all sides by a curtain. There are also two small nightstands, and a sturdy, functional, but undistinguished mahogany dresser.

The chambermaid maneuvers the heavy tray onto one of the small bedside tables and the Queen, who unhesitatingly describes herself as "a real morning person," chatters brightly about the weather. On the tray is a tea service for one: two small silver pots, Royal Crown Derby bone china teacup and saucer decorated in one of Her Majesty's favorite floral patterns, a napkin bearing the monogram EIIR (Elizabeth II Regent), and a few biscuits.

Her Majesty always serves herself this all-important first cup of Darjeeling or occasionally Earl Grey (two lumps of sugar with milk trucked in fresh from the royal herd at Windsor Castle), then savors it while listening to the news on BBC Radio 4. The maid throws open the bedroom curtains, then draws the Queen's morning bath.

The Queen, who has a fondness for knee-length, floral-print Liberty of London nightgowns, puts on her favorite chenille robe and pads to the bathroom in bare feet. While she bathes, the maid lays out her wardrobe for the day—all preselected and tagged by her dresser and confidante Angela Kelly, who also chooses which one of the Queen's two hundred purses will best go with her outfit. What is actually in the Queen's handbag, along with those magnets for picking up stray pins that might injure her corgis? Since she routinely powders her nose at the dinner table—a practice that some people find surprising—the Queen always carries a treasured metal makeup case Philip made for her as a wedding gift. She also carries lipstick—in 1952 Elizabeth II commissioned her own shade called "the Balmoral Lipstick" to match her coronation robes—which she applies frequently throughout the day. In addition to a small selection of family snapshots and a number of good luck charms from her children—the Queen is unapologetically superstitious—Her Majesty's handbag includes a small tube of mints, several crossword puzzles to while away the time spent traveling from one appearance to another, doggie treats, a fountain pen (she refuses to use a ballpoint), sunglasses, reading glasses, a small mirror, a diary and address book—and often a tiny camera she might suddenly whip out to take photos of other world leaders. To keep from having to place her purse on the floor, the Queen also carries a small white suction cup with a hook on it. When the occasion arises, she sticks the suction cup to the underside of a table and hangs her purse from it. "Very handy, don't you think?" she said to one startled guest at a luncheon in Yorkshire.

Almost as revealing is what she *doesn't* carry in her purse: credit cards, car keys, cash, or a passport—she has never required one because, as the Queen, she issues all UK passports. Every other member of the Royal Family, including Prince Philip and Charles, requires a passport to travel abroad.

At eight-thirty, Elizabeth joins Prince Philip for breakfast in the first-floor dining room overlooking the palace gardens. Often Philip, who gets up an hour earlier than his wife, has breakfast alone in his own private dining room down the hall. (Elizabeth and the Duke of Edinburgh maintain separate dining rooms, sitting rooms, bedrooms, and bathrooms.) But today he is here to wish his wife of sixty-eight years happy birthday with a peck on both cheeks.

The Queen's breakfast menu rarely varies: Special K or oatmeal brought to the table in Tupperware containers, crustless whole wheat toast with orange marmalade, a single boiled egg, and small bowls of prunes, apricots, and macadamia nuts. While Elizabeth sips her tea, she scans the papers piled on her breakfast table. On top is her favorite publication, the *Racing Post*, followed by the *Daily Mail*, the *Daily Express*, the *Mirror*, the *Daily Telegraph*, the *Times*, and *Thoroughbred Owner and Breeder*.

She reads them all. "I don't read the tabloids," the Duke of Edinburgh said. "I glance at one. I reckon one's enough. I can't cope with them. But the Queen reads every bloody paper she can lay her hands on!"

Philip does not even attempt to speak to the Queen when she is immersed in her racing results and the day's tipsheets. He drinks his black coffee—the Prince is not a fan of tea in the morning—and proceeds to down a full English breakfast of fried eggs, fried mushrooms, bacon, sausages, scones, and oatcakes with honey. At one point, he breaks a tiny piece off a scone, crumbles it, walks over to the window, and places the crumbs in a bird feeder just outside the window.

At 9:00 a.m., the Queen's Piper marches to his customary spot in the garden just beneath the dining-room window and begins to play a strained rendition of Rodgers and Hammerstein's "People Will Say We're in Love" from the 1943 Broadway musical *Oklahoma!* It has been one of the Queen's favorite tunes since she was a teenager.

Elizabeth puts her papers down and walks to the window. To Major Rodgers's undisguised delight, both she and Philip are smiling down at him. Unfortunately, the Queen's Piper cannot hear her gamely humming along, trying to keep up with his wheezing bagpipes.

Oklahoma! opened on the West End in 1947, and she and Philip saw it when they were dating. According to Elizabeth's governess and friend Marion Crawford (who, like the Queen Mother, never stopped calling her young charge "Lilibet"), "People Will Say We're in Love" was Elizabeth and Philip's song. "After he started taking her out," Crawford remembered, "Lilibet would often ask the band at restaurants where they dined to play 'People Will Say We're in Love' for her." Elizabeth and Philip fell in love while slow dancing to the tune, and were married that November. At the time, long before Charles and Diana and William and Kate, theirs was the Wedding of the Century.

For a few blissfully free moments, Elizabeth is lost in her memories. Such moments of queenly reverie are rare; Her Majesty's hectic schedule aside, she has never been one for introspection. But since the death of the Queen Mother, friends and royal household staff alike have noticed what her cousin Margaret

Rhodes called "a change in the Queen's mood . . . a kind of serenity. I think in a funny way, perhaps, the death of the Queen Mother had quite a huge effect on the Queen . . . in a way that she could come into her own as the head of the family and as the senior royal lady."

If the Queen felt more than a little intimidated by her mother, Elizabeth was always—to borrow Diana's nickname for her mother-in-law—"Top Lady" in everyone else's eyes. Now, as the world celebrates her ninetieth birthday, she knows precious time is running out. The Queen may not share Camilla's night terrors about what lies ahead for the monarchy once she is gone, or Kate's deceptively guileless sense of youthful optimism—in short, the firm if unstated belief that William will prevail, and sooner rather than later. But the Queen is keenly aware that to preserve the institution that she has embodied longer than anyone, hard choices must be made—and that royal egos will be badly bruised in the process.

The Queen's Piper ends with a flourish, then marches off. Her Majesty claps in appreciation, then turns from the window and heads back down the hall. As she walks toward her bedroom, she beckons to her "moving carpet" of corgis and dorgis to come along. Willow, Holly, Vulcan, and Candy all swarm at their mistress's feet, yapping happily.

It is time to get dressed for the Trooping the Colour parade, and for all the celebrations that will follow. Perhaps more than at any time in her life, she knows who she is, what she represents, the power she still has to stir the world's imagination, and what she must do with that power. She also knows that, after spending more time on the world stage than anyone in history, male or female, she has achieved an almost mythic status that transcends mere fame.

Milestone events like this official birthday, overflowing with pageantry and pomp, are an important part of the royal equation. "I must be seen," Elizabeth has always been fond of saying, "to be believed."

Let us not take ourselves too seriously. None of us has a monopoly on wisdom.

—THE QUEEN

2

"IT WILL BE THE MOST APPALLING SHOCK"

HIGH IN A FIG TREE IN KENYA

FEBRUARY 6, 1952

Clad in safari jacket and jeans, binoculars firmly in hand, she climbed to the observation platform shortly before dawn and waited for the rhinos to come. This was Princess Elizabeth's long-delayed honeymoon trip to Africa, and while her husband, the Duke of Edinburgh, preferred to sleep in, she was not about to miss the sight of wild game gathering at the watering hole to drink some fifty feet below. In the meantime, she and Philip's private secretary, Michael Parker, gazed in wonder at the sight of the equatorial sun beginning its ascent on the horizon.

Just as everything began to turn an eerie, shimmering pink, a white eagle darted out of the sky. For a moment, it seemed as if it might dive down and attack Parker and the royal Princess, but instead it just made lazy circles above them before flying off toward the sun. "That was very strange," Elizabeth said at the time, unaware that it was at that moment that her father died at Sandringham—and she became queen at age twenty-five.

"Because of where we were," said Pamela Hicks, a lady-in-waiting on the trip, "we were almost the last people in the world to know." Their hotel in Kenya, Treetops, was nothing more than a series of structures built among the branches of a giant fig tree smack in the middle of the jungle. It was considered too dangerous for most tourists, who ran the risk of being attacked by wild animals coming to the salt lick at the base of the tree. It was also deep in rebel territory, and would actually be burned down during the bloody Mau Mau uprisings a year later.

It would be more than four hours before the news reached Parker, who told Philip immediately. "It will be the most appalling shock," said Philip, who believed like everyone else at the time that the King's lung cancer treatment had been successful and he was on the road to recovery. King George had actually spent an enjoyable day shooting pheasant at Sandringham, and after a pleasant, upbeat dinner with his wife and Elizabeth's sister Margaret, went to bed at 10:30 p.m. Several hours later, however, he suffered a pulmonary embolism and died in his sleep. He was fifty-six.

The BBC was already broadcasting the news when Philip walked into Elizabeth's hotel room and broke the news to her. The Prince would recall that she looked "pale and worried," but did not cry. Philip took his wife through the garden down to the nearby Sagana River, where they walked slowly up and down the riverbank while he spoke words of comfort and reassurance to her.

Not long after, she was sitting bolt upright at the desk in her hotel room, pen in hand, while Philip sat on the sofa, calmly reading the *Times*. Whenever anyone in their party expressed their condolences, Elizabeth apologized for having to cut the trip short. "I'm so sorry we've got to go back," she said. "It's ruining everybody's plans."

When Elizabeth's private secretary, Martin Charteris, asked what name she wished to be known by as monarch, she looked puzzled. "My own, of course—what else?" she replied, apparently forgetting that her own father's real name was Albert ("Bertie" to his family).

Later, on the twenty-four-hour flight home to London, Elizabeth would leave her seat several times to cry privately in the bathroom. But for now, she could not afford the luxury of self-pity. Whatever feelings of grief she had, Parker observed, were buried "deep, deep inside her." Instead, sitting at her desk suspended in a fig tree in Kenya, she jotted down notes, fired off cables, and wrote letters in her loopy script—seizing her destiny, as Lord Charteris put it, "with both hands."

No one knew what to expect—not even the then Prime Minister Winston Churchill, who wept at the news of the King's passing and wondered aloud if Elizabeth was up to the task. "I don't even *know* her," he complained. "She's only a child!"

Yet Elizabeth had already proved she was no pushover. When Philip insisted that their children be given his family name—Mountbatten (the Anglicized form of "Battenberg")—Elizabeth followed Churchill's advice and stood up to her husband, officially proclaiming that they would carry on the Windsor name. "Are you telling me," he demanded in front of the Prime Minister, "that I am the only man in the country not allowed to give his name to his children? I'm nothing but a bloody amoeba!"

Philip had reason to be particularly sensitive when it came to surnames. The Duke had been given his mother's Battenberg family name by default. It could have been much worse. Princess Alice of Battenberg, a schizophrenic who was once committed to a mental institution, could have left her son with the unwieldy Teutonic surname Schleswig-Holstein-Sonderburg-Glucksburg. To avoid ruffling the feathers of their English cousins after World War I and during the years leading up to World War II, it was agreed that Elizabeth's future husband should technically have no surname at all, and simply be known as Prince Philip of Greece and Denmark.

Philip's wife embraced her fate with a fervor that surprised even the most ardent monarchists. She was, after all, the young mother of two: Charles was three when she became queen, his sister Anne not yet two. Andrew would arrive in 1960 and youngest child Edward in 1964. Lady Airlie, a close friend of Elizabeth's grandmother, Queen Mary, echoed the sentiments of many when she urged the new queen's handlers "not to kill the poor little girl" by loading her down with too many royal engagements. Even the Queen's physicians urged her to avoid all but a handful of important engagements and devote most of her time to raising her children.

Elizabeth, ever the dutiful daughter, would have none of it. As a way to further suppress her grief and to honor her father's memory, she threw herself into her new job. From this point on, the mother Charles had known would become little more than a phantom—a distant, formal figure who treated him with chilly detachment.

As small children, Charles and his sister, Anne, would see their mother twice a day—at 9:00 a.m. and again shortly before dinner—for a grand total of thirty carefully allotted minutes.

(Originally, the Queen saw her children for only fifteen minutes on Wednesdays, but she moved her weekly audience with the Prime Minister from five-thirty to six-thirty so she would have time to tuck Charles and Anne into bed.)

In an apparent effort to loosen things up a bit, Elizabeth did make one significant change in royal protocol when it came to the children. Although the Queen Mother and her own sister, Princess Margaret, were required to curtsy or bow in Elizabeth's presence, her young children were no longer required to. "It's silly," Elizabeth told her private secretary. "They're too young to understand what's going on." Yet as heir to the throne, Charles grew up feeling unloved and essentially ignored. For the most part, all of Elizabeth's offspring spent their childhoods in the company of nurses, nannies, and governesses in the six-room nursery on the palace's second floor.

Charles later remembered how his mother seemed to simply vanish without any real explanation for months on end. When the Queen returned from one of her early Commonwealth tours, the little boy yearned for a hug from his mother. Instead, when he rushed up to greet her, the Queen said, "No, not you, dear," and returned to the business of greeting grown-up dignitaries first. When it was finally Charles's turn, she bent over, shook his hand, and—without uttering a word—resumed talking to the officials who were there to welcome her home.

Although Charles's governess, Mabel Anderson, was a no-nonsense disciplinarian, he formed a deep personal attachment to her. "At least," he later observed, "she was there for me."

Charles could scarcely turn to his father for comfort. If anything, Philip was even more distant and unloving than his wife. In later years, he would go on record describing his father as rigid, authoritarian, cold, bullying, and "undemonstrative—incapable of sensitivity or tenderness." (The Duke of Edinburgh was apparently quite capable of being demonstrative with members of the opposite sex, however. He had a particular fondness for actresses and showgirls, and his affair with one—British theater star Pat Kirkwood—was rumored to have lasted more than twenty-five years.)

Elizabeth was well aware of her husband's roving eye. Early on during the courtship, she was within earshot when one of Philip's dancing partners—a particularly naive young aristocrat—proclaimed loudly that it was "terribly uncomfortable dancing with Philip. That torch [flashlight] he insists on carrying in his pocket keeps jabbing me in the stomach. I've heard the other girls complain about it, too."

Although her parents' marriage had been a close and happy one (George VI described his wife to his elder daughter as "the most marvelous person in the world in my eyes"), Elizabeth knew this was the glaring exception. After all, it was her playboy Uncle David's insistence on marrying the twice-divorced American Wallis Simpson that resulted in his abdication and led to Elizabeth's ultimately becoming queen. Infidelity remained par for the course in royal circles, and given her husband's Viking good looks, it was scarcely realistic to think that he would remain entirely faithful.

In any event, she was far too busy attending to the business of being a modern monarch—The Firm's chairman and CEO. Elizabeth established her own daily schedule as soon as she returned to London from Africa as queen, and it would remain virtually unchanged for the remainder of her sixty-plus-year reign.

Her first order of business each day was attending to the infamous dispatch boxes that required her attention whether she was in residence at Buckingham Palace, Windsor, Balmoral, Sandringham, or even aboard the royal yacht *Britannia.* Made by the discreet London-based leather goods company Barrow and Gale, the red boxes were the size of small suitcases and bore the royal insignia along with the words THE QUEEN embossed in gold. They could only be opened with the Queen's key and three others in the possession of her private secretary and his two deputies. (All were actually refurbished boxes that had previously been used by the Queen's father. In the fall of 2015, Elizabeth became emotional when she discovered that an anonymous Barrow and Gale craftsman had scrawled "God Bless and Keep Safe Their Majesties" inside one of the boxes made for George VI shortly after his brother's abdication thrust him onto the throne in 1936.)

The red boxes all contained paperwork directly pertaining to her schedule—from the opening of Parliament and state visits to hospital walkabouts and wreath-layings. More daunting were the ministerial boxes that arrived on her desk each morning from the Foreign Office. Each was chockablock with confidential cables, intelligence reports, cabinet minutes, documents requiring her signature, and dispatches that were meant to keep the monarch up to date on government affairs and conditions throughout Great Britain, the Commonwealth, and the world at large.

By ten each morning, Elizabeth met with her private secretary—the first of her eight private secretaries as Queen was Sir Alan Lascelles—to briefly go over the day's schedule. Although Her Majesty's staff included more than 350 full-time members and around 250 part-time or honorary positions, fewer than a dozen could lay claim to having regular contact with her.

Twenty minutes after being briefed by her private secretary, the Queen returned to the elaborately carved desk in her study, pen in hand, trying to get a head start on the day's paperwork. One of George VI's hobbies was needlework, and she sat on an eighteenth-century Chippendale chair with a seat cushion embroidered by her father. Her desk was cluttered with framed family photographs, boxes of stationery, and mementos—all of which staff members were instructed not to touch. There was also a large vase brimming with fresh-cut flowers brought in from the palace's extensive gardens each day.

There were overstuffed sofas, comfortable chairs, and along one wall a large Hepplewhite bookcase crammed with volumes ranging from biographies of prominent figures in British history to Agatha Christie mysteries and books on gardening. There would be changes over the years—the wallpaper, for example, would go from a calming blue green to apricot then back to blue green—but one thing would remain constant throughout the Queen's reign: At or near her feet there would always be at least one corgi, usually snoring.

Early in the day she methodically plucked envelopes from a basket on her desk—some of the two or three hundred letters written to the monarch each day—quickly scanned them, and then scribbled notes about how each letter should be answered by her ladies-in-waiting. In addition to feeling an obligation to respond to people who "often write such personal things," Elizabeth believed these letters offered a valuable daily snapshot of what was going on in the minds of her subjects—a look into what was "worrying people."

Beginning around 11:00 a.m. on most weekdays, the Queen was also called upon to receive the credentials of newly appointed ambassadors, bid farewell to departing envoys, and give what amounted to a brief private audience to a wide range of high commissioners, senior military personnel, jurists, clerics, artists, scientists, and visiting dignitaries from throughout the Commonwealth. These always took place in the palace's cavernous, coral-accented Bow Room, where, once the Queen gave the signal, two footmen threw open the twelve-foot-high doors to announce the next awestruck visitor.

Equerries had already briefed each guest on the proper protocol: Take a single step into the room, curtsy or bow, take three more steps into the room, bow or curtsy once more, shake the Queen's hand only after she has extended her hand, then wait for her to begin the conversation. Elizabeth, having already been briefed on each guest, usually confined the encounter to a ten-minute standing chat, although sometimes a visitor would be asked to sit with her in one of the room's damask-covered Louis XVI settees. She would signal the end of each conversation by extending her hand to the guest, at which point an equerry would politely lead that person away in preparation for the next visitor.

Every day just before lunch, the Queen downed the same bracing cocktail—two parts Dubonnet and one part gin over two ice cubes, with a single slice of lemon. Occasionally she hosted a half-dozen or so luminaries—"meritocrats" from the worlds of literature, religion, the arts, education, business, medicine, and sports. The brainchild of Prince Philip, these lunches were designed to keep the Queen abreast of what was going on in the world beyond palace walls. The fact that none of the guests knew each other or had anything in common added to what the noted photographer and artist Cecil Beaton described as the Queen's "underappreciated sense of mischief."

Usually, however, Elizabeth had her midday meal alone. Grilled

Dover sole on a bed of wilted spinach was a particular favorite, or perhaps chicken served with fresh vegetables and cheese from the royal farm at Windsor Castle. Lunch seldom lasted more than forty-five minutes, and if she didn't have to leave the palace to unveil a plaque or make a speech (she averaged around four hundred such engagements each year), the Queen was back at her desk by 1:00 p.m., hard at work on the royal boxes. At two-thirty, she normally went for a long walk with her corgis in the palace gardens. This was the Queen's principal "alone" time—only the royal gardeners were permitted in the vicinity when Elizabeth emerged for her walk, and even they were told not to speak or even look at her.

With the exception of the occasional fitting or primping by her hairdresser, the next two hours would often be devoted to brief meetings with members of her Privy Council followed by another stab at the seemingly bottomless royal dispatch boxes. At 5:00 p.m., the Queen dropped everything for teatime. A butler wheeled in the silver cart heaped with scones, muffins, gingerbread, and tiny cakes as well as crustless, round-cut sandwiches—usually watercress, egg mayonnaise, ham with mustard, and cucumber.

The Queen insisted on brewing and pouring her own Darjeeling, then nibbled on one or two sandwiches as she crumbled pieces of the muffins in her hand and placed them on the carpet for her ever-present corgis. Not that she neglected her own sweet tooth; Her Majesty had a weakness for honey and sponge teacakes, as well as "jam pennies"—tiny raspberry jam sandwiches cut into circles the size of an English penny.

After she saw the children off to bed and then had her weekly meeting with the Prime Minister, the Queen was presented with a brief summary of the day's activities in Parliament, written by one of the government's Whips. Elizabeth, determined to keep abreast of all political developments in her country, read these six-hundred-word reports on the spot.

Before dinner at 8:00 p.m., the Queen enjoyed another Dubonnet and gin cocktail. Occasionally, she would opt for a gin martini, neat. In her liquor preferences, Elizabeth was following the example set by the Queen Mother, who reluctantly moved out of Buckingham Palace and into her own quarters at nearby Clarence House.

In the course of a day, the Queen Mother usually consumed a Dubonnet and gin, a martini, two or three glasses of wine, champagne (usually Veuve Clicquot), port, and even the occasional beer. When she traveled, her ladies-in-waiting hid bottles of gin in hatboxes so that the Queen Mother could take a nip before each public appearance. (Many years after her daughter became queen, at a luncheon thrown at the Windsor Guildhall to celebrate her hundredth birthday, the Archbishop of Canterbury made the mistake of accidentally picking up the Queen Mother's wineglass. "Hey!" she snapped. "That's mine!")

Early in her reign, Elizabeth often dined in the evening with Philip, the Queen Mother, or other family members. But as time progressed, if she wasn't hosting a state dinner or attending a glittering command performance, Her Majesty often settled on supper served on a tray in front the television set in her sitting room. The cuisine remained fit for a Queen, regardless of the setting. A typical dinner might consist of pheasant shot at Sandringham, or perhaps salmon or venison shipped in from Balmoral Castle. The Queen's favorite desserts: chocolate biscuit cake, and especially the white peaches grown in her greenhouses at Windsor.

After dinner, she returned to the dreaded dispatch boxes, often working on them until well past midnight. Whenever she felt overwhelmed, she often called her closest confidante, her mother. It was a standing joke inside the Royal Family that these phone calls placed through the palace switchboard required operators to say the following words to the Queen Mother: "Good Evening, Your Majesty. Her Majesty is on the line for Your Majesty."

....

IF WINSTON CHURCHILL INITIALLY HARBORED doubts about Elizabeth's ability to handle the job, they were dispelled virtually overnight. During their weekly meetings in the opulent Bow Room—Churchill always showed up in a top hat and frock coat—the young Queen not only charmed the crusty statesman, but she impressed him with her grasp of important issues and her eye for detail. Once, when she asked him what he thought about that day's urgent dispatch from Britain's ambassador in Iraq, Churchill realized he had overlooked it. Dashing back to his offices after the meeting, he finally read the cable—and was mortified to discover that its contents were in fact extremely important.

The young Queen and the aging Prime Minister went on to develop a deep and lasting bond, in large part due to their shared love of horses. While both the Queen and her prime ministers were sworn to secrecy about what was said during these weekly audiences—no notes were ever taken and no one else was present—Churchill conceded that they talked "mostly about racing, and polo." For her part, the Queen conceded decades later that of all her audiences, the ones with Churchill were by far her personal favorite. Winston was, she said, "very obstinate" but "always such fun."

To postwar Britain and the world outside its borders, Elizabeth was an entirely new breed of monarch: a vibrant, poised, intelligent wife and mother who, along with her beguiling young family, was already breathing new life into a musty, male-dominated institution. "It was a thrilling time," Paul McCartney remembered. "I grew up with the Queen, thinking she was a babe. She was beautiful and glamorous."

So, too, was the Queen's only sibling. Princess Margaret was just twenty-one when Elizabeth became queen. With her blue-violet eyes, raven hair, and hourglass figure, Margaret already boasted a well-deserved reputation as the headstrong, hell-raising, defiantly decadent flip side to her dutiful elder sister. A denizen of London's nightclub scene who liked to be photographed with a long cigarette holder, Princess Margaret had what Cecil Beaton called a "sex twinkle" that made her "irresistible to the press and of course a thorn in the side of the establishment."

For all the young Queen's budding statesmanship that so impressed the legendary likes of Winston Churchill, the first real crisis thrust upon her had nothing at all to do with the worlds of politics or international relations. It involved Princess Margaret's complicated romantic life—the first in a cavalcade of Royal Family missteps, scandals, and misadventures that Elizabeth would have to wrestle with and, sadly, that would come to define her reign.

Margaret, at the time third in line to the throne behind Prince Charles and Princess Anne, had fallen in love with Peter Townsend, a dashing Royal Air Force Group Captain who shot down eleven German planes during the Battle of Britain. Self-effacing and matinee-idol handsome, Townsend had worked for the Royal Family for nearly a decade, first as an equerry and later as Deputy Master of the Household—a post that placed him in charge of arranging all private engagements for the Royal Family.

Unfortunately, Townsend was also sixteen years older than Margaret and the divorced father of two young sons. Once Townsend's final divorce decree was granted, he and Margaret went directly to Elizabeth and informed her that they wished to marry. To do so, they would need the consent of the sovereign.

The very next day the Queen's private secretary, Alan Lascelles, briefed her on what such a marriage would mean. Most important, the Church of England—of which Elizabeth II was head—would not recognize it. (The Church refused to remarry anyone whose marriage had ended in divorce, regardless of their status in society.) Moreover, divorced people continued to be shunned in royal circles—banned from all functions at the royal palaces, and even aboard the royal yacht.

There was more. Churchill stepped in to make the case that, should something happen to the Queen and Prince Philip when their children were still minors, Margaret might be a logical choice to serve as regent. He also reminded Elizabeth that her sister was right behind the Queen's own children in the line of succession—"Just a car crash away," Churchill liked to say, "from the throne." Given Margaret's importance in the royal scheme of things, Sir Winston continued, her marriage to a divorced commoner could cause a rift within the Commonwealth, since parliaments in those countries might reasonably conclude that such a marriage was unsuitable. Churchill flatly informed the Queen that, if her sister insisted on marrying, she would have to renounce any claim to the throne.

Elizabeth, spurred on by her firm conviction that there was no place for divorcees in the Royal Family, concocted a scheme of her own. Convinced that the romance would cool off if she could put distance between her mercurial sister and the dashing Townsend, the Queen suggested he be reassigned to serve in the British embassy in Brussels as air attaché. The couple agreed, believing that, once she turned twenty-five, Margaret was free to marry without her sister's approval.

But that was not the case. The headline-grabbing love affair between the Princess and the war hero stretched on another agonizing two years, and soon Elizabeth was consulting with the new prime minister, Anthony Eden, on how best to handle the delicate matter. With both the Church of England and Parliament opposing the marriage, the Queen was in no position to grant her sister's wish.

At Windsor Castle the Princess was told that if she insisted on marrying Townsend in a civil ceremony, a Bill of Renunciation would be placed before Parliament, stripping Margaret of all her rights, privileges, and income. It was not a sacrifice the Princess was willing to make.

Concerned that Townsend might still put up a fight, the Queen secretly enlisted the help of the Queen Mother. "I know what a great decision you have to make fairly soon," the Queen Mother wrote Margaret, "and I beg you to look at it from every angle, and to be quite sure that you don't marry somebody because you are sorry for them."

Defeated, she phoned Townsend in tears. "We reached the end of the road," he later wrote. "Our feelings for one another were unchanged but they had incurred for us so great a burden that we decided, together, to lay it down."

On October 27, 1955, Margaret informed the Archbishop of Canterbury of her decision. Four days later, she announced in a statement that was submitted to the Queen for her approval that any prospect of marriage with Townsend had ended. "I would like it to be known," Margaret's statement read, "that I have decided not to marry Group Captain Peter Townsend. Mindful that Christian marriage is indissoluble and conscious of my duty to the Commonwealth, I have resolved to put these considerations before others."

Although Elizabeth had never intended to allow the marriage to take place and had deftly maneuvered behind the scenes to thwart it, she appeared to sail above the controversy. Even Margaret, who felt that she had been misled to believe that at twenty-five she was free to marry anyone she wished, blamed the Queen's senior staff and not her sister. Ironically, within just a few years attitudes toward divorce would change dramatically. In 1978, Princess Margaret's eighteen-year marriage to photographer Anthony Armstrong-Jones (later Lord Snowden) would end, making her the first royal to divorce since Henry VIII. By the end of the century, three of the Queen's own children would be divorced.

From Berlin to the Cuban Missile Crisis to Vietnam to the assassinations of John F. Kennedy, Martin Luther King, and Robert Kennedy to the rise of the counterculture, the 1960s were a time of unparalleled political and social upheaval. Yet, remarkably, during the first thirty years of Elizabeth's reign the Royal Family was relatively untouched by scandal—a streak that was broken in 1981 when news of Prince Andrew's steamy affair with American soft-porn actress Koo Stark hit the tabloids, earning Elizabeth's second son the sobriquet "Randy Andy."

There were early exceptions, to be sure. During the Profumo spy scandal of the early 1960s, speculation arose that a member of the Royal Family was the infamous "naked waiter" who served drinks at a sex party wearing only a hood over his head and a pink ribbon tied to his genitals. (In fact, it turned out to be a top cabinet minister.) Of more direct concern to the Queen was her sister's continued unpredictable behavior. Princess Margaret kept making headlines with her freewheeling lifestyle and a string of rumored lovers that included Mick Jagger, Peter O'Toole, Peter Sellers, and Warren Beatty.

Fleet Street wasted no time holding up the wild princess as a prime example of decadence and moral decay among members of Britain's aristocracy. "The upper classes," noted journalist Malcolm Muggeridge wrote at the time, "have always been given to lying, fornication, and corrupt practices."

For all the aggravation Margaret undoubtedly caused her, the Queen never scolded or pressured Margaret to change. It was enough that, in order to avoid a constitutional crisis, Elizabeth did not hesitate to stand in the way of her own sister's one true chance at happiness.

"Of course as sisters the Queen and Princess Margaret loved each other very much, without doubt," their cousin Margaret Rhodes said. "But the Queen always puts duty first. Always."

....

Strange, but I never felt intimidated in his presence, never.
I felt from the beginning that we were two peas in a pod.

—CAMILLA

....

3

“I AM SO DESPERATE, CHARLES. PLEASE LISTEN TO ME!”

SMITH’S LAWN NEAR WINDSOR CASTLE

AUGUST 1971

“That’s a fine animal, sir!” Charles was sliding off his sweat-soaked mount at Smith’s Lawn near Windsor, and turned to see the young blonde in a green Barbour jacket and painted-on jeans standing apart from the rest of the awestruck onlookers. “I thought,” she continued brightly, “you played wonderfully well.”

The scene around the royal enclosure was too familiar to Charles: scores of comely young women, the highborn daughters of Britain’s elite, all smiling broadly and hoping to catch the Prince’s eye. Charles recognized all of them—with the exception of the one young woman audacious enough to break away from the pack and call out to the Prince directly.

Camilla Rosemary Shand stood out from the leggy, shapely,

meticulously groomed young "Windsor Club groupies" who routinely threw themselves at him, yet he was instantly charmed by her brash self-assurance. He wandered over and started up a conversation about their shared love of horses in general and polo in particular. To one spectator, the couple looked "completely relaxed in each other's company."

At this time in Charles's life, someone to talk to was precisely what he needed. His isolated, loveless childhood had been followed by what Charles later referred to as a "prison sentence" at Gordonstoun, the spartan Scottish boarding school Philip had chosen for his son. Even when it snowed, Gordonstoun's mostly middle-class students began each day with a shirtless run topped off with an icy shower. Charles's classmates, not wanting to be accused of sucking up to the future king, alternately teased, shunned, and bullied him.

At Cambridge University, where he studied archaeology, history, and anthropology, the awkwardly stiff Royal who had been called "sir" since he was named Prince of Wales at age ten made few friends. Now that he was about to embark on a seven-year tour of duty as an officer in the Royal Navy with a stint aboard the guided missile destroyer HMS *Norfolk*, Charles felt more than ever in need of a confidant.

Mummy and Papa were not about to change any time soon. Philip showed only thinly veiled contempt for his son, and the Queen worried that perhaps he was too sensitive. (Later, while serving aboard the HMS *Jupiter*, Charles broke down over the phone while telling his mother that a young seaman under his command had been killed in a car crash. "Charles," she told her private secretary, "must really learn to be tougher.")

There had always been only one person with whom Charles

could share his deepest thoughts: his adored great-uncle Lord Louis Mountbatten of Burma, the legendary World War II hero who later served as Viceroy of India and First Sea Lord. Convinced that his great-nephew would make a superb king, "Dickie," as Mountbatten was called in royal circles, invited Charles to spend long stretches of time at Broadlands, his imposing estate in Hampshire.

At Broadlands, Mountbatten (whom Charles called "Grandpapa" even though Mountbatten was his great-uncle) also undertook his own scheme to put a member of his household on the throne alongside Charles. Lord Louis introduced the Prince of Wales to dozens of suitable young women, most significantly his granddaughter (and Charles's cousin) Lady Amanda Knatchbull. Since she was only fourteen at the time, the other women were to amuse Charles until Amanda came of age.

"In a case like yours," Mountbatten bluntly advised Charles, "a man should sow his wild oats and have as many affairs as he can before settling down." Not surprisingly, women beat a path to Charles—they were literally delivered to his doorstep by aides wherever he happened to be—and, by his friends' reckoning, the Prince of Wales obliged scores of them.

But Mountbatten made it clear to his young charge that these women were not to be seriously thought of as marriage or even mistress material. "For a wife," he told Charles, "you should choose a suitable, attractive, sweet-charactered girl before she has met anyone else she might fall for." Mountbatten also told his grandnephew not to marry until he was thirty.

By arranging for Charles to conduct his more serious trysts at Broadlands, Mountbatten was also in the enviable position of being able to vet each candidate. "Grandpapa is the one person I can trust completely," Charles said, "to have my interests at heart."

Soon there would be someone else he could learn to trust, implicitly. At a dinner party not long after their encounter among the horsy set at Smith's Lawn, Lucia Santa Cruz sidled up to Charles and whispered in his ear, "I have found the perfect girl for you!"

The stunning daughter of Chile's ambassador to Great Britain, Santa Cruz spoke from experience. The Prince of Wales allegedly lost his virginity with her when he was a first-year student at Cambridge. Santa Cruz vanished, but within a matter of moments reappeared with Camilla at her side.

"Your Highness," Santa Cruz said, "I would like to present Miss Camilla Shand."

"Yes," Charles answered with a nod and a smile, "I believe we've already met."

Camilla, who at twenty-four was sixteen months Charles's senior, curtsied. Then she said, without missing a beat, "My great-grandmother and your great-great-grandfather were lovers. So how about it?"

While other ancestors were responsible for amassing the family's fortunes with shrewd real estate investments in London's Mayfair and Belgravia districts, Alice Keppel, the notorious mistress of King Edward VII, had been Camilla's role model since childhood. So firmly entrenched was Keppel as King Edward's mistress that Queen Alexandra summoned her to her husband's bedside as he lay dying. Witty, kind, beautiful, and unflappable, Keppel conducted her affairs right under the nose of her husband, George. "My job is to curtsy first," she once explained of her role as royal mistress, "and then jump into bed."

Although Alice Keppel met an ignominious end—in 1946 she died of cirrhosis of the liver—Camilla boasted about her great-grandmother's exploits even as a child. Fellow pupils at the aptly named Queen's Gate boarding school near Kensington Palace remember ten-year-old "Milla" waltzing into class and grandly ordering the other children to bow before her. "My great-grandmother was the lover of the King," she proclaimed. "We're *practically* royalty."

Actress Lynn Redgrave, who was a few years ahead of Camilla at Queen's Gate, recalled that "landing a rich husband was the top of the agenda. Camilla . . . wanted to have fun, but she also wanted to marry well because, in her mind, that would be the most fun of all."

It was Camilla's boisterous sense of humor and utter lack of self-consciousness that made her a favorite of both sexes—but especially the boys. It also helped that the other girls did not feel threatened by Milla when it came to looks. "If she'd been very beautiful," Redgrave said, "I imagine it would have been a different story."

A lantern-jawed tomboy, Camilla nevertheless attracted more male interest than any girl at the school. Her secret: "She could talk to boys about things that interested them," said Carolyn Benson, another Queen's Gate alumna. "She was never a girls' girl. She was always a boy's girl." By the time she graduated at sixteen, Camilla exuded what Benson called a "sexy confidence over men. She was quite a flirt."

From Charles's standpoint, what added vastly to Camilla's appeal was her ingrained love of the country life. Whenever she could, Camilla fled home to The Laines, the Shand estate fifty miles south of London in rural East Sussex, to join her sister Annabel and brother Mark in their favorite family pastime—foxhunting. Sibling rivalry among the Shand children was intense, however. Remarkably, Mark Shand later admitted that when he was a child he "loathed Camilla with such passion" that he tried to "murder her" by stabbing her in the neck with a penknife—which could have changed the course of history. Mark, who later became a noted playboy, travel writer, and conservationist, botched the job and ended up accidentally stabbing himself.

There was the requisite year at finishing schools in Geneva and Paris before Camilla returned to London to work briefly as a receptionist at a decorating firm—and collect the $1.5 million inheritance from a relation she barely knew. During this time, Camilla shared a flat in central London with two other aristocratic young women.

It quickly became apparent that, as a flatmate, Camilla was far from fastidious. Camilla's room looked "like a bomb had gone off in it," said her roommate Virginia Carrington, daughter of Lord Carrington. "As soon as she walked in the door, her coat and shoes and everything else hit the floor—and that's where they stayed until someone else came to pick them up." If Camilla was an unrepentant slob, it didn't seem to bother the people around her. Camilla, explained Carrington, "was so sweet it was impossible to be angry with her. She was like a big, boisterous puppy."

Besides, the real business at hand was landing a rich husband, which Camilla's flatmates promptly did: Virginia Carrington bagged Camilla's real estate tycoon uncle, Lord Aschcombe, and Jane Wyndham married Winston Churchill's grandnephew, Lord Charles Spencer-Churchill.

Asked why she hadn't been quite so fortunate, Camilla shot back: "I'm holding out for a king, like my great-grandmother did."

....

THE NIGHT THEY WERE INTRODUCED by Charles's former lover, the Prince was instantly charmed by the toothy, somewhat rough-around-the-edges country girl. Soon, Charles was bringing Camilla along on his trips to Broadlands. Not only did Mountbatten approve, but he made certain that Camilla was always given the Portico Room at Broadlands. "Now I don't want you to get any ideas," Charles joked with Camilla, "but this is the room where my parents spent their wedding night."

Lord Mountbatten was thrilled with his grandnephew's new paramour—although he cautioned Charles not to think of Camilla as anything more than a temporary diversion. According to his private secretary John Barrat, Mountbatten "knew that Camilla would make a perfect mistress for Charles until his granddaughter was of marriageable age."

In the meantime, Charles and Camilla weren't exactly hiding their relationship from the public. In the months before Charles began his naval career, they were photographed at nightclubs and restaurants throughout London, giving rise to speculation that Charles might soon pop the question.

"For the Prince, real life began with Camilla," said Charles's friend, Argentinean polo player Luis Basualdo. By the time Charles shipped out aboard the HMS *Minerva* on an eight-month tour of duty in the Caribbean in early 1973, he and Camilla were close enough to have pet names for each other: Fred and Gladys, after two characters played by Peter Sellers in Britain's popular radio program *The Goon Show.*

They exchanged passionate letters for months, so when Charles learned of Camilla's sudden engagement to Major Andrew Parker Bowles that spring, he was understandably shocked. Parker Bowles, a player on the Prince of Wales's polo team, had dated Princess Anne and was considered a rising star in the elite Blues and Royals regiment. He wasn't exactly a prince, but the

Parker Bowles family seat was Donnington Castle in Berkshire, and his father was a distant cousin and close friend of the Queen Mother. The Queen knew of the Parker Bowles family long before Camilla joined it; at fourteen, Andrew had been a page at her coronation. She also knew that Parker Bowles had a well-deserved reputation as an insatiable womanizer, and that he had bedded the wives of numerous peers.

The couple exchanged vows in the Guards Chapel near Buckingham Palace, with the Queen Mother (a longtime friend of the Parker Bowles family) and Parker Bowles's onetime girlfriend Princess Anne among the guests (Princess Margaret skipped the ceremony but made the reception). "At the time Camilla had no illusions about marrying Charles," Brooks-Baker said. "The most she hoped for was to continue as the royal mistress. But for that she had to be married, and Andrew Parker Bowles met all the requirements. Besides, from what I understand she was as besotted with Andrew as she was with Charles."

Charles took it well. When Camilla gave birth to a son, Thomas Henry *Charles*, on December 8, 1974, the Prince agreed to be a godfather. As might have been expected, rumors flew that the boy was actually Charles's son. While the remote possibility existed, the fact is that Charles was at sea off the coasts of Australia and New Zealand during the time Tom would have been conceived. (Four years later, Camilla would give birth to a daughter, Laura Rose.)

For the Prince of Wales, the rest of the decade was a blur of sexual activity. He romanced the tony likes of Georgina Russell, daughter of Great Britain's ambassador to Spain; the Duke of Wellington's daughter, Lady Jane Wellesley; Lady Tryon; Lady Victoria and Lady Caroline Percy, daughters of the Duke of Northumberland; Lady Cecil Kerr, daughter of the Marquis of

Lothian; Lady Leonora Grosvenor and Lady Jane Grosvenor, both sisters of the Duke of Westminster; Louise Astor, daughter of Lord Astor of Hever; Lady Charlotte Manners, daughter of the Duke of Rutland; Lady Camilla Fane, daughter of the Earl of Westmorland; Lady Henrietta FitzRoy, daughter of the Duke of Grafton; Bettina Lindsay, daughter of Lord Balneil; Davina Sheffield, granddaughter of Lord McGowan; brewery heiress Sabrina Guinness (who had already had relationships with Mick Jagger, Jack Nicholson, Rod Stewart, and David Bowie), and Fiona Watson, daughter of Lord Manton. Fiona distinguished herself from her rather staid fellow aristocrats by posing nude for *Penthouse* under an assumed name.

....

NOT ALL OF CHARLES'S WOMEN were plucked from Britain's upper classes. In 1974 he was so smitten with Laura Jo Watkins, the daughter of American Admiral James Watkins, that he invited her to his maiden speech in the House of Lords. For months he secretly dated the actress Susan George, best known for her turn opposite Dustin Hoffman in the film *Straw Dogs*.

Then there were the dozens of women introduced to him by friends like Luis Basualdo. Charles's polo chum drove around the countryside picking up tenant farmers' daughters—"some seventeen or younger, but I told them to tell Charles they were nineteen"—giving them one hundred pounds (the equivalent in 2015 to well over $1,500) and delivering them to the Prince at Lodsworth House, the Sussex estate owned by Basualdo's father-in-law. One girl, who worked in a local butcher's shop, "looked like she was fourteen but she was probably eighteen. Stunning," Basualdo recalled, "a dead ringer for Mia Farrow."

Basualdo would bring Charles as many as four girls at a time for the purpose of playing sex games at Lodsworth House. Although the Prince preferred that the girls not be drunk, Basualdo made certain they had had a few drinks before meeting him.

Prince Charles's favorite nocturnal game was "Murder in the Dark," with Basualdo playing the murderer, Charles the detective, and the girls the victims. Groping about with the lights off, Charles was supposed to pinch the girls in the nose to make them scream. Instead, he would "find a girl, pinch her somewhere naughty, and then start kissing her. It was dark, so he'd throw them on sofas and have sex with them, there and then."

According to Basualdo, who was also Christina Onassis's on-again, off-again lover, the two men "shared dozens of girls. Of course I asked some of them what he was like in bed. They would laugh and tell me he was good. I never heard any complaints." Charles was worried that he might be caught with an underage girl, however, and asked Basualdo to bring him "society girls of twenty-one or twenty-two."

One of these was a young Colombian socialite. Their tryst took place at Basualdo's house in London's swank Belgravia district. "They were so noisy," he said. "The headboard was banging, banging—it woke up the rest of house. Next time I saw Charles he was apologetic but laughed."

Most of these encounters continued to take place near the polo grounds in Sussex, in Lodsworth House. "We had a massive attic furnished with sofas and a big bed," Basualdo said. "It became his bolthole. I said he could make as much noise as he wanted." There, Charles would come in from playing polo and announce loudly: "Ahem, I'm just going upstairs to take a bath"—which, added Basualdo "was his euphemism for sneaking a lady upstairs."

At one point, the Prince's polo teammates, well aware of what he was up to after nearly every match, sneaked into the attic while he was making love to a girl. When he chased them out, they locked the attic door from the outside—trapping him inside. Charles pounded on the door for thirty minutes before Basualdo showed up to let him out. "Do not ever do that to me again," he shouted. "Do you understand?"

One of his longest and least-known affairs began just weeks after he attended the christening of Tom Parker Bowles. "There was one girl who managed to remain very nearly anonymous," said Stephen Barry, the prince's longtime valet. "The Prince saw more of her than anyone realized. Her name was Janet Jenkins, and she was a Welsh girl living in Canada."

Blonde, thirty-year-old Jenkins was in fact the receptionist at the British consulate in Montreal, and within hours of their first meeting they made love in her apartment while the Prince's bodyguards stood outside in the hallway. During that and all subsequent encounters, Charles and Jenkins did not use birth control, and it remains unlikely that the Prince of Wales ever considered using contraception with any of his lovers. "Neither of us," Jenkins conceded, "thought of using protection." (Inevitably, this laissez-fair attitude toward birth control led to numerous unsubstantiated rumors of abortions and illegitimate children—including Janet's son Jason, who was born on June 13, 1984, just nine months after one of Jenkins's sexual encounters with the Prince of Wales. Jenkins, who listed her husband as the father on Jason's birth certificate, denied that her son was the product of her affair with the future king.)

Over the years, Charles wrote a series of lengthy, torrid love letters to Jenkins, and rearranged his schedule on several occasions so that he could fly to Montreal to be with her. "He always included official functions," she later recalled, "so that no one suspected a thing."

No one except Camilla, whose polo club chums kept her abreast of all the significant players in Charles's love life. Another was Lady Sarah Spencer, who stuck by Charles even after he abandoned her in the middle of a date to make love to his Colombian bombshell.

At this point, Sarah's younger sister also hovered in the wings. Lady Diana Spencer had just returned from a year at the exclusive Swiss boarding school Institut Alpin Videmanette when she met the Prince of Wales for the first time in a muddy field at Althorp, the Spencers' thirteen-thousand-acre estate in Northamptonshire.

In the end, Charles unceremoniously dumped Sarah Spencer for socialite Cristabel Barria-Borsage. The Venezuelan beauty later claimed that in bed, Charles insisted on being called Arthur—as in King Arthur.

Throughout it all, "Gladys" was always just a phone call away from "Fred." After he left the Royal Navy, Charles turned to Camilla—not the Queen—for advice on what to do with the rest of his life. Her Majesty had let it be known through channels that he might be appointed Governor-General of Australia, if that were to his liking.

Charles chafed at the notion of being his mother's proxy Down Under. The job was essentially ceremonial, and he knew that he faced a lifetime of ribbon-cuttings and hospital walkabouts. Instead, Camilla urged the Prince to make his mark in the nonprofit world, lending his name to a wide range of charities that reflected his personal interests. The result was the Prince's

Trust, which over the course of the next several decades would raise hundreds of millions of dollars for a wide range of British charities.

Like his frugal mother, who told the chef at Buckingham Palace to reuse the lemon wedges that had not been squeezed at royal banquets, Charles also kept a close eye on his personal finances. For more than six hundred years, the Duchy of Cornwall—135,000 acres of farmland, forests, waterfront, and commercial property encompassing Cornwall and twenty-one other counties—had been generating tax-exempt revenue that flowed directly to the future monarch. In addition, Charles received the tax-free net income from the Duchy's extensive investment portfolio. (By 2016, the yearly sum would exceed $45 million.)

In August 1979, Camilla comforted a weeping Charles when IRA terrorists blew up Lord Mountbatten's fishing boat off the coast of Ireland, killing Mountbatten and two others, including Mountbatten's fourteen-year-old grandson. Determined to keep his promise to his great-uncle, he proposed marriage to Mountbatten's granddaughter Amanda Knatchbull after she turned twenty-one, only to have her reject him.

In the wake of Mountbatten's death, Charles struck up a romance with high-strung Scottish heiress Amanda ("Whiplash") Wallace. Charles proposed to the cameo-perfect Wallace—twice. Wallace was still mulling over the second proposal when, during a birthday party for the Queen Mother, she became enraged over the fact that he never left the side of his former girlfriend Camilla.

Wallace had reason to be miffed. Charles had just purchased Highgrove, a country manor in Gloucestershire, from Member of Parliament Maurice Macmillan, son of former Prime Minister

Harold Macmillan. Located two hours west of London, Highgrove also happened to be a twenty-seven-minute drive from Bolehyde Manor in Chippenham, home to Mr. and Mrs. Andrew Parker Bowles.

Camilla realized, of course, that on his way to Highgrove Charles occasionally made a detour to the home of Lady Dale Tryon, stylish socialite and fashion designer and the only other woman who might justifiably lay claim to being the Prince of Wales's mistress. Nicknamed "Kanga" by the future King for her Australian roots and her bouncy personality, Lady Tryon shared the Prince's bed with Camilla off and on for a period stretching over twenty years. More important, Camilla knew that, with Lord Mountbatten gone, Kanga was the only other person in the world Charles trusted implicitly.

"He would ring out of the blue," Tryon said later of the "comfort stops" Charles made at her estate, "and say he would be passing by and would I mind if he stopped in." Tryon always greeted him with a glass of whisky, and then, she said, "we'd chat before making ourselves more 'comfortable.'"

Neither woman had any illusions about marrying Prince Charles, but unlike Camilla, Lady Tryon was not about to remain in the shadows. "Kanga was Australian and much less uptight than the rest of that set," veteran royals correspondent James Whitaker said. "She wanted everyone to know that she was the Prince of Wales's mistress. It was hard for her to keep her mouth shut and play along. But it wasn't easy—not even for her."

....

SOME OF THE SAME FRUSTRATIONS would be felt even more keenly by the next young woman to step into Charles's life. Lady

Diana Spencer was just nineteen and a part-time kindergarten teacher (the employment agency she signed up with also sent Diana out on the odd housecleaning job) when she met Charles a second time at a barbecue in the summer of 1980. They were seated next to each other, and soon the conversation turned to Mountbatten's funeral. "You looked so sad as you had to walk down the aisle," Diana told the Prince. "I have never seen anything so sad before. My heart bled as I saw you so, and I thought; 'That is not right, you are completely alone, you should have someone with you who you trust.' "

Charles was moved by the young woman's spontaneous and clearly genuine expression of sympathy. Diana's innate sense of compassion was rooted in her own desperately unhappy childhood. From the beginning, she felt unloved and unwanted. Following the births of her sisters Jane and Sarah and a son who lived only ten hours, Diana's parents were so determined that their next child be a boy that they did not even bother to pick out a girl's name. When a third daughter was born, it took them a week to arrive at the name Diana Frances. Another three years would pass before the birth of Diana's brother Charles, the male heir they had so desperately desired.

Diana was only six when her mother walked out on the family. Left to be raised by a succession of sadistic nannies—one routinely struck Diana on the head with a wooden spoon, another banged Diana's and her brother's heads together whenever they misbehaved—Diana cried herself to sleep "every night. But in the end I think it helped me become a better person. I can appreciate other people's pain because I've experienced it."

Like so many British schoolgirls, Diana had had a serious crush on the Prince of Wales. A portrait of Charles hung over her bed.

"She had pictures of him everywhere," remembered Diana's piano teacher Penny Walker. "Diana *adored* him."

Their casual encounter at the barbecue might well have amounted to nothing if Charles, now thirty-two, hadn't been under pressure from his domineering father to find a bride. He turned to the two people he trusted most—Camilla and Kanga Tryon—to come up with a proper wife for England's future sovereign.

Without hesitation, Camilla invited Kanga to meet with her at Bolehyde Manor, where the two royal mistresses were, claimed Tryon, "most civilized toward each other." At Camilla's suggestion, they each wrote down the names of women they thought would make suitable brides for Charles. They each came up with three names, but, Kanga said, "the only name Camilla and I both came up with was Diana Spencer, so she went to the top of the list."

"She is just lovely—a true English rose," Tryon told Camilla. "And she is going to look marvelous in a tiara."

Camilla smiled in agreement. "Yes," she added, mulling over their choice. "Of course, she's very young. She's very shy, too, and sweet. A little frightened I think. I don't think she'll be causing any trouble." ("How wrong can you be?" Tryon laughed when she recounted the exchange years later.)

After the Prince's two mistresses named Diana as their top pick for a royal bride, Diana's name was added to the royal calendar. Charles and Diana's first date was a performance of Verdi's *Requiem* at the Royal Albert Hall followed by a cold buffet in Charles's private quarters at Buckingham Palace. Later, Charles invited Diana to spend a weekend of sailing at Cowes, the picturesque seaport town on the Isle of Wight, followed by the most prized invitation of all: the chance to join the Prince for fishing, hiking, and other country pursuits at the Royal Family's favorite and decidedly most rustic venue, Balmoral Castle.

For all their considerable powers of persuasion, Charles's mistresses at first could not convince him that the shy girl with the upward glance was the one. They got some assistance in the unlikely form of two key figures whom Diana would ultimately come to view as her mortal enemies: the Queen's private secretary Robert Fellowes, who was married to Diana's sister Jane, and the Queen Mother, whose most trusted lady-in-waiting was Diana's grandmother, Lady Fermoy.

Unlike nearly all other candidates for the position, Diana possessed what was regarded as the most important qualification. "All my friends had boyfriends but not me," she later said, "because I knew that I had to keep myself tidy for whatever was coming my way."

"First on the list was virginity," Brooks-Baker said of three basic requirements a royal bride would have to possess. "Second was the ability to do the job. Third, she must be seen to have the potential to bear heirs to the throne." Those heirs, descended from one of England's oldest families, the Spencers, would turn out to be more authentically British than the Teutonic Windsors.

....

FOR MONTHS, CAMILLA HAD BEEN worried about the psychological toll all the pressure to wed an heir was having on the man she loved. Philip routinely harangued his son about the immediate need to produce an heir, and after each tension-filled conversation with his father, Charles turned to Camilla for consolation. Camilla was the woman he loved, he told her, and she was the woman he wanted to marry. Certainly Parker Bowles, who was now seventy-six hundred miles away in Rhodesia to assist in that country's transition to full independence as the state of Zimbabwe, had given Camilla grounds for divorce. In his short time in Africa, Camilla's faithless spouse had already cheated on his wife with two different women—affairs that were duly chronicled in Britain's unslakable tabloid press.

Charles urged Camilla to leave her husband—the first step, perhaps, in a process that might somehow eventually lead to marriage for "Fred" and "Gladys." They both knew, of course, that this was impossible. Camilla also had her own interests in mind. While she held no place at court—the Queen and her mother heartily disapproved of Charles's "friendship" with Mrs. Parker Bowles—Camilla did not wish to be seen as another Wallis Simpson coming between a future king and his destiny.

Nevertheless, Charles continued to stall, leaving a bewildered Diana to wonder if he would ever pop the question. Hounded by reporters, Diana became increasingly desperate. "She came through the door one day and burst out weeping," one of her roommates recalled.

"He won't ask me," she cried. "I don't understand. Why won't he ask me?"

Convinced by Camilla that Diana was too young and unaffected to suspect anything—and that if Diana did find out about their affair she would simply accept it as a fact of royal married life—Charles asked the Queen for her approval. Elizabeth, evidently unaware of all the behind-the-scenes intrigue, was delighted; she and the rest of the Royal Family were fond of Diana, and particularly impressed with how she had handled the press.

Charles was about to ask Diana to be his wife in late February when his prized racehorse Alibar suddenly collapsed while being exercised and died. Diana immediately drove to the stables to commiserate with Charles, only to discover that he had already turned to Camilla for comfort.

Several days later, Charles summoned Diana to the Parker Bowles estate. There, in the gardens of Bolehyde Manor with Camilla peering from behind a curtain on the second floor, Charles asked Diana to marry him. "Yes, please," she answered, and in a spontaneous burst of enthusiasm that left Charles taken aback, threw her arms around him.

The Queen threw a dinner party at Windsor to celebrate, and two days later the happy couple showed off her eighteen-carat sapphire and diamond engagement ring to the press.

"Are you in love?" a reporter asked them.

"Of course," Diana replied indignantly. But even now, Camilla was never far from Charles's mind, and he weighed his words carefully. "Whatever 'in love' is," he snickered. Charles conceded to one friend that he was definitely not in love, but that he was going to marry Diana anyway because she had "all the right qualities."

Soon Charles was preparing to depart on a five-week solo tour of Australia, New Zealand, Venezuela, and the United States. Camilla had offered to keep an eye on Diana while he was gone, and toward that end invited her to dinner at Bolehyde Manor. Diana noticed the invitation, written in longhand by Camilla and referencing the pending wedding. The invitation was dated prior to the day Charles proposed—clear evidence that Camilla was in on the planning.

Charles, unhappy that he was being forced into a marriage he clearly had no enthusiasm for, wasted no time whittling away at his fiancée's self-confidence. Slipping his arm around her waist, he pinched some skin and cracked, "Oh, a bit chubby here, aren't we?"—a remark that sent Diana into a downward spiral of depression and bulimia. Forcing herself to vomit five or six times a day, Diana's waist eventually shrank from twenty-nine to twenty-two inches.

At one event, he chastised her for wearing a chic black dress to a charity event in London. "Only mourners wear black," he sniffed. The remark was heard by Monaco's Princess Grace, who ushered her into the ladies room, bolted the door, praised her fashion sense, and then listened patiently to Diana's misgivings about becoming Princess of Wales. "Don't worry," Princess Grace said, laughing. "It will get a lot worse!"

Around the same time, before he left for Australia, a playful Diana was sitting on Charles's lap in his Buckingham Palace office when a call came through from Camilla, who wanted to say goodbye. Diana instinctively left the room so that Charles and Camilla could have a private conversation. Later, Diana said that moment left her "heartbroken," for it was then that she realized she had a serious rival in Camilla.

As the wedding drew near, Diana—who had always been "Duch" (short for "Duchess") to family and friends—grew increasingly desperate. Two days before the wedding, she discovered a diamond bracelet Charles had made for Camilla with the intertwined initials F and G, for Fred and Gladys.

"I can't marry him, I can't do this," she told her sisters on the eve of the wedding.

"Well, bad luck, Duch," they said, pointing out that tens of millions of dollars' worth of souvenirs bearing the likeness of the newlyweds had already been sold. "Your face is on the tea towels so you're too late to chicken out."

1

2

3

Elizabeth had already reigned as Queen for twenty-three years when Prince Charles and Camilla got together after a polo match in 1975. During a break in their affair, he met the only movie star he claimed to have a serious crush on—Barbra Streisand.

4

5

6

7

A lifelong horsewoman, the Queen rode sidesaddle during the Trooping of the Colour parade even after blank rounds from a revolver startled her mount in 1981. She began taking a carriage during the ceremonies six years later.

8

It was just for laughs when Diana smashed a prop bottle over her husband's head on the set of the film *The Living Daylights* in 1989. But Diana was already begging the Queen to end Charles's affair with Camilla. The Queen Mother, standing between Elizabeth and Diana on the royal balcony at Buckingham Palace, disliked Diana but detested Camilla.

10

The great-granddaughter of Edward VII's mistress, Camilla prided herself in carrying on the family tradition. When her prince was unavailable, Camilla ran errands, smoked by the pool, and—in true aristocratic fashion—rode to the hounds.

11

12

13

14

Diana's death in a Paris car crash on August 31, 1997, shocked the world and nearly toppled the monarchy. Stunned, the Queen took to the airwaves in an attempt to win back her subjects.

15

16

After two years as the most hated woman in Britain, Camilla made her first public appearance with Charles at London's Ritz Hotel in 1999. It was another year before the Queen, whose holographic image loomed large at an art gallery visited by Charles, finally agreed to meet her son's mistress.

17

Grandeur at Windsor. On December 19, 2004, the Queen (standing center left at the table) hosted one of the several state banquets held at Windsor Castle and Buckingham Palace each year. This one was to honor French president Jacques Chirac.

18

The Queen seems to be having problems with the ostrich feathers in Camilla's hat as the newlyweds leave St. George's Chapel at Windsor Castle. At the time, 93 percent of the public opposed Camilla's becoming queen, and Charles promised she wouldn't be. He has since reneged.

After a polo match, Prince William gives his new stepmother a kiss. Despite the grief she caused Diana, both William and Harry embraced Camilla as the love of their father's life.

19

20

Touring India in March of 2006, Camilla sat on a throne to watch the Rajasthan Parade in Jaipur. She nearly collapsed twice from the heat. Camilla, Prince Philip (left), and the Queen were in high spirits at a Buckingham Palace banquet honoring Norway's King Harald V.

21

Kate Middleton got William's attention modeling lingerie in a St. Andrews University fashion show in 2001, but they broke up six years later. "Waity Katie" hit the London clubs, joined an all-women rowing team, and acted as if she just didn't care. The strategy worked.

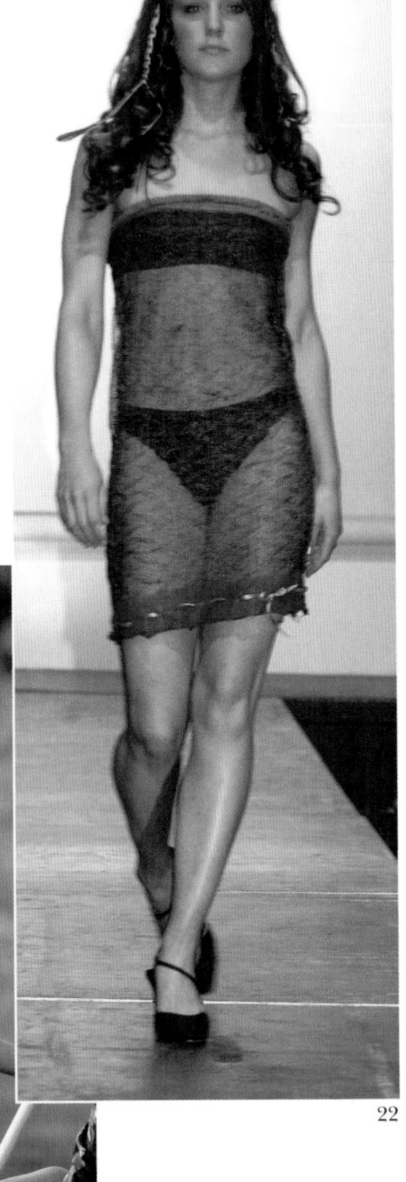

22

23

....

THE WEDDING OF THE TWENTIETH Century took place on July 29, 1981, at St. Paul's Cathedral and was witnessed by a worldwide television audience of 750 million people. Feeling like "a lamb to the slaughter," Diana walked down the aisle knowing all eyes were on her. But as she approached the altar, her eyes were trained on Camilla—"pale gray, veiled pillbox hat, saw it all, her son Tom standing on a chair . . ."

Another guest, Charles's Canadian paramour Janet Jenkins, watched Camilla closely as well. For years, their shared lover had always talked to Jenkins about "how wonderful Camilla was—he never spoke of Diana." Jenkins knew that Charles "was in love with only one woman and that was Camilla. She was pulling the strings and the levers, definitely."

At the wedding, Jenkins was "fascinated to get a look at this woman he preferred to his gorgeous young bride. Camilla had this cool, Cheshire cat grin as she watched them march down the aisle. She just seemed so delighted with the whole arrangement."

From the very start, Diana later said, "there were three of us in this marriage, so it was a bit crowded." Yet when she looked at Camilla on her wedding day, something "clicked" inside her. "I desperately wanted it to work. I desperately loved my husband, and I wanted to share everything together. . . . Here was a fairy story that everyone wanted to work."

As far as Camilla was concerned, the fairy story was working splendidly—just as she planned it. Both she and Kanga Tryon were convinced that in Diana they had a pretty, guileless, malleable child who would bend to the ways of her elders. "Diana is a very sweet girl," Camilla told Harold Brooks-Baker, "and she will give Charles beautiful children." Diana's friend Lady Elsa Bowker even recalled Camilla, whose passion for horses was surpassed only by the Queen's, favorably comparing the Princess of Wales to a "beautiful brood mare."

Willingly, even eagerly casting herself in the role of royal mistress, Camilla had already proven herself adept at maneuvering courtiers, courtesans, and even members of the Royal Family like so many pieces on a chessboard. Everyone was right where she wanted them—or so Camilla believed. "Diana moved into Kensington Palace like she was supposed to," Elsa Bowker recalled, "and they told her to do what they said, what the Queen wanted."

Diana had other plans. "They thought of me as a blank slate," Diana told Lady Bowker, "and they didn't expect someone like me could possibly have a mind of her own. They were wrong."

"YOU'RE CRYING WOLF," CHARLES SHOUTED as he stormed through the main hall and out the front door of Sandringham in his riding clothes. "I'm not going to listen. You're always doing this to me." His wife, now three months pregnant with their first child, stood on the second-floor landing and was vowing to throw herself down the main staircase. "I am so desperate, Charles," she pleaded. "Please listen to me!"

Over the years, Diana's unhappiness over Charles's affair with Camilla would drive her to slash her wrists with a razor, stab herself in the chest with a pocketknife, and hurl herself against a glass display case, cutting herself badly in the process. This, however, was arguably the most spectacular—and dangerous—action she had ever taken to get her husband's attention.

The Queen and Princess Margaret were on the main floor, overhearing everything as the bitter quarrel that started in the couple's upstairs rooms spilled into Sandringham's entrance hall. A blood-chilling scream, followed by the sound of a tumbling body, and the Queen came running to find her daughter-in-law in a heap at the foot of the stairs.

The Queen was, Diana later said, "absolutely horrified. She was so frightened." Before any footmen arrived, Princess Margaret comforted Diana while the Queen, trembling, called for medical help. Incredibly, Charles just kept right on walking—out the front door and twelve minutes down the road to the stables of the Royal Stud. He would eventually learn that, although the bruises on Diana's lower abdomen were of concern to her gynecologist, tests showed the fetus had not been harmed.

To the outside world, all appeared well in Camelot. A blue-eyed, seven-pound, one-and-a-half-ounce heir was born at 9:03 p.m. on June 21—an induced labor timed not to interfere with the Prince's polo schedule—and the world rejoiced at the arrival of the future king. No one was more pleased than the Queen, who could breathe easier now that—regardless of her son's dogged refusal to give up Camilla—the future of the monarchy was assured.

Unlike his own father, who had been playing squash with an equerry when Charles was born, the Prince of Wales was at his wife's side throughout the delivery. At the moment their son was born, Charles whispered to his wife, "Fantastic, beautiful. You are a darling."

Yet there was still little they could agree on, including the name of their first child. She preferred the trendy Oliver or Sebastian.

He wanted to call their newborn Arthur or Albert (after Queen Victoria's husband). After a week, they settled on William Arthur Philip Louis Windsor.

Diana was surprised at how easily her stiff, obstinate, even cruelly detached husband took to fatherhood. Although neither he nor Diana ever contemplated changing a diaper—that task was strictly the responsibility of no-nonsense nanny Barbara Barnes—he often volunteered to give Baby William his bottle and rock him to sleep.

Not that the new family dynamic made him a more caring spouse. When asked what he gave Diana for her twenty-first birthday on July 1—just ten days after giving birth—Charles replied curtly, "Some flowers and a hug."

The undeniable joys of motherhood notwithstanding, Diana continued to battle chronic depression and bulimia—and not entirely because of her husband's infidelity. By this time, Diana was the most photographed, imitated, celebrated, admired woman in the world. She was both an avatar of fashion and a courageous humanitarian whose personal touch—Diana was the first to dispel unfounded fears about the disease by embracing AIDS patients, for example—made her the "People's Princess."

If Diana was unquestionably the glistening jewel in the Windsor crown—the one person who had breathed new life into the monarchy—the Queen's Men in Gray never let her know it. In fact, Diana's every move was monitored, her every action strictly controlled. She could count on stinging rebukes from the Palace virtually every day—negative comments on what she did, said, or wore that were classified under the general heading of "constructive criticism."

Some of the fault-finding came directly from Elizabeth. Diana told her bodyguard, Ken Wharfe, that at one point the Queen demanded that she drop AIDS from her list of personal crusades. "Why don't you," she asked her daughter-in-law, "get involved in something a little more pleasant."

The Princess of Wales, still vexed by feelings of worthlessness rooted in her childhood, took it all very personally. "I think Diana was very angry and annoyed that the Queen could not see what she was doing," Wharfe said. "Diana felt a member of the Royal Family should be involved with campaigns to find a cure for AIDS."

"All I want is one 'Well done,' that's all," Diana said. None was forthcoming. To cope, she turned to spiritual advisors, psychic healers, astrologers, and psychiatrists who prescribed large doses of Valium. Nothing worked. One friend, Lord Palumbo, witnessed the "crying, sobbing, wailing for two or three hours until her black mood had run its course." Then she would charm and delight a crowd at some public event "as if there had been no darkness at all."

Despite the strains caused by his continued devotion to Camilla, Charles longed for a daughter, and toward that end was intent on resuming what he called the royal couple's "breeding program." When Diana told Charles about the second pregnancy, it struck her as odd that he took it in stride. They had sex sporadically if at all during this period. "Diana told me chances for intimacy were limited. I took her to mean nonexistent," said Lady Bowker. Diana could only say, provocatively, that the blessed event was occurring "as if by a miracle."

Blocked by Camilla from forging an emotional connection with her own husband, Diana took lovers of her own. One, Captain James Hewitt, had been Diana's riding instructor at Kensington Palace. Although he would initially claim that he and Diana had not met until after Harry's birth, ginger-haired Hewitt changed his story in 2005, claiming under hypnosis that their affair had begun in earnest shortly after William's birth in June 1982. In early 1984, he received an urgent call from the Princess. "I'm pregnant, James," she told him.

Perhaps Charles was too busy to remember precisely whom he slept with, or when. What neither Diana nor Camilla knew was that, less than three months earlier, Charles had secretly resumed his affair with Janet Jenkins at Highgrove. "We slipped back into that familiar intimacy," Jenkins said, "that predated the marriage." When Jenkins married a wealthy Canadian businessman that December, she was already three months pregnant.

Diana, unaware that Jenkins was back in the picture, took some consolation in the fact that Charles was a doting father. Despite all the hours spent with other women and a schedule packed with walkabouts, charity events, and groundbreakings, the Prince clearly reveled in spending time with the rambunctious toddler his parents called "Wills."

As her second pregnancy drew to a close, Diana was hopeful that the dark cloud of gloom that had always hung over the marriage had begun to recede. The last six weeks before Harry's birth, Charles and Diana were "very, very close to each other—the closest we've ever, ever been and ever will be."

When Henry Charles Albert David was born on September 15, 1984, she called Hewitt from the hospital to tell him it was a boy—minutes before the happy news was announced to the world at large.

The child, she told him, clearly hoping to elicit a response, had red hair.

....

CHARLES, WHO HAD HOPED FOR a girl and was well aware of Diana's infatuation with Hewitt, took one look at Harry and snapped "Oh, God, it's a boy. And he even has red hair."

This was the moment, Diana later said, when "something inside me closed off."

Diana's mother, Frances Shand Kydd, was also aware of the rumors concerning Hewitt. When Charles continued to complain at the christening that Harry had "rusty hair," Shand Kydd knew what he was implying. "You should just be happy," she reminded him, "that your son is healthy." Unaccustomed to being lectured in such a manner, Charles refused to have any further contact with his mother-in-law.

As Harry grew to look less like a Windsor and more like Hewitt, Camilla wondered aloud to an old family friend if the rumors could be true. At the point Harry was conceived, Charles was spending nearly all his time—or at least so Camilla thought—with his mistress, not his wife. In the end, she tamped down whatever suspicions she may have had. Charles was utterly devoted to both his sons, and any scandal involving Harry's paternity would only tear the Prince of Wales—not to mention the monarchy—apart.

William was five and Harry not yet three when Charles moved more or less full-time into Highgrove—away from the city-loving Diana and just twelve minutes from Middlewick House, the eighteenth-century manor Camilla and Andrew Parker Bowles now called home. From this point on, things took an almost comical cloak-and-dagger turn as Charles and Camilla plotted and schemed, clumsily, to conceal their affair from Diana.

On those days when Diana was at Highgrove, Charles would crawl out of his bed to tryst with Camilla just inside the garden walls. Then Charles would creep back into his room, put on a new pair of pajamas—and leave his valet, Ken Stronach, a pile of dirty clothes to deal with.

"There was mud and muck everywhere," Stronach recalled. "They'd obviously been doing it in the open air."

On other occasions, when Diana remained in the city, Stronach was instructed to treat Camilla as mistress of the house. A guest room was assigned to her, but after midnight the Prince of Wales would switch off the elaborate alarm system guarding his room so that Camilla could sneak in. Stronach was told to mess up the bed in Camilla's room so that the servants would think she had slept in it.

Stronach also had orders to personally examine all glassware to make sure there were no lipstick traces, and to empty all ashtrays that the chain-smoking Camilla might have used. Charles always kept a framed photo of Camilla at his bedside; packing it away was on Stronach's growing list of things to do whenever Diana popped in to Highgrove.

Wielding his considerable influence to make sure that Parker Bowles's assignments kept him far from home for weeks or months at a time, Charles frequently called on Camilla at Middlewick House. Once Royal Protection officers alerted Camilla that the Prince was on his way, all lights at Middlewick House were switched off so he could pull inside Middlewick's driveway without being spotted—a bit of espionage Camilla's servants called "The Blackout." Since Charles always slept in Camilla's room and then departed before daylight, they called him "The Prince of Darkness."

On one occasion, Diana arrived at Highgrove unannounced to find Charles's room staged with props: a half-eaten snack, an empty glass of sherry, a folded TV guide with shows circled in pencil—all designed to make it look as if he had just stepped out.

"I mean, *really*," she screamed before collapsing on his bed with laughter.

It wasn't really a laughing matter to Diana, though, and she let Charles know. The Prince was stony and evasive, but when she could corner him their arguments escalated quickly. "Do you know who I am?" he demanded during one shouting match.

"You are a fucking animal!" was Diana's blunt reply. Doors slammed, crockery and glassware flew indiscriminately, and during one spat an angry Charles hurled his heavy boots against a wall. The couple's respective bodyguards worried where this all might lead. It was already well established that Diana suffered severe bouts of depression that led her to harm herself. Now Charles was telling royal lawyer Lord Arnold Goodman, "I have nothing to live for." Goodman went so far as to label the Prince of Wales as "suicidal"—a result of the severe depression he felt over the unraveling of his marriage and the impact it was having on his children. "We went through Highgrove and locked up all the firearms," a Royal Protection officer said. "We didn't want anyone getting shot. They were so angry, it was a real possibility."

The children were already caught in the crossfire. When Diana, weeping after a particularly bitter row, locked herself in the bathroom, ten-year-old William slipped tissues under the door. "Mummy, don't cry," he told her. "I hate to see you sad."

Camilla commiserated with her lover, but reassured him that Diana would eventually accept the status quo. "Camilla felt that somehow Diana hadn't caught on to their little game," a friend of both women said, "and that if she had, she would play by the rules as all royal wives have."

Kanga Tryon believed Camilla was convinced that "Diana had no choice, that she'd just grow up. What the hell was she going to do? Divorce was not an option. No one thought the Queen would ever allow it."

Camilla was at her younger sister Annabel's fortieth birthday party, chatting with Charles and another male guest downstairs, when the party turned very quiet. Suddenly Diana appeared in the room. "Okay, boys," she said, "I'm just going to have a quick word with Camilla and I'll be up in a minute." They shot out of the room, Diana later said, "like chickens with no heads." She sensed "all hell breaking loose" among the partygoers upstairs, and she was right. Charles had no idea what his unpredictable wife was up to, and he feared the worst.

Charles's wife got straight to the point. "Camilla," she said, "I would just like you to know that I know exactly what is going on between you and Charles. I wasn't born yesterday."

Camilla's hands were trembling; the ice in her vodka and tonic clinked loudly. Had she obeyed proper protocol, the woman Diana derisively called "The Rottweiler" would have curtsied the moment Diana entered the room. Aside from being the most famous woman on the planet, Diana outranked every woman in the realm except for the Queen and the Queen Mother.

Instead, Camilla demanded to know why Diana refused to simply look the other way. "You've got everything you ever wanted," she said pleadingly. "You've got all the men in the world to fall in love with you and you've got two beautiful children. What more do you want?"

Taken aback by Camilla's impudence, Diana shouted back,

"I want my husband. I'm sorry I'm in the way, I obviously am in the way and it must be hell for both of you but I do know what is going on. Don't treat me like an idiot."

Curiously, the confrontation between the two women did not have the intended consequences. Rather than feel contrite, Charles saw Camilla as the victim, and upbraided Diana for her "monstrous" behavior. While a devastated Diana wept over the hopelessness of her situation, Camilla now saw in Diana a worthy adversary. If the Princess could not be mollified, then a formal separation was indeed possible—and with it the possibility of even more time with Charles. "Charles does not like to be pushed," Janet Jenkins said. "Diana pushed too far, and Camilla took advantage of that."

No matter. The twentieth century had entered its final decade, and Diana was now intent on seeing her son William crowned the next monarch—not Charles. Toward that end, she would wage a public relations campaign to discredit her husband.

Part of the plan involved portraying Charles as an uncaring, uninvolved father.

....

THE WORLD KNEW OF DIANA'S love for her children; their trips to theme parks, movie theaters, and fast-food restaurants—all designed to give William and Harry something akin to a "normal" childhood—were well documented by the press. So, too, were visits to hospitals and homeless shelters that Diana hoped would instill in the young princes a sense of compassion and civic responsibility.

Less well-publicized was Charles's own warm and nurturing relationship with his sons. Like his parents before him, the Prince eschewed public displays of affection, deeming them undignified, unmanly, and, in the words of one courtier, "unworthy of a royal personage. They are all that way. Prince Philip is the worst."

Yet behind closed doors, Charles clearly relished the time spent with his frisky young sons. When William and Harry were toddlers, he got down on the floor for playtime, read them bedtime stories, and even joined them in the bath, commanding a fleet of toy boats and yellow rubber ducks.

As the boys grew older, Diana engaged them at least twice a week in ferocious, to-the-death pillow fights. Not to be outdone, Charles concocted a game called Big Bad Wolf. The rules: Papa stood in the center of the room, and William and Harry would try to get out. As they scrambled for the door, Charles snatched them up and tossed them on the couch. Then they'd bolt for the door again, only to be sent flying by Big Bad Wolf Papa—much to their squealing delight. Similar games were played during summer weekends at Highgrove, with Papa alternately tossing his sons into the pool, carrying them on his shoulders, and challenging them to furious splash-fights.

Charles was so smitten with the boys that he wanted to buck royal tradition and not send them to boarding school at the age of eight. Instead, he told Diana he wanted William and Harry to simply continue at Wetherby, the day school located at Notting Hill Gate, just five minutes from Kensington Palace. "I think sending small children to boarding school is an appalling tradition—singularly British," agreed Penelope Leach, the noted British child care expert. "Eight is awfully young for any child to be away from his parents."

But Diana, claiming that Royal Protection officers felt it would be easier to protect the boys at boarding school, signed William up for Ludgrove, an exclusive school in Wokingham, Berkshire. There William, and later Harry, slept eight to a room in spartan dormitories with peeling paint on the walls and cold, bare wooden floors. There was no television, not even radio.

"I wanted them to stay home where I could spend time with them," Charles told Janet Jenkins. "I know Diana was upset about sending them off to Ludgrove, but it was more important to her that I be shown who had the power. She wanted to hurt me by sending the boys away, and she did."

Amazingly, the public was largely unaware of the rancor within the royal marriage until May 1991, when tabloid reporters made note of the fact that Charles and Camilla just happened to be vacationing in Florence, but without their spouses. "They were so used to getting away with it in England," celebrity photographer Ron Galella said, "but the European press, especially the Italians—those guys don't let anything get by."

A turning point came the following month, when Diana was lunching with a friend at her favorite London restaurant, San Lorenzo, and Charles was once again cozying up to Camilla at Highgrove. William and his classmates had been practicing on the putting green at Ludgrove when one of the other boys took a wild swing and accidentally clocked the young Prince full-force in the forehead. Knocked cold, with blood spurting from the wound in his head, William was taken in a police car to nearby Royal Berkshire Hospital.

According to Highgrove housekeeper Wendy Berry, Charles was "white with shock" at the news. Both he and Diana rushed to William's bedside, then accompanied him as he was transferred by ambulance to London's Great Ormond Street Hospital. There, he was to undergo an operation that would check for bone splinters and fully ascertain the damage. The operation required twenty-four stitches and left William with a permanent four-inch-long scar running horizontally above his left eye.

Diana held William's hand as he was wheeled into surgery and waited until neurosurgeon Richard Hayward emerged to pronounce the seventy-five-minute operation a success. Charles, however, was nowhere in sight. He had consulted with Camilla and they both agreed there was nothing to be accomplished by his remaining at Great Ormond Street Hospital. Leaving his son in the hands of the professionals, he had gone ahead with plans to attend a performance of *Tosca* at Covent Garden, telling his guests in the royal box that William's condition was "not too bad." From the opera, he took a train to an environmental conference in North Yorkshire.

Meanwhile, a distraught and exhausted Diana, still concerned that the injury might have some lingering effects—primarily infection leading to epilepsy or meningitis—stayed with William at Great Ormond Street. "Her reaction to William's accident was horror and disbelief," said Diana's friend James Gilbey. "By all accounts it was a narrow escape. She can't understand her husband's behavior."

Neither could the British public, which was quickly consumed with rage over what it saw as Charles's callous indifference to the well-being of his own son. WHAT KIND OF DAD ARE YOU? screamed the headline in the next day's *Sun*.

....

CAMILLA HAD SERIOUSLY UNDERESTIMATED HER rival. According to Jenkins, Charles's mistress told him that Diana was "cold and calculating" in her ability to manipulate public opinion, to get the press to "tell the story she wants to tell, whether it's the truth or not."

"Cold" was the adjective that Diana most often used to describe her husband—and his family. It seemed to Diana that William and Harry, now nine and seven respectively, were just beginning to get an inkling of what she meant. "Diana used to say, 'They are all so cold. They have no heart,'" her friend Lady Elsa Bowker said. During visits to Buckingham Palace, Windsor, Sandringham, even Balmoral, the little princes now seemed to pay more attention to the fact that every grown-up without exception—including generals in uniform and important government leaders like the Prime Minister—bowed to Granny. More than that, most of them seemed tense and apprehensive around her.

"William and Harry could see them all bowing, everyone afraid to do or say the wrong thing in Her Majesty's presence," Bowker continued. "Their grandfather Prince Philip having to walk behind their grandmother—for two small boys, it was very intimidating." It was indeed a lesson, but one that Diana was determined they learn, even at this early date.

The brothers began to understand that "it was more than just respect for the Queen that made people bow and scrape," Bowker said. "It was fear."

I have no idea what to say to her.

—THE QUEEN, AFTER DIANA WEPT TO HER ABOUT CHARLES AND CAMILLA

....

If anything ever happens to me, do you think they'll think of me as another Jackie Kennedy?

—DIANA, TO ROYAL MILLINER PHILIP SOMERVILLE

....

You don't know how to behave when someone is making such a mess. You want to help them mend, but how to do it?

—ELIZABETH II, TO LADY PATRICIA BRABOURNE, ABOUT DIANA

....

All my hopes are on William now.

—DIANA, TO TINA BROWN AND ANNA WINTOUR

4

"THAT WICKED, WICKED WOMAN"

WINDSOR CASTLE

3:00 P.M., FRIDAY, NOVEMBER 20, 1992

HER MAJESTY'S FORTY-FIFTH WEDDING ANNIVERSARY

She stood in Wellingtons and a hooded macintosh, shock and anguish etched on her face as she watched the orange-red flames blaze high above her beloved castle. She covered her mouth as if to stifle a scream as the roof above the state apartments collapsed with a deafening roar. A helmeted fireman standing next to her could offer no words of comfort.

Hours earlier, the Queen was about to accept the credentials from diplomats at Buckingham Palace when Prince Andrew called with the news that a conflagration was consuming Windsor. During extensive renovations, a spotlight left on by a worker had touched a curtain in the Private Chapel, and the resulting fire had spread to more than one hundred rooms, including the State

Dining Room, the Green Drawing Room, the Octagon Dining Room, the Crimson Drawing Room, and the Grand Reception Room. Scores of volunteers pitched in to rescue as much as possible of the furniture, paintings, artifacts, and other valuables, and when it was all over the Queen herself ventured inside to retrieve whatever personal items she could.

"It was the most shaken I ever saw her," her private secretary, Robert Fellowes, said. The Queen Mother (known affectionately as "the Old Queen" by downstairs staff) invited her daughter ("the Young Queen") to stay with her that night at Royal Lodge, the Queen Mother's residence in Windsor Park. The next week, in a letter addressed to "Darling Mummy" (the Queen Mother addressed her letters to the Queen "My Darling Angel"), Elizabeth thanked her for taking her in the day of the fire. "It made all the difference to my sanity," she wrote, "after that terrible day."

It was more than just one terrible day, of course, that had left the Queen to deal with unfamiliar feelings of doubt and even shame. The fire at Windsor Castle seemed to be divine retribution for a Royal Family run amok.

....

IT HAD ALL BEGUN WITH the disintegration of Prince Andrew's marriage to the spirited redhead who once called herself Diana's best friend, Sarah Ferguson. Starting in January, the scandal would reach its zenith that summer of 1992 when the *Daily Mirror* ran photos of a topless Duchess of York having her toes sucked while vacationing on the French Riviera by her American "financial advisor," thirty-seven-year-old John Bryan.

Fergie recalled that, over breakfast at Balmoral the day the *Mirror* story hit the stands, the Queen and her guests sat "eyes wide and mouths ajar." The Duchess of York had been "exposed for what I truly was. Worthless. Unfit. A national disgrace." The Queen, who often lost her temper but seldom flew into a rage, was "furious" with Fergie and let her know it. This display of anger "wounded me to the core," Fergie said, "all the more because I knew she was justified."

By the time the toe-sucking scandal erupted, the Palace was already reeling from that spring's release of Andrew Morton's bombshell book *Diana: Her True Story*. Essentially dictated to Morton by Diana herself—a fact that would not come out for years—the book recounted in graphic detail Diana's bouts with suicidal depression caused by her unfeeling husband and his scheming mistress.

The Queen was determined to save Charles's marriage for the sake of the children and to avoid a constitutional crisis. It was possible, Palace legal advisors initially pointed out, that Charles would have to relinquish his claim on the throne if he insisted on divorcing his wife. Diana and Charles were summoned to Windsor Castle for an emotional meeting with the Queen—whom Diana was told to always call "Mama"—and Prince Philip. Diana later told Paul Burrell that, when she and Charles raised the possibility of splitting, the Queen instructed them to "learn to compromise, be less selfish, and try to work through your difficulties for the sake of the monarchy, your children, the country, and its people."

Neither the Queen nor Diana—nor Camilla, for that matter—were aware that, while the realm was still reeling from the disclosures in Andrew Morton's book, Charles was enjoying another illicit rendezvous with Janet Jenkins at Highgrove. For more than four hours, Jenkins, whose son, Jason, was now eight, held

Charles's hand and listened patiently as the Prince complained bitterly about his relentlessly demanding wife and the toll their rancorous breakup was taking on the children. Charles was, Jenkins recalled, "consumed with worry over the psychological health of the boys—how all the fighting and bitterness would affect them in later life."

When he was done, Charles and his Canadian mistress tumbled into bed together—"the last time we were sexually intimate," said Jenkins, who insisted that at that point she was unaware that Camilla was still in the Prince's life. Jenkins later conceded that it was "ironic" that Charles was "cheating on his mistress with me!"

....

FOUR DAYS AFTER THE DUCHESS of York's humiliating romp through the pages of the *Daily Mirror*, the tabloids were filled with titillating transcripts of an intercepted cellphone conversation between Diana and her car-dealer friend James Gilbey. He called her "Squidgy"—which provided a convenient label for the scandal—and, more than fifty times, "Darling." He also repeatedly insisted that he loved her, while Diana gushed that Gilbey made her "go all jellybags."

But most damaging was what she had to say about "His Nibs" (Charles) and the way she was being treated by the Queen even though her celebrity, charitable pursuits, and personal popularity had undeniably bolstered the monarchy's image. She told Gilbey she felt "really said and empty. Bloody hell. After all I've done for this fucking family." Her life inside the royal cocoon, Diana told Gilbey, was "torture."

According to Ken Wharfe, the Squidgygate conversations had actually been intercepted by UK intelligence, then repeatedly broadcast widely by Charles's allies inside the government to insure a private citizen would pick it up—which is precisely what happened. This was all done, Wharfe added, "knowing that it would eventually reach the media."

Morton's tell-all book, Fergie's toe-sucking scandal, and now "Squidgygate"—it all left the monarch reeling, although she never let on to anyone but those closest to her. "Can you imagine," she asked her friend Lady Patricia Brabourne, "having two daughters-in-law like this?"

Nevertheless, Diana had actively sought guidance from the woman she jokingly referred to as "Top Lady." She often appeared at Buckingham Palace on the spur of the moment, waiting in the page's vestibule until the Queen could find a moment to speak with her.

Once inside the Queen's study, Diana poured her heart out to her mother-in-law. "Mama," she said on one occasion, "sometimes he calls Camilla from the bathtub. I listened at the door. Do you know what he said to her? 'Whatever happens, I will always love you.' "

Then Diana cried, the Queen later told Paul Burrell, "nonstop." When a weeping Diana, clearly at the end of her rope, simply asked, "Mama, what do I do?" the Queen threw up her hands. "I don't know *what* you should do," she answered. "Charles is hopeless."

The Queen knew that she was being of no help at all to her heartbroken daughter-in-law. "I tried to reach out to Diana many times," she later told Burrell. Referring to the two women's polar opposite styles, the butler tried to explain to Her Majesty that she "spoke in black and white. The princess spoke in color."

To the outside world, Diana radiated self-assurance. At a Westminster Abbey service marking the fiftieth anniversary of the Battle of El Alamein, she glared daggers at Camilla, who tried to avert her eyes as she slunk back into her pew. Fleet Street, seizing this rare opportunity to publish photos of the two women at the same event, had a field day comparing the sleek young princess to her dowdy rival. Diana's "eyes were wide, bright, and open," reported the next day's *Daily Mail,* and she wore a "jacket of silvery gray and a tight-fitting white skirt." By contrast, Camilla was "a funereal figure—pale, thin, and hair flecked with gray, in shapeless, somber blue." Camilla and Diana were, the paper's correspondent concluded, "the twin faces of war—the dullness of defeat and the radiance of victory."

The Royal Family had always been, in essence, the world's longest-running soap opera. Yet the proliferating Windsor family scandals were turning out to be far more than merely embarrassing. They were clearly undermining public support for the monarchy. This became painfully evident when a grassroots campaign was launched to force the Queen, and not the taxpayers, to pay for repairs to still-smoldering Windsor Castle.

For months, the Men in Gray had been urging the Queen to open the state rooms at Buckingham Palace—a move she had resisted on the grounds that, said a senior official, it would lift "the veil too much on the mystery of the monarchy." Now that money from admission fees was needed to pay for the repairs to Windsor, she reluctantly agreed.

To mollify critics in Parliament who felt the monarchy had grown far too expensive for a nation in the midst of an economic downturn, she also agreed to voluntarily pay taxes on her private income from the Duchy of Lancaster. Charles would also pay taxes on his Duchy of Cornwall income—again, strictly voluntarily.

For the time being, the Queen was conveying the image of a more open, modern, and forward-looking monarch who was not afraid of change. In opening portions of Buckingham Palace to the public, she also tapped into a new and significant revenue stream that wound up raising 70 percent of the $59.2 million it eventually took to restore Windsor Castle.

Just four days after the fire, the Queen, suffering from the flu and running a temperature of 101, spoke to a Guildhall gathering in honor of her fortieth year on the throne. Looking pale and haggard, her voice raspy from the smoke she had breathed in at the scene of the fire, she told the crowd that "1992 is not a year in which I shall look back with undiluted pleasure. In the words of one of my more sympathetic correspondents, it has turned out to be an *annus horribilis.*"

The capstone was yet to come. Now that separation or even divorce seemed inevitable, Elizabeth II worried about what impact it would all have on the succession. She recalled too well the chaos that surrounded her uncle's decision to marry Wallis Simpson, and the abdication that forced her reluctant father into a job that was so stressful it killed him. Now she worried that by divorcing, Charles was putting his own claim to the throne in peril. "History," she told Archbishop of Canterbury George Carey, "is repeating itself."

The Queen also talked to Carey about her very real concern that Charles intended to wed Camilla. "I saw despair," the Archbishop recalled. "She thought Charles was in danger of throwing everything out the window by rejecting Diana and forging another relationship." In this scenario, Camilla was cast in the role of Wallis Simpson, the Duchess of Windsor.

To ensure that a divorce would not spell the end for Charles, the Queen asked Prime Minister John Major to consult with the Archbishop, the Lord Chancellor, and the Foreign Secretary. Since there was really no precedent for this situation, they concluded only that it was "unlikely" in modern times that a divorce could prevent Charles from becoming king.

Just eight days after the Windsor fire, Charles—whom Diana now regularly referred to as either "the Great White Hope" or "the Boy Wonder"—was eagerly awaiting the arrival of William and Harry at Sandringham for his annual three-day shooting party when Diana canceled at the last minute. Unable to spend another tension-filled weekend with her Windsor in-laws, she took the boys to Highgrove instead.

This was the breaking point for Charles. Unwilling to let Diana continue to dictate the terms of his access to the young princes, he made the decision to call it quits. Once the shooting party was over, he drove to Kensington Palace and asked her for a separation. "You have left me with no choice," he told her. "I've already told the Queen and she approves."

Diana's first concern was for William and Harry. On December 3, she rushed to Ludgrove to warn William and Harry that news of the separation would soon be everywhere. What she told her eldest son at the time would be critical to his understanding of the institution of marriage—and would ultimately redound to the stability of the crown.

"I put it to William, particularly," Diana remembered, "that if you find someone you love in life, you must hang on to it and look after it and if you were lucky enough to find someone who loved you, then you must protect it."

William wept when Diana told him that, although she still loved Charles, she could no longer live under the same roof with him. As heartbreaking as the moment was, Diana felt a weight lifted off her shoulders as she drove her racing green Jaguar XJ-S back to Kensington Palace. "From Day One I always knew I'd never be the next queen," she said. "No one ever said that to me, I just knew it. . . . I just had to get out."

Just as she was convinced she would never become queen, Diana believed her astrologer's prediction that Charles would die before his mother and never become king. Taking solace from polls in the *Daily Mail*, the *Sunday Times*, and other publications showing that the vast majority of Britons wanted William as their next king, Diana said she had been training her son for the job all along. "I want William to lead from the heart," she said, "not the head."

Perhaps. But when Prime Minister John Major stood in the House of Commons on December 9, 1992, to announce the separation, he made it clear that the royal couple had "no plans to divorce and their constitutional positions are unaffected." He went on to insist that "the succession to the Throne is unaffected by it. There is no reason why the Princess of Wales should not be crowned Queen in due course."

It was impossible to imagine, of course, that Charles and Diana could ever go through the motions of a coronation, much less reign together harmoniously as King and Queen of England. But as her *annus horribilis* drew to a close, the Queen held out hope for a reconciliation—and a resolution to Charles's obsession with

"That Wicked, Wicked Woman," Her Majesty's shorthand for Camilla Parker Bowles.

....

THE NEXT YEAR, SADLY, WOULD be even worse. In January, it was Charles's and Camilla's turn to embarrass the sovereign. This time, tabloids had a field day with transcripts of an intimate cellphone chat between the clandestine lovers. A ribald snippet:

CAMILLA: Mmmmmm, you're awfully good at feeling your way along.

CHARLES: Oh stop! I want to feel my way along you, all over and up and down you and in and out.

CAMILLA: Oh!

CHARLES: Particularly in and out. . . .

CAMILLA: I can't start the week without you.

CHARLES: I fill your tank!

CAMILLA: Yes you do.

CHARLES: Oh, God, I'd just live inside your trousers or something. It would be much easier!

CAMILLA (laughing): What are you going to turn into? A pair of knickers? Oh, you're going to come back as a pair of knickers?

CHARLES: Or God forbid, a Tampax. Just my luck!

CAMILLA: You are a complete idiot! Oh, what a wonderful idea.

CHARLES: My luck to be chucked down the lavatory and go on and on forever, swirling round the top, never going down!

CAMILLA: Oh, darling!

It came as no surprise that press and public focused on Charles's expressed desire to be reincarnated as Camilla's tampon. But there were serious moments, as well:

CHARLES: Your great achievement is to love me.

CAMILLA: Oh, darling, easier than falling off a chair.

CHARLES: You suffer all these indignities and tortures and calumnies.

CAMILLA: Oh, darling, don't be so silly. I'd suffer anything for you. That's love. It's the strength of love. Night night.

Charles then reverted to his lecherous self, offering to hang up by "pressing the tit"—a British term for button.

"I wish," Camilla replied in her most sultry voice, "you were pressing mine."

Harry was too young to quite comprehend what was going on, but William was another matter. Diana's friend Vivienne Parry pointed out that "children don't want to know that their parents are doing it. It's out of the question. So when it's obvious that your parents *are* doing it—and with different people—it's a bit disturbing."

William managed, in time-tested Windsor tradition, to conceal whatever feelings he may have had from classmates, teachers, and most significantly, his own family. Both princes continued to put on a resolutely upbeat front when Fleet Street reported that Diana had placed more than three hundred harassing calls to the home of another boyfriend, art dealer Oliver Hoare.

The Princess denied this, claiming that Charles's allies were concocting another tale to make her look mentally unbalanced. In fact, it was eventually established that the harassing calls were made by a teenage boy feuding with one of Hoare's sons—but too late to undo the damage to Diana's reputation.

In the ensuing months there was an uninterrupted stream of newspaper stories linking Diana to a variety of men, including British businessman Christopher Whalley, rugby player Will Carling (his wife accused Diana of ruining her marriage), Canadian rocker Bryan Adams, and suave American billionaire Theodore Forstmann.

There were countless other male admirers, from electronics tycoon Gulu Lalvani to legendary tenors Placido Domingo and Luciano Pavarotti. She also had a schoolgirl crush on Tom Cruise, who invited Diana to bring William to watch him film *Mission Impossible* at Pinewood Studios. She told her hairdressers Natalie Symonds and Tess Rock that she wouldn't mind if Cruise's then-wife Nicole Kidman was "out of the way. Nicole keeps giving me dagger eyes."

Diana also said she "adored" then President Bill Clinton and found his "southern drawl" to be "incredibly sexy." She was surprised, however, how nervous he seemed to be in the presence of the First Lady. Hillary, she told Symonds and Rock, "certainly is the one who wears the pants in that family."

The Princess of Wales was also smitten with King Constantine's eldest son, Prince Pavlos. When Pavlos married American heiress Marie-Chantal Miller, Diana was "devastated," said Symonds. Diana was convinced she would never be Queen of England, but, she said, "there's no reason I can't be Queen of Greece."

In the end, the man who won Diana's heart was chubby, chain-smoking Pakistani heart surgeon Hasnat "Natty" Khan. She became so obsessed with Khan that she donned scrubs to watch him perform operations at London's Royal Brompton Hospital. The couple also had a code name for Diana to leave whenever she called to speak to him while he was doing his rounds. "Please tell Dr. Khan," she would tell the receptionist, "that Dr. Allegra is trying to reach him."

"She became so devoted to Hasnat," Symonds recalled, "that she said she at last began to understand the undying love Prince Charles shared with Camilla. She was wildly in love, totally obsessed by Dr. Khan."

The affair with Khan was tempestuous, even by Diana's standards. Yet Khan was, Diana told her friend Tess Rock, "everything to me—the love of my life. . . . He's got no money, I'll have to keep him, but I've got a thing about doctors."

Neither the young princes nor the Queen, who saw no constitutional repercussions, seemed particularly rattled by stories of Diana's extramarital exploits. Diana even kept William, whom she often referred to as a "deep thinker" and "my little wise old man," up to date on some of the most intimate details of her love life. "Diana had both a mother-and-son relationship and a mother-and-husband relationship with William," her friend Roberto Devorik said. Diana told Devorik she had "very private and very profound" conversations with William, and that he was "an extraordinary moral support."

According to her friend Rosa Monckton, Diana told William "more things than most mothers would have told their children. But she had no choice. She wanted them to hear the truth . . . rather than read a distorted, exaggerated, and frequently untrue version in the tabloid press."

Nevertheless, others who were close to the Princess wondered if it was appropriate for her to describe her feelings—sometimes in unsettlingly graphic terms—for men other than their father. In addition to seeking dating advice from her own young son, Diana talked to William about his father's utterly passionate devotion to Camilla, the Palace's continued efforts to silence her, and her "spiritual journey" that embraced everything from astrology, Tarot cards, and crystals to hypnotherapy, homeotherapy, aromatherapy, herbal medicine, reflexology, and feng shui.

As she stepped up her visits to pediatric cancer wards, AIDS patients, victims of domestic abuse, substance abusers, and the homeless, the Princess of Wales found herself leaning more heavily than ever on her son. "I pay attention to people, and I remember them," she told William. "When I cup my hands around the face of someone suffering, they are comforting me as much as I am comforting them."

Perhaps, but the strain on William was beginning to show. "Diana often cried on Prince William's shoulder—literally and figuratively," said one friend. "William's role was really more alternative husband than son. It was a heavy burden for anyone, but especially someone so young."

For all the pressure she put on her son, the Princess nonetheless worried about William. She told her friend Richard Greene that the young Prince had "deep feelings and an understanding far beyond his years," and that he was "an incredibly sensitive soul. He needs," she added, "to be protected."

Inevitably, Diana asked William if he approved of her marrying Dr. Khan, a Muslim. His succinct and oft-repeated reply: "Mummy, you have to do what makes you happy."

The Queen did not share William's opinion, however. Although Diana wanted to marry Khan and have two daughters by him, she also "knew that to marry a Muslim would create enormous problems for William and Harry," Elsa Bowker said. Accordingly, she tried to keep the Khan affair under wraps—literally—by smuggling him into Kensington Palace in the trunk of her butler's car. Nevertheless, the Palace soon got wind of it.

When she was informed that Diana was giving serious thought to marrying Khan, the Queen consulted with the Archbishop of Canterbury and her advisors about the possible ramifications. It was highly unlikely that the Church of England would recognize any such union, and even more unlikely that the Men in Gray would tolerate a Muslim's becoming stepfather to Britain's future king. "The Queen seldom shows her feelings," said one Member of Parliament who was asked to weigh in, "but in this case it was clear that she felt the Princess of Wales had finally lost her mind completely." Either that, he continued, or "Princess Diana was determined to bring down the monarchy." Either way, the Queen, who once felt sympathy for her daughter-in-law, now viewed Diana as "the enemy."

It was a sentiment that had been shared by most of the Queen's relatives since the separation. Prince Philip refused to even acknowledge Diana's presence at William's eleventh birthday party. Princess Margaret, one of the few senior Royals who was genuinely fond of Diana and frequently spoke up in her defense at family gatherings, felt compelled to join the other Windsors in turning her back on the rebel Princess.

Now that Diana was intent on airing The Firm's dirty linen in public and at the same time portraying the Royal Family as cold and unfeeling, Her Majesty was determined to retaliate. Knowing that it would deeply wound Diana, the Queen hastily added the names of Andrew Parker Bowles and his wife, Camilla, to the list of those fortunate few invited inside the royal enclosure at Ascot. (Even then, the Queen refused to be introduced to Camilla.)

It was not long, however, before the Queen found herself dealing with a crisis not of Diana's making. On June 29, 1994, the Prince of Wales inexplicably went on national television to admit to veteran broadcaster Jonathan Dimbleby that he had committed adultery. He claimed he had been "faithful and honorable" to his wife until their marriage became "irretrievably broken down, us both having tried."

The TV interview, intended to generate interest in Dimbleby's forthcoming authorized biography of the Prince, infuriated the Queen and the public alike. The headline in the *Daily Mirror*: NOT FIT TO REIGN. Diana couldn't have been more thrilled.

The same night Charles made his disastrous admission of infidelity, a radiant Diana attended a charity event at London's Serpentine Gallery wearing a daring black chiffon cocktail dress by designer Christine Stampolian.

Fleet Street promptly dubbed it "the Revenge Dress."

....

FOR A BRIEF TIME, THE heat was off Charles after *Princess in Love*, Anna Pasternak's book detailing James Hewitt's affair with Diana, hit stores in September of 1994. In it, the former soldier and riding instructor shared the steamy details of his six-year affair with the Princess of Wales—leading Fleet Street to brand Hewitt "the Love Rat."

Again worried about the impact on her sons, Diana later recalled that she "ran to them as fast as I could." William, twelve, greeted her with a box of chocolates. "Mummy, I think you've been hurt," he said. "These will make you smile again."

Charles was soon back in the line of fire. The release of Dimbleby's *Prince of Wales: A Biography* in October 1994 sent more shock waves through Buckingham Palace. In it, he complained bitterly about his unhappy childhood, portraying Prince Philip as insensitive, callous, and overbearing, and his mother as cold, distant, and aloof.

The Queen and Philip were both wounded by the way Charles characterized them in the book. But nothing was so devastating to William and Harry as their father's claim that he never loved their mother and only married her because Prince Philip forced him to do it.

"Imagine being told that your parents never loved each other," Diana said. "How do you think poor Wills and Harry must feel?"

When William asked if it was true, his eyes "pierced my heart like a dagger," Diana said. "I just wanted to cry." Later, at Highgrove, William confronted his father. "Why, Papa?" he wanted to know. "Why did you do it?" Before Charles could answer, Wills bolted from the room.

In the midst of the brouhaha, Charles fled to the United States on a long-planned, ten-day U.S. goodwill tour. When he arrived in Los Angeles on October 31, 1994, it was the first time he had set foot in the City of Angels in twenty years.

Back in 1974, Charles was a twenty-six-year-old officer aboard the HMS *Jupiter* when his ship docked in San Diego. During a side trip to Los Angeles, he was offered his pick of Hollywood stars to meet but was only interested in one: Barbra Streisand. "I'm sure they thought I'd say Raquel Welch," Charles told his valet, Stephen Barry, "but I said Barbra Streisand. I wanted to meet the woman behind the voice." He was no less a fan of her acting, having seen *Funny Girl* no fewer than three times.

Given the predilection of most Windsor men for leggy showgirls and buxom starlets, it may have struck the casual observer as odd that Prince Charles had for years harbored a crush on Streisand. A framed photo of Barbra had hung on the wall of his room at Cambridge University; after graduation, he relocated the photo to his private quarters in Buckingham Palace. "Barbra Streisand," he told Barry, "is my only pinup."

At the time, Streisand was on a Columbia sound stage dubbing dialogue for *Funny Lady,* the sequel to *Funny Girl,* and hating every minute of it. Still, the royal visit was a publicity windfall for Columbia, which roped off an area of the studio and invited fifty press photographers to snap away as the Prince and the superstar stiffly shook hands.

That first encounter was awkward, even by Charles's standards. "She appeared to be rather nervous," he said, "and kept asking me endless questions in a rather tight-lipped fashion." The photo session lasted a few minutes, and afterward the couple drifted off to a corner to chat privately over coffee.

The Prince wanted to stay and "really get to know her," but Streisand begged off, saying she had to get back to work. "I think I caught her on a bad day," said Charles, who was unaccustomed to being treated so curtly by a member of the opposite sex. "She had very little time and appeared very busy."

Years later, Streisand learned that Charles had felt slighted during their first meeting. "Who knows?" she cracked. "If I'd been nicer to him, I might have been the first *real* Jewish princess."

No matter. If anything, their first brief meeting under the klieg lights fanned his interest. "People look at me in amazement when

I say she is devastatingly attractive and with a great appeal," the Prince of Wales wrote in his journal. "But I *still* contend she has great sex appeal after meeting her."

On April 25, 1994, Charles attended a Streisand concert at Wembley Arena in London, and she sang "Someday My Prince Will Come" in his honor. Just six months later Barbra, fresh off a string of high-profile love affairs, was among the scores of A-List Hollywood stars who showed up for a gala honoring the Prince of Wales on November 2, 1994. Not long after the gala, Streisand had a secret rendezvous with Charles at his suite in the secluded Bel-Air Hotel. When word of the meeting got out, the official explanation was that Barbra Streisand and Prince Charles enjoyed "a private tea." Harold Brooks-Baker noted that Charles had had "private teas" with "a long procession of women over the years. From what I understand, he was absolutely besotted with Barbra Streisand. Did anyone ever turn Charles down? Not to my knowledge."

The Prince and the Superstar would hook up again ten months later, this time after Streisand flew to London to attend a dinner for Charles's favorite preservationist organization, the Foundation for Architecture. Fresh off a scorching affair with Angelina Jolie's father, Academy Award–winning actor Jon Voight, Barbra somehow managed to remain under the radar in England. When Elton John arrived at Highgrove for a private dinner, he was "surprised" to find Streisand there—and neither Diana nor Camilla anywhere in sight.

"The Prince and Miss Streisand were very affectionate toward each other," a Highgrove staff member recalled. Another housekeeper described Charles and Barbra as acting "quite flustered" when she surprised them in Charles's study.

According to Lady Elsa Bowker, Diana "knew that Charles was infatuated with Miss Streisand. She would not have been surprised if they had an affair." As for Camilla: "She would have been absolutely *thrilled*—that would have excited her, I think."

In March 1995, Camilla quietly divorced Andrew Parker Bowles after twenty-two years of marriage. By that time, of course, she had been carrying on her affair with the Prince of Wales off and on for twenty-three years.

....

RUMORS WERE NOW RAMPANT THAT another, significantly more historic divorce was imminent, but the Queen was still convinced that reconciliation of some kind might be possible. "The Prince and Princess have no plans to divorce," a Palace spokesman said. "That remains the position."

In the meantime the Queen, fearing that the avalanche of scandals was seriously undermining the monarchy in the eyes of her people, gave serious thought to a future without King Charles. "Divorce seemed more and more likely," a courtier said, "and a divorced man had never been crowned king."

The picture became even murkier if a divorced Prince of Wales insisted on marrying a divorced Camilla Parker Bowles. "It would have been easy if their spouses were dead," James Whitaker said, "because then Charles and Camilla could be considered widower and widow in the eyes of the Church of England." But Diana and Andrew Parker Bowles were, at least for the moment, still very much alive.

All of which made the role William was destined to play all the more important. Now that he was enrolled at one of the world's most elite prep schools, Eton, William was that much closer to Granny. From wherever he stood at Eton, William could look up and see the medieval cluster of turrets, granite keeps, Gothic arches, and granite battlements that jutted up on a hill just across the Thames—Windsor Castle.

By the time William enrolled in Eton in the autumn of 1995, there were few traces of the damage done by the fire that had ripped through Windsor three years earlier. Even as artisans put the finishing touches on the renovation, the splendor of Windsor was undeniable. From St. George's Chapel, where Knights of the Garter are installed with much ceremony and pomp, to the Grand Vestibule showcasing hundreds of antique firearms, the castle's interior is as opulent as its exterior is forbidding.

Here, too, resides one of the world's great art collections: paintings by Rubens, Van Dyck, Canaletto, Gainsborough, Lawrence, Hogarth, Reynolds, Rembrandt, and Holbein line the walls, as well as a six-foot-high malachite urn given to Queen Victoria by Czar Nicholas I and six Gobelin tapestries. From the parapets, however, one cannot ignore the cooling tower of a nuclear power plant rising in the distance, or the passenger jets flying low as they make their approach to Heathrow. (Passengers on one of these flights were treated to Princess Diana donning the uniform of a Virgin Airlines flight attendant, then getting on the plane's public address system to offer some commentary: "If you look out the window to your right now, you'll see Granny's place.")

From her bedchamber, the Queen could see more than just power plants and jets screaming overhead. She had a clear view of Eton's redbrick chimneys, wrought-iron gates, Gothic turrets, and mullioned windows. Founded by Henry VI to train young scholars for another institution of higher learning he established, King's College, Cambridge, Eton had been preparing the sons of Europe's most influential families for life on the world stage for 558 years. History, as George Orwell once famously proclaimed, was "decided on the playing fields of Eton."

Where Charles had been by turns teased and shunned by the other, less aristocratic boys at Gordonstsoun, Wills fit in well with the sons of Arab sheiks, barristers, political leaders, bankers, financiers, and British nobles who made up Eton's student body of thirteen hundred. Like his schoolmates, Wills strolled Eton's manicured lawns in stiff white collar, striped trousers, and a swallowtail coat. Unlike them, he was shadowed by a nineteen-member security detail and carried his own transmitter for tracking purposes.

At exactly 3:50 p.m. every Sunday, a car picked William up at school and drove down Eton High Street, past the Home on the Bridge restaurant and the 581-year-old Cockpit pub, then over the small span linking Eton to the village of Windsor. Just as often, William, accompanied by two guards packing Heckler and Koch machine pistols, walked to Windsor Castle—a journey of less than seven minutes on foot.

Once at Windsor Castle, William proceeded directly to the Oak Drawing Room for tea with the Queen at 4:00 p.m. Diana had, of course, taken pains to give her children "an understanding of people's emotions, people's insecurities, people's distress, and people's hopes and dreams." But it was left to the Queen to school William on what it meant to be a modern monarch—Chairman of "The Firm."

The future king was accustomed to Granny's efforts at trying to sneak a history lesson in wherever she could—a letter from

Thomas Cromwell to Henry VIII, perhaps, or notes from her own first meeting with Winston Churchill. But like any grandmother, Elizabeth was eager to know what was happening in William's life—how his studies were going, what sporting events he was competing in, who his friends were and what they were like. Since, like all Windsors, they shared a passion for horses, the Queen also quizzed William on how his polo was progressing—at fifteen he was just starting to play—and talked to him about which of her thirty thoroughbreds would be racing this year.

The Queen's focus was on molding a future king, so she was more likely to ignore Harry's misconduct while making William toe the line. Once, while riding at Balmoral, William suddenly took off alone, leaving his groom—and his security detail—scrambling to catch up. Later, back at the castle, "the Queen tore a strip off Prince William," a member of the household staff recalled. This rare fit of royal pique was, added the staffer, "only out of concern for his safety."

Diana was concerned for her son's emotional well-being when she drove to Eton on November 19, 1995, to warn him that she had done a television interview that was airing on the respected BBC public affairs program *Panorama* the following night.

"I didn't," she said, "want it to catch you by surprise."

....

SHE HAD TOLD THE MEN in Gray the same thing five days earlier, on Charles's forty-seventh birthday. Diana neglected to share any important details with them—certainly not that, in order to avoid detection, compact cameras had been smuggled into Kensington Palace to enable reporter Martin Bashir to conduct a wide-ranging three-hour-long interview with the embattled Princess.

The resulting material was cut down to a compelling fifty-five minutes, and scheduled to air on November 20—the forty-eighth wedding anniversary of the Queen and Prince Philip. Through the Men in Gray, the Queen asked for at least a preview. It was a request Diana flatly denied.

Speaking in hushed tones and looking up from heavily mascaraed lashes, Diana might either have been in total control or teetering on the verge of a meltdown as she answered Bashir's questions. There was universal agreement that, purely from a media standpoint, the Princess of Wales had delivered what veteran broadcaster Barbara Walters called "a superb performance." Although the Queen could not bring herself to watch—her advisors were instructed to take notes and report back to her—William did, seated alone before the television set in the headmaster's study at Eton.

The Queen had rightly suspected Diana's motives in launching a sneak attack. It was not enough that Diana believed her astrologer's prediction that Charles would predecease his mother. In light of the whispering campaign portraying her as mentally unstable, the Princess of Wales believed she needed to commence the kind of media offensive that called into question whether her husband was fit to rule.

First, Diana spoke calmly about her reasons for doing the interview, claiming the Prince of Wales's camp was portraying her as someone who "should be put in a home of some sort," and that the Royal Family simply dismissed her as "sick, unstable . . . an embarrassment." She then unburdened herself about her eating disorders, her suicidal depression, the Palace conspiracy against her ("there is no better way to dismantle a personality than to isolate it"), and her own decision not to "go quietly. . . . I'll fight to the end."

She also discussed Camilla ("There were three of us in this marriage, so it was a bit crowded"), and her own affair with James Hewitt ("Yes, I adored him, yes, I was in love with him"). But what most upset the Palace were the scathing broadsides she leveled at Charles and the Royal Family. Diana speculated that the "top job" would "bring enormous limitations to him, and I don't know whether he could adapt to that." She felt Charles would find the role of monarch "suffocating."

As for herself, Diana wanted "the man in the street" to know she would "always be there for him." She did not wish to be the next Queen of England, she insisted, but instead wanted only to reign as "the Queen of People's Hearts. . . . Someone," she added, "has got to go out there and love people and show it." No one in the Palace, she said, "is streetwise in any way—nor do they want to be. They don't believe they should relate to the world, the real world of today. . . . They want me and my children to behave as if we were still in Victorian England."

Nevertheless, Diana also made a point of asserting that she did not want a divorce, and that she saw "a future ahead—a future for my husband, a future for myself, and a future for the monarchy."

When he came down to collect William, the housemaster found the young Prince sitting on the sofa, his eyes red from crying. Although his father had said on national television that he never loved Diana, he never mentioned Camilla's name or professed his love for her. William and Harry had never even met their father's longtime mistress. But the boys knew Hewitt as their riding instructor and had once been deeply fond of him. To hear that their mother had been in love with someone they had once trusted was doubly upsetting for William and his brother.

It was not Diana's only miscalculation. In this round of the Game of Crowns, Diana had, as planned, scored a major public relations victory. A Gallup Poll conducted immediately after the *Panorama* interview was aired showed that three-quarters of the people approved of Diana's performance, 84 percent found her to be honest, and 85 percent believed that she should serve as a kind of roving ambassador of goodwill for the United Kingdom.

Moreover, she had cast significant doubt on Charles's future. Now no fewer than 46 percent of Elizabeth II's subjects felt her eldest son was worthy of the crown. This was the figure that Diana most wanted to see. In a series of maneuvers that evoked all the serpentine intrigue of the court of Henry VIII, Diana was using the media to push Charles out and her son forward as the person best suited to succeed Elizabeth. Diana did not mention that she would likely play a major role in the reign of William V, helping to forge a new, more relevant, populist, and compassionate monarchy as the power behind the throne.

Diana had, unfortunately, seriously overplayed her hand. "This was a sneak attack on the monarchy, there's no other way to describe it," said a Clarence House staffer. "Diana was right about one thing—she could not be controlled. And the Palace cannot ever relinquish control."

The day after the interview aired, the Queen told Prime Minister John Major and the Archbishop of Canterbury that she was cutting Diana loose from The Firm. While Her Majesty sat down at her desk to compose the letter that would change the course of royal history, Diana flew to New York to accept a Humanitarian of the Year Award from United Cerebral Palsy. Radiant in a shimmering sleeveless, low-cut black evening gown, the Princess showed no sign of concern as she cheerfully mingled with the likes of Colin Powell, Barbara Walters, and her friend Henry Kissinger.

....

DURING THIS WHIRLWIND VISIT TO the United States, Diana had one particular reason to be pleased. The Princess and her friend the Duchess of York had often openly fantasized about marrying John F. Kennedy, Jr. For Diana, the connection ran deeper. She had always admired Jackie, and would later say that she hoped William might turn out as well as John when it came to handling the pressures of public life. When Jackie died of lymphoma in May of 1994, Diana wrote condolence letters to both Caroline and John, telling them that their mother had been her role model.

Diana and Kennedy finally arranged to meet at her suite in the Carlyle Hotel on Madison Avenue, ostensibly to talk about the possibility of doing an interview for John's magazine *George*. For years, the Carlyle had served as JFK's base of operations in New York; Jackie and her children lived at the hotel during their postassassination transition from Washington to an apartment on Fifth Avenue, and John still spent weekends there when he wanted to escape from the pressures of being *People* magazine's "Sexiest Man Alive."

After Diana entered the Carlyle through its main entrance on East Seventy-sixth Street, John entered undetected through an unmarked side door on East Seventy-seventh—one of the many ways in and out of the hotel President Kennedy had used to elude the press. Diana's private secretary, Patrick Jephson, later described the meeting between these two iconic figures as "brief and businesslike." Conversely, Diana's spiritual advisor, Simone Simmons, insisted the Princess told her flatly that she and JFK Jr. "ended up in bed," that their encounter was "pure lust" and "pure chemistry," and that Kennedy was "an amazing lover—a ten, the tops."

Diana's butler, Paul Burrell, insisted that she and JFK Jr. were never lovers. At the time Kennedy, who had already had affairs with the high-profile likes of Madonna, Sarah Jessica Parker, and Daryl Hannah, was involved with Calvin Klein public relations executive Carolyn Bessette. Although Kennedy went on to marry Bessette, neither seemed particularly interested in being faithful to the other. For his part, Kennedy was coy about his interaction with the Princess of Wales. "Diana had the most unusual upwards glance, really seductive," John told his friend William Noonan. "The most unusual blue eyes . . ." A one-night stand with the Princess was "certainly not out of the question," another friend said. "Sometimes he talked a blue streak about the women he slept with—all the lurid details—but with certain women, he could be very closed-mouthed. He had lots of secrets."

Diana came crashing back to earth soon enough. On December 12, 1995, the Queen wrote Charles and Diana individually, asking—or more to the point instructing—them to seek an "early divorce" that would be "in the best interests of the country." Both letters were signed "With love from Mama."

"Diana was crushed," said one of her closest confidants. "She did not want a divorce. She viewed the Queen as a friend, but the Queen had had enough of scandal." During a meeting with the Queen, she aired a variety of concerns—from her reluctance to give up her "HRH" status to her concern over the possibility of Charles's marrying his mistress and Camilla becoming stepmother to her sons. The Queen made it clear that she believed Charles had no intention of remarrying.

Curiously, Diana also told the Queen that she worried about Charles and William flying together; if something happened and their plane went down, she worried that Harry could not bear all the responsibility that would then fall on his shoulders. Her Majesty assured her that this was unlikely; she also understood the true cause of Diana's worry. The long-dormant rumors that had swirled about Harry were sprouting up again now that he was growing up to look less and less like a Windsor and more like a Hewitt. If, through some quirk of history, Harry did wind up on the throne, it could precipitate a constitutional crisis unlike any that had gone before. It was, after all, through a quirk of history—the abdication of Edward VIII to marry his American mistress—that Elizabeth wound up queen.

Charles and Diana met at St. James's Palace, which the Prince of Wales now called home, on February 28, 1996. In an obvious effort to make it appear as if she—and not the Royal Family—was in charge of the proceedings, Diana issued a statement to the effect that she had agreed to Charles's request for a divorce, that she would still be involved in all decisions relating to the children, and that she would retain her title.

Once again, the Queen was forced to rein in her daughter-in-law. Elizabeth issued a statement of her own, making it clear that no issues were resolved until the sovereign said they were. After four months of tough negotiations, the divorce was finalized on August 28, 1996. Diana received a lump-sum cash payment of $22.5 million as well as $600,000 a year to maintain her offices.

She retained all of her titles—Princess of Wales, Duchess of Cornwall, Duchess of Rothesay, Countess of Chester, Countess of Carrick, Baroness Renfrew—but volunteered to give up "Her Royal Highness" status after William told her he didn't care what she was called. "You're Mummy," he shrugged.

Diana leaked details of her conversations with the Queen, strongly implying she had been pressured to give up her royal designation. The Queen put out a statement of her own stating that this was "categorically" untrue. "The decision to drop the title is the Princess's and the Princess's alone."

Diana seized the opportunity to ramp up her image as the most glamorous philanthropist the world had ever known. She took steps to streamline her operation, scaling back the one-hundred-plus charities she actively supported to a more manageable five: the Leprosy Mission, the National AIDS Trust, the Royal Marsden Cancer Hospital, a homeless charity called Centrepoint, and the Great Ormond Street Children's Hospital. In addition, she remained patroness of the English National Ballet.

Diana also took it upon herself to focus global attention on the human suffering wrought by land mines. The Queen in particular was astonished by video of Diana walking through minefields in Angola and Bosnia—brave actions that helped lend a sense of urgency to the anti–land mine treaty eventually signed by more than 120 nations. Elizabeth, knowing how devoted William and Harry were to their mother, praised Diana for her courage but cautioned her not to take "any unnecessary chances."

Diana was concerned for her safety, but not because she risked being obliterated by a land mine. After opting to go it on her own without Royal Protection officers, the Princess was driving her green Audi convertible through London's Knightsbridge district when her brakes failed as she approached a traffic light. Her car plowed through the intersection before rolling to a stop. The incident left Diana shaken, but, incredibly, unharmed. "The brakes of my car have been tampered with," she wrote in separate notes to her friends Simone Simmons, Lady Annabel Goldsmith, Lady Elsa Bowker, and Lucia Flecha de Lima. "If something happens to me it will be MI5 or MI6." MI5 and MI6 are Britain's domestic and foreign intelligence agencies.

Diana let it slip to her voice coach and confidant Peter Settelen in 1992 that a close friend had already been assassinated by MI6—or at least that's what she believed. Five years earlier, Diana's loyal bodyguard, Barry Mannakee, was fired when it was strongly suspected that he and the Princess were having an affair. Not long after, a car suddenly pulled out of an alleyway, striking his motorcycle. "And he was killed," she told Settelen. "And I think he was bumped off. . . . He was the greatest fella I ever had."

....

BACK IN OCTOBER 1993, DIANA sat down at her desk in Kensington Palace and wrote a letter that outlined in eerily prescient detail what she thought might ultimately happen to her—but not before railing against her husband and the Palace. "I have been battered, bruised, and abused mentally by a system for years now," she wrote. "Thank you Charles, for putting me through such hell and for giving me the opportunity to learn from the cruel things you have done to me."

In her letter, Diana described "this particular phase" in her life to be "the most dangerous. My husband is planning an accident in my car, brake failure and serious head injury in order to make the path clear for Charles to marry."

Scotland Yard later confirmed that in the letter, which Diana told her butler Paul Burrell to keep "just in case," the Princess identified someone other than Camilla as Charles's choice for a second wife—and future queen. According to Diana, the Prince of Wales wanted to "marry Tiggy. Camilla is nothing but a decoy, so we are all being used by the man in every sense of the word."

In the four years since Charles's and Diana's separation was announced, Alexandra "Tiggy" Legge-Bourke had been serving as royal nanny whenever William and Harry spent time with their father. It was an arrangement that irked Diana from the very beginning. "I don't need a substitute father for the boys when they're with me," the Princess complained. "So why does Charles need a substitute mother when they're with him?"

If Charles was looking for a Diana substitute, in many ways, Tiggy Legge-Bourke fit the bill. The daughter of a Welsh aristocrat and a wealthy merchant banker, the nanny grew up on her family's six-thousand-acre estate, Glanusk Park, and was even sent to the same Swiss finishing school Diana had attended. A tall, stunning, outgoing thirty-year-old with a hearty laugh to match her big personality, Tiggy also believed in having fun with her royal charges at zoos, amusement parks, movie theaters, arcades, and country fairs when she wasn't smothering them with kisses and hugs. Unlike the decidedly urbane Diana, Legge-Bourke was, like Charles and Camilla, a dyed-in-the-wool country girl who loved to hike, fish, ride, and shoot.

After a brief stint as a kindergarten teacher—another thing she shared with Diana—Tiggy started her own nursery in central London. Legge-Bourke named the school "Mrs. Tiggy-Winkle" after the hedgehog in Beatrix Potter's *The Tale of Mrs. Tiggy-Winkle.*

From then on, the nursery school teacher with the privileged past was simply "Tiggy."

Diana's resentment of the role Tiggy played in her young sons' lives grew markedly in the coming years. Her solicitor, Lord Mishcon, later confirmed that Diana was convinced that "Camilla was not really Charles's lover, but a decoy for his real favorite, the nanny Tiggy Legge-Bourke."

"It's the Men in Gray," Diana told Lady Elsa Bowker. "They're trying to brainwash my boys so they will forget me . . . I won't let it happen."

P. D. Jephson, Diana's private secretary, went so far as to warn Legge-Bourke that Charles and the Princess of Wales had no compunction about using their children as unwitting pawns in their seemingly never-ending power struggle. She might, he cautioned the new nanny, find herself caught in the crossfire.

Tiggy responded with a shrug. "Doesn't bother me," she said. "I'm just the nursery maid, guv."

Tiggy ran, swam, rode, and roughhoused with William and Harry. She was also assigned a bedroom adjacent to the boys' rooms at Sandringham, St. James's Palace, Balmoral, and Highgrove. Those pillow fights that had once been a nightly ritual for Diana and her sons were now part of their nightly ritual with Tiggy.

Newspapers were soon filled with photographs of Harry sitting on Tiggy's lap, or the nanny tousling William's hair as he walked off a muddy polo field. When Tiggy referred to the princes as "my babies" in the press, Diana made it clear she had had enough. In a flurry of letters to her estranged husband, the Princess of Wales demanded that Tiggy's role in their sons' lives be drastically curtailed. Diana asked, among other things, that "Miss Legge-Bourke not spend unnecessary time in the children's rooms . . . read to them at night, nor supervise their bath time."

Camilla shared Diana's distaste for Tiggy. Although the nanny served the dual purpose of freeing Charles to spend time with his adult friends while at the same time being a thorn in Diana's side, Charles's mistress referred to Tiggy as simply "the hired help." She also came up with another nickname for the curvaceous nanny, who had a penchant for wearing skin-tight riding britches and hip-hugging skirts: "Big Ass."

Like it or not, Tiggy wasn't going anywhere. During a meeting at Kensington Palace in October 1995, Diana voiced many of the same concerns she had harbored about her safety to her solicitor, Lord Mishcon, and two of his associates—only this time with a new and significant twist. Diana told Lord Mishcon that "the Queen would be abdicating . . . and the Prince of Wales would then assume the throne." Mishcon went on to say that Diana was "convinced that there was a conspiracy that she and Camilla would be put aside." At the time, he recalled, "I could not believe what I was hearing."

Diana was initially told by her spies inside the Palace that "The Abdication Plan" called for the Queen to relinquish the throne in April 1996—more specifically, on the monarch's seventieth birthday. By then, Diana believed both she and Camilla would have been "set aside" by British intelligence operatives, leaving Charles free to marry her sons' nanny. This would pave the way for King Charles III to be crowned alongside his "Queen Alexandra" (Tiggy's real name).

Diana told Mishcon and solicitors Rae and Sandra Davis that

she, on the other hand, was pushing to have the Queen force Charles out of the line of succession so that William could assume the throne as quickly as possible. This, Diana said, was the "ideal solution" to the problem of keeping the monarchy alive in the twenty-first century. Since William was only thirteen at the time, Diana wanted Prince Andrew, the Duke of York, to serve as Regent until the boy turned eighteen. Presumably, Diana felt the Queen, having by then permanently sidelined Charles, would be amenable to having her second son take temporary control.

Whenever the abdication issue was raised, advocates pointed to the example set by Queen Juliana of the Netherlands, a distant cousin and close friend of Elizabeth who relinquished her crown in 1980 at age seventy-one. But in that instance, Juliana was handing off the crown to her popular daughter, Beatrix. Polls continued to show that, in the wake of so many embarrassing scandals, Britons were not ready to see Charles on the throne. By a margin of two to one, they wanted William to succeed his grandmother. "It was simply too tumultuous a time," Lord Mishcon said, "for the Queen to simply walk away." Since Elizabeth was only seventy and Charles a relatively youthful forty-seven, "it wasn't really a difficult decision for her to make."

Faced with Tiggy's unfettered presence in her children's lives, Diana took matters into her own hands. During the Waleses' annual Christmas party for one hundred of their staff members at London's Lanesborough Hotel, Diana strolled over to Tiggy and muttered, "So sorry to hear about the baby." The rumor that Legge-Bourke had aborted Charles's baby—now broadcast among the Prince of Wales's closest friends—was enough to send Tiggy running from the party in tears. Tiggy went so far as to have her solicitor threaten to sue if the Princess didn't retract her statement and apologize. Diana never did. Shortly before the tawdry tale became public, Patrick Jephson resigned as Diana's private secretary. He later explained that he was "simply shocked" that Diana had "exulted in accusing Legge-Bourke of having had an abortion."

As Tiggy's influence over Charles and the boys increased, Diana became more convinced than ever that a royal conspiracy was afoot. She told Lord Mishcon that factions loyal to Charles were plotting with the Men in Gray to assassinate not only her but the Prince's longtime mistress. "Camilla is in danger," she told Lord Mishcon. "They are going to have to get rid of us both."

(Maggie Rae, another of Diana's lawyers, believed "it was very clear that Princess Diana thought she was going to be killed." Lord Mishcon was so concerned that he took detailed notes of Diana's concerns, which he gave to British authorities just three weeks after the Paris crash that took her life. Incredibly, police suppressed Lord Mishcon's account for six years, until the final official inquest into Diana's death in 2003.)

The Queen also took note of Tiggy's high-profile relationship with Charles and her grandsons. While Legge-Bourke was clearly a positive and stabilizing influence at a chaotic time in the boys' lives, Her Majesty was well aware of the impact it was all having on Diana's state of mind—and on the Royal Family's rapidly deteriorating public image. At one point, according to a courtier, she shared her concerns with Charles, urging him to consider scaling back the nanny's responsibilities or "risk forcing Diana's hand."

In the meantime, Camilla had grown increasingly confident in her role as chatelaine of Highgrove. So self-assured, in fact, that she insisted on sitting next to Janet Jenkins when Jenkins was invited back to Highgrove in 1996. Charles's other mistress found Camilla "absolutely charming. Either she didn't know that Charles and I had been lovers or she didn't care, because she treated me wonderfully."

Another of the Prince of Wales's mistresses had not fared so well. Battling substance abuse, Kanga Tryon checked into a treatment center called Farm Place in 1996, only to suffer a mysterious fall from a third-floor window. She suffered a fractured skull and a broken back, and from this point on was confined to a wheelchair. A year later Kanga, who like Diana was convinced her husband had been plotting to kill her, was committed to a mental institution. Not long after, she died after a minor medical procedure. She was forty-nine.

In March 1997, Diana seized on a second opportunity to get rid of Tiggy during William's confirmation at Windsor Castle. The Princess complained loudly to Charles when Tiggy, who was put in charge of the guest list, omitted the names of several Spencer relatives. By this time, Diana and Charles were getting along so well that he felt obliged to take action. Within three weeks, Tiggy was out of the picture—at least for the time being.

Oddly, once the divorce became final, the animosity that had defined their marriage was replaced with acceptance, respect, even affection. The turning point, Diana later said, was the day she and her ex-husband proudly looked on as William enrolled at Eton. Now they were on the phone with each other several times a week, usually kibitzing about their boys. When her friend Tess Rock visited the Princess of Wales at Kensington Palace, she crossed paths with Charles. "Did you see Charles?" Diana gushed. "Guess what? He was wearing the sweater I gave him for his last birthday. I was so touched."

Diana had even begun to accept—even admire—the enduring bond between Charles and Camilla. Now that she had begun giving advice to fifteen-year-old William about what to look for in a mate, the Princess of Wales could think of no better examples than her ex-husband and his mistress. "When you find a true, deep love like that," Diana told William, "it's a precious thing. You've got to hold on tight to it." This did not mean she felt warmly toward Camilla per se; rather than hating "The Rottweiler," Diana viewed her husband's mistress with a kind of bemused indifference.

Diana's romantic life, meanwhile, was a shambles. "When I was born I was unwanted," she famously said. "When I married Charles I was unwanted. When I joined the Royal Family I was unwanted. I want to be wanted." After she pressed Natty Khan to marry—going so far as to ask Paul Burrell to secretly arrange for a Roman Catholic priest to do the job—Khan angrily accused Diana of leaking stories about their romance to the press. Khan stormed out of Kensington Palace, then called back to apologize.

Confused, Diana fled to one place she said people are "always on my side"—the United States. There, she appeared at a benefit for the Red Cross, had breakfast at the White House with First Lady Hillary Clinton, attended *Washington Post* publisher Katharine Graham's eightieth birthday party, showed up at a preview party for an auction of her gowns at Christie's (this had been William's fund-raising idea), and visited with her friend Mother Teresa at an AIDS hospice in the Bronx—the last time the planet's two most famous humanitarians would ever see each other.

Just days after returning to London, Diana celebrated her thirty-sixth birthday as guest of honor at a gala marking the Tate Gallery's centennial. Prime Minister Tony Blair, who had been consulting with President Bill Clinton about what role Diana might play on the world stage, invited her to discuss the matter with him at Chequers, the PM's official country estate. To her delight, Blair told Diana that he wanted to send her on a number of foreign assignments as Britain's roving goodwill ambassador. She left feeling that "at last" she had found someone who "will know how to use me." She also told friends that she found Blair "quite sexy."

This new job for Diana had already been approved by the Queen, despite the fact that she knew Charles would be, in the words of a Palace staffer, "green with envy. He had always been pushed aside by people wanting to get close to Diana, and now it looked as if she was going to upstage him forever." Or at least until he became king.

Diana remained convinced, of course, that this would never happen—certainly not as long he insisted on keeping company with the massively unpopular Camilla. In one week, Charles was throwing a fiftieth birthday party for Camilla at Highgrove. The highly publicized private event, to which no other members of the Royal Family were invited, was for all intents and purposes Charles's first public declaration of love for Camilla. "This trial balloon," Harold Brooks-Baker said at the time, "will determine whether Prince Charles is on shaky ground or not." He went on to say that if the public showed signs of accepting Camilla, "you can be certain attempts will be made to make a marriage possible, because today—given the opposition of the Church, the Queen, and Parliament—it is not."

At this point, the public's attitude toward Camilla had already softened considerably. Polls now were showing that one in five Britons had changed their minds about Camilla, and fully 68 percent felt that Charles should be free to marry his longtime mistress. The vast majority, however, could not yet bring themselves to accept a future "Queen Camilla."

Nor, apparently, could Tony Blair, Diana's most important friend and ally in the government. Although the Queen and the Archbishop of Canterbury had the ultimate say, the Prime Minister would also have to sign off on any marriage plan. "He certainly has the right of veto," said British constitutional expert Ben Pimlott, "if he thinks it will be damaging to the country or the constitution."

Diana hoped the best for Charles and Camilla but sensed that the party would be a public relations fiasco. "Wouldn't it be funny," she cracked, "if I jumped out of the cake in a bathing suit?"

Hasnat Khan, meanwhile, was more convinced than ever that Diana was leaking details about their affair to Fleet Street. Not long after Diana's summit with Tony Blair at Chequers, Khan again confronted her at Kensington Palace, reducing her to tears. True to form, on July 11, 1997, he apologized with a dozen red roses—but this time, Diana had had enough.

That same day, she departed London with William and Harry for the palatial Saint-Tropez estate of Mohamed Al Fayed.

....

"AL FAYED?" THE QUEEN LOOKED up from the note she had just been handed and squinted at her private secretary over rimless reading glasses. Robert Fellowes, who also happened to be Diana's brother-in-law, swallowed hard. The Queen's tone always went up an octave or two at times like these, making her sound less like a monarch and more like the schoolgirl she was during the Blitz. "*Really*? She can't be serious. *Al Fayed*?"

There were, in fact, few more controversial figures in Great Britain than the Egyptian-born self-made billionaire entrepreneur. Over a span of three decades, Mohamed Al Fayed had managed to acquire a number of British icons: Harrods department store, royal shirtmaker Turnbull and Asser, several apartment buildings on London's Park Lane, the Fulham Football Club, Scotland's pink-walled fourteenth-century Balnagown Castle, and the satirical magazine *Punch*, to name a few. To underscore his love of all things British, Al Fayed also maintained a personal fleet of sixty-four Rolls-Royces.

None of it mattered. Al Fayed was stopped at every turn in his quest for respectability. Denied British citizenship, spurned by most of British society, he was considered a boorish arriviste by every aristocratic family but the Spencers.

The Queen was livid, and not just because the Princess of Wales had accepted Al Fayed's standing invitation to visit his Saint-Tropez mansion. Under the terms of the divorce agreement, Diana was required to obtain the Queen's permission in writing before taking either William or Harry out of the country.

It was too late to do anything about it now; Diana and the young princes were already aboard Harrods' Executive Gulfstream IV jet bound for Nice. Once there, they would board the Egyptian mogul's 195-foot yacht *Jonikal* for the five-hour trip to Al Fayed's $17 million compound overlooking the Mediterranean.

Two days later, Diana's affair with Al Fayed's forty-two-year-old son Dodi began with a food fight aboard the *Jonikal*. The yacht's chief stewardess, Debbie Gribble, remembered that they were "chasing each other and laughing and giggling like a couple of kids."

Following Diana's turbulent affair with Khan, William encouraged his mother to pursue the relationship with the fun-loving, high-living Emad "Dodi" Fayed. (In pursuit of a career as a Hollywood producer—Dodi was executive producer of the Academy Award–winning *Chariots of Fire*, as well as *Hook*, *F/X*, and *The Scarlet Letter*—he dropped the "Al" in Al Fayed.) Over the next few days in Saint-Tropez, the Princess and the playboy spent long hours talking mostly about Diana's hopes and dreams. Unlike the other men in her life, Fayed had perfected the art of listening to women. "Dodi could make you feel," a former girlfriend said, "like you were the center of the universe." Soon it became clear to Gribble that "something had passed between them. Suddenly they seemed to fit as a couple."

For the rest of July and into August, Diana and Dodi were virtually inseparable. When they weren't sharing cozy evenings in Kensington Palace or at his luxurious apartment in Mayfair, they were being photographed sunbathing and kissing aboard the *Jonikal*.

The Queen, Charles, Camilla, and for that matter the rest of the world were riveted by the tabloid saga of Diana and her improbable new love. Indeed, Camilla's birthday party—Charles's much-ballyhooed proclamation of love for the "other woman" in his royal love triangle—was completely overshadowed by Diana's Mediterranean escapade.

Although Dodi showered Diana with attention, affection, and gifts (a Bulgari ring, a gold Cartier Panthère watch, a diamond bracelet), she told friends like Lana Marks, Rosa Monckton, and Annabel Goldsmith that marriage was the farthest thing from her mind. "The last thing I need is a new marriage," she said. "I need it like a bad rash on my face."

The Queen was not so sure. She worried that Mohamed Al Fayed was seeking the ultimate revenge for being snubbed by the British establishment by marrying into the Royal Family. As the father-in-law to the Princess of Wales—and potentially grandfather to children who would be half-siblings of William and Harry—Al Fayed would gain more social status than he might otherwise have dreamed possible.

That August of 1997, William and Harry joined their father and the Queen at their beloved Balmoral Castle in the Scottish Highlands. Diana figured that they were "out killing something" whenever she tried to reach them on the phone, and she was invariably right. If they weren't angling for trout in the River Dee, they were either hunting the red deer that were indigenous to the region or gunning down dozens of pheasants, grouse, and ducks—often in a single morning.

The Queen regarded Balmoral as a magical place. It was here that, at the age of seventeen, she shot her first stag. (Although Diana shot her first stag at thirteen, she detested killing in all its forms and found the country life "immensely dull.") Although Elizabeth no longer hunted—she shot her last stag in 1983, in a glen now called "the Queen's Corry"—she loved nothing more than riding the estate's narrow trails on horseback or traipsing through the muddy landscape with a brace of corgis swarming at her feet.

A trained mechanic who worked in a motor pool during World War II, the Queen also enjoyed getting behind the wheel of a Land Rover and taking it for a spin across the Highlands terrain. Her Majesty never wore a seat belt and, in the words of her cousin Margaret Rhodes, usually drove "like a bat out of hell." Most days at Balmoral, the Queen would drop in on the all-male hunting parties at some point to see how they were progressing. On these occasions, corgis were seldom seen. When the menfolk raised shotguns to blast away at the birds that were flushed out of bushes and trees at Balmoral and Sandringham, the Queen stood behind them, flanked by Labradors and cocker spaniels—her "gun dogs."

Midday, the Queen often presided over an elaborate picnic lunch sans servants, setting the places herself ("She has to have it absolutely right," said frequent guest Anne Glenconner) and then listening intently to the princes' tall hunting tales over a gin and tonic and plates of cold roast chicken. Once the Queen had finished, she cleared the table with the help of her grandsons, then donned rubber yellow kitchen gloves to scrub the dishes before putting them away. "You think I'm joking but I'm not," said Tony Blair, recalling one of his "intriguing, surreal, and utterly freaky" weekends with the Royal Family at Balmoral. "The Queen asks if you've finished, she stacks the plates up and goes off to the sink."

While the Windsors enjoyed their country pursuits in Scotland, five hundred miles to the south a psychic named Edward Williams walked into the South Wales police station at 2:12 in the afternoon and told police he had a premonition that Princess Diana was going to die. He had previously predicted—correctly—that Ronald Reagan and Pope John Paul II would be victims of failed assassination attempts. The log of the department's Special Branch investigative unit recounted Williams's August 27, 1997, visit in detail, and described him as appearing to be "quite normal." Williams realized he could have been dismissed as the "local nutter," but felt he had to "do *something* . . . the feeling that Diana was in danger didn't leave me."

Three days later, Charles penned a letter to "My Dearest Diana," asking if Harry, already held back one year, should stay an additional year at Ludgrove before joining William at Eton. No intellectual match for the Heir, the Spare had been struggling with his grades. The Prince signed the letter "Lots of love, Charles," and then told his secretary to put it on Diana's desk at Kensington Palace so she would have it as soon as she returned to London.

She had been separated from William and Harry for more than a month now, and all Diana could think about now was getting home to her children. She told one American friend, Richard Greene, that she believed she was destined to reform the monarchy ("Yes, I believe in destiny"). But towering above all other considerations was her sons' happiness.

Stopping over in Paris on the way to London, Diana and Dodi were staying on the Place Vendôme in the Hotel Ritz, which happened to be owned by Dodi's father. Harry's thirteenth birthday was in a matter of weeks, and since she could not face the army of reporters camped outside, Diana asked a hotel staffer to pick up the Sony PlayStation he had asked for.

Late that afternoon, Prince William called from Balmoral. If Diana had been thinking of marrying Dodi, as Fleet Street speculated and the Queen deeply feared, she would have talked it over with her "little old wise man"—the one person whose opinion on all such things she valued most—William. She didn't. Instead, the conversation centered on Harry, and whether a photo opportunity being set up at Eton to mark the beginning of William's third year there would make the Spare feel awkward and "ignored."

They talked about other things as well in that final twenty-minute phone conversation—how many game birds he and Harry bagged that day, what a great shot Grandpapa Philip was, how fast Granny drove, how they were looking forward to spending time with her in London before returning to school, the Sony PlayStation Mummy was giving Harry for his birthday. William also asked if he and Harry could meet her when she arrived at Heathrow—a homecoming that was sure to create a scrum of photographers at the airport.

"Of course," the Princess instantly replied. In stark contrast to her in-laws' stiff formality, Diana was famous for running to her children and sweeping them up with bear hugs and kisses. She also knew that those heartwarming images would again be splashed across the front pages of newspapers worldwide. After cavorting with Dodi on the Riviera and in Paris, Diana wanted to remind the Queen, Charles, and the world at large of her place in the Royal Family—and, as the mother of a future king, her role in shaping the monarchy. "Diana was Merlin—an absolute wizard—when it came to manipulating the media," said veteran *Times of London* correspondent Alan Hamilton, a favorite of the Royal Family. "The Queen, in particular, was in awe of this."

As for Charles, relations with his ex-wife had warmed to such an extent that he was preparing to make his first public appearance with Diana since they enrolled William at Eton nearly six months earlier. The royal yacht *Britannia*, which cost nearly $20 million a year to run, had become such a symbol of royal excess at the taxpayers' expense that the Queen made what for her was a painful personal decision to decommission the vessel. In October, the 412-foot ship was to begin its farewell tour around Britain, and, fittingly, the Prince of Wales was to board at Cardiff. Diana was ecstatic when Charles invited her and the boys to join him. For reasons both personal and strategic, the Princess was happy to "be seen in public as a family again. I know it will please the Queen."

Elizabeth was glad to hear that Diana was finally returning to England, and hoped that the adventure with Dodi—and any future connection to Mohamed Al Fayed—was over.

While Charles prepared to return to London with William and Harry, the Queen stayed behind at her beloved Balmoral.

"It's nice," she said, "to hibernate for a bit."

Be careful, Paul. There are powers at work in this country about which we have no knowledge.

—THE QUEEN, TO PAUL BURRELL

....

My darling, what is going to happen to us now?

—CAMILLA TO CHARLES, ON HEARING NEWS OF DIANA'S DEATH

5

"THE QUEEN WANTS TO KNOW: WHERE ARE THE JEWELS?!"

ST. ANDREWS COLLEGE

MARCH 27, 2002

"Prince William is out there," one of the student models said, sending a palpable ripple of excitement through the crowd backstage. One of the models was not surprised; Kate Middleton and the Prince were already friends, and she knew he wasn't about to miss St. Andrews University's annual Don't Walk charity fashion show sponsored by Yves Saint Laurent. Kate had also told William that she was making her debut on the runway to conquer her inhibitions, and he promised to be there with a few of their mutual pals to lend moral support. In fact, the Prince paid two hundred pounds for a front-row seat.

As with everything else she did, Kate took considerable care in deciding which garment to wear—and, just as important, how to wear it. She settled on a sheer black, gold, and green piece with blue ribbon trim. What she didn't know at the time was that the piece (total cost for materials: fifty dollars) had been made two years earlier by budding designer Charlotte Todd for a college project titled, appropriately enough, "The Art of Seduction."

Slipping into a bandeau bra and black bikini panties, Kate started to pull the shift over her head, resting the top just above her breasts so that the hem hit her midthigh. "No, no, that's not right. It's a skirt, a floor-length skirt," a dresser said, handing her a black blouse. "Here, this goes on top. Put this on."

Kate refused. "I like it this way," she insisted, studying herself in the mirror. "This is much sexier."

Moments later, she strode out confidently in what looked like a naughty negligee, chestnut curls bouncing on her bare white shoulders. William clapped and cheered the loudest, but Kate did not break her model-serious pose for an instant. When she returned to the catwalk in white lace bra and white lace panties, the Prince and their friends, fortified with champagne, whooped and whistled.

"It was a side to her we didn't know existed, and it was a turning point in people's perception of her," said their classmate and friend Jules Knight. "Everyone took note, including Will."

Their first meeting more than six months earlier had been awkward, and mercifully brief. Kate remembered that when they first met at their dormitory, St. Salvatore's, she "turned bright red and sort of scuttled off, feeling very shy about meeting him."

Yet, like the young women who accounted for a 44 percent surge in applications to St. Andrews in the fall of 2001, Kate was at the Scottish university for that very purpose—to meet (and perhaps even someday marry) the future King of England. Like so many English schoolgirls of her generation—and more than a few Americans—Kate had a crush on Princess Diana's handsome young son. Her bedroom at Marlborough College, the exclusive boarding school she attended not that far from Camilla's house in Wiltshire, was dominated by a color photo of William and Charles at Balmoral.

Kate—until she turned fifteen she was nearly always called Catherine—kept track of William's hectic royal schedule online and on television. She also lapped up every newspaper story, magazine article, and juicy gossip column tidbit about the young Prince. "You cannot tell me anything about Prince William," she once told a schoolmate, "that I don't already know."

Kate's obsession mirrored that of her mother for William's father, the Prince of Wales. Carole Goldsmith was six years older than Diana, and like the future Princess of Wales, dreamed of marrying the Queen's eldest son. Unlike the Spencers, the Goldsmiths were decidedly working class—two-fisted, hard-drinking denizens of County Durham's coal fields in northeastern England. Kate's great-great-great-grandfather was thrown in jail for public drunkenness in 1881; her great-grandmother Edith, left to raise six children in a condemned flat following the death of her husband, worked long hours at a pickle factory. Most of Kate's maternal ancestors succumbed to influenza, scarlet fever, and cholera, or fell on the battlefield during World War I.

Things were considerably more promising on her dad's side of the family. The Middletons were related to Academy Award–winning actor Sir John Gielgud; author and illustrator Beatrix Potter; Britain's leading Shakespearean actress, Ellen Terry; and—through seventeenth-century statesman Sir Thomas Fairfax—even to the Royal Family. (Known as "Black Tom" because of his swarthy complexion, Fairfax played a key role in the restoration of the monarchy and the return of Charles II to the throne in 1660.) Kate and William were, it turned out, fifteenth cousins.

By the late nineteenth century, Kate's Middleton forebears had amassed a fortune worth $50 million in today's dollars, only to squander it all long before Michael Francis Middleton was born in 1949. There would, however, be a new Middleton fortune—this time thanks to the driving ambition of Kate's Goldsmith relatives.

Given her impoverished background, it was understandable that Kate's grandmother, Dorothy Harrison Goldsmith, would grow up with deep-seated doubts about her place in society. According to her niece Ann Terry, Dorothy developed expensive tastes to impress the neighbors and burdened her struggling housepainter-husband Ronald with the cost.

By the time Carole arrived in 1955, her mother had earned the nickname "Lady Dorothy"—despite the fact the family was still struggling to make ends meet at their cramped, unheated council flat in London's downscale Southall district. The public housing project where they lived was directly under Heathrow's flight path—not unlike Windsor Castle. "We really never stopped to think," Carole later told a neighbor, "that those same planes were flying over the Queen's head, too." (At Windsor, guests were often surprised when the Queen nonchalantly ticked of the names of the aircraft roaring overhead. "That one's a 777. No, I'm wrong . . . Airbus!")

When Carole was eleven and her brother Gary not quite two, the Goldsmiths managed to relocate to a comfortable three-bedroom home in Norwood Green, a more affluent section of the west London borough of Ealing. Still very much a working-class girl with neither the means nor the desire to attend college, Carole graduated from high school in 1974 and went straight into the British Airlines flight attendant program. "Back then, air travel was really quite glamorous compared to the way it is today," recalled another retired BA stewardess who, like Carole, wore the airline's dark-blue uniform of knee-length skirt, blazer, and pillbox hat. "It was a dream job for a young girl—we got to fly all around the world." The pay "was awful, really, for all the hours you had to work. But there were other compensations."

The "other compensations" included the opportunity to cull a rich husband from the ranks of well-heeled businessmen who flew first class. It really didn't matter, the former BA flight attendant admitted, "whether they were already married or not."

Finding love even closer to home, Carole fell in love with a fellow British Airways employee, a young flight dispatcher six years her senior. Following in the footsteps of his father, who had served in the RAF during World War II, Michael Middleton originally hoped to become a pilot. Instead, like Carole, he joined the ranks of British Airways' flight attendants. From there, he became a dispatcher, and by the time he met Carole Goldsmith in 1977, Mike Middleton was in charge of ground operations at Heathrow and collecting a hefty salary.

"Love at first sight?" asked Carole, "Yes, absolutely!" Mike remembered being impressed not only by her "incredible beauty" but also by her "keen intelligence, her passion for life, and her sense of humor. From the very beginning, we laughed a *lot*."

After living together for a year—first in a modest flat, then in a small brick house in the village of Bradfield Southend—Michael and Carole were wed on June 21, 1980, at Buckinghamshire's picturesque twelfth-century Church of St. James the Less, just down the road from Windsor Castle. Apparently not wanting to expose the upper-middle-class Middletons to the working-class relations on their side of the family, Carole and Dorothy excluded all but two out of more than twenty Goldsmiths from the guest list. "Carole," a cousin said, "was a lot like her mother in that way."

Neither Carole nor Michael could have imagined how elevated their social status would ultimately be when Catherine Elizabeth Middleton was born on January 9, 1982, at the Royal Berkshire Hospital in Reading. The entire world would take note of another birth six months later, when Prince William arrived, curiously enough, on June 21—the Middletons' second anniversary as a married couple.

Carole embraced full-time motherhood with gusto. Catherine was twenty months old when sister Philippa ("Pippa") arrived, followed by their brother James in 1987. A born organizer, Carole did not hesitate to sign up for all the parent committees at nearby St. Peter's Church preschool. Of all her many talents, one stood out: Mrs. Middleton had a special knack for assembling the fancifully decorated goodie bags stuffed with candy, toys, trinkets, and other treats that are handed out at children's birthday parties. Word spread, and soon the other mothers in Bradfield Southend were paying Carole to make the goodie bags for their children's parties.

It didn't take long for Carole to expand the scope of her services, offering to plan and then oversee the parties themselves. Three months after she gave birth to James, she took the plunge and launched Party Pieces, a mail-order business that supplied anything and everything needed to throw a proper children's party: balloons, streamers, glitter, paper plates, plastic utensils, party hats, costumes, even fireworks.

Within months, thousands of orders poured in. Michael quit his job at British Airways to pitch in, and soon Catherine and

Pippa were posing for brochures and ads. A neighbor remembered Catherine "in her sparkly princess dress and little rhinestone crown, watching Princess Diana on the television and imitating her."

Meantime, the family income soared. Where Carole's parents could never have afforded to send her to a private school, the Middletons effortlessly paid the $20,000 a year it took to send seven-year-old Catherine to St. Andrew's School in the nearby town of Pangbourne. Catherine excelled at both sports and academics, and—not surprisingly given her established fondness for playing dress-up—sang the lead in the school's musical productions.

During one of those performances, captured on video, Catherine plays the lead in the Victorian melodrama *Murder in the Barn.* In one eerily prophetic scene, a fortune-teller informs Catherine's character that she will marry a rich, handsome stranger.

"Will he take me away from here?" she asks.

"Yes," replies the fortune-teller, "to London."

Eventually, the hero of the play asks her to marry him. "Yes, it's all I've ever longed for," Catherine gushes. "Yes, oh, yes, dear *William.*"

Thanks in large part to Carole's canny decision to set up a Party Pieces website in 1992, the company was soon employing thirty people to fill orders at the company's new, greatly expanded headquarters in Ashampstead Common, Berkshire. With an annual gross income exceeding $3 million, the Middletons were now able to purchase Oak Acre, a baronial, six-bedroom, brick-walled Tudor-style estate next to the privately owned Bucklebury Estate.

In the fall of 1995, the Middletons sent their tall (Catherine always towered over most of her friends as a child), skinny, and awkward thirteen-year-old elder daughter to Downe House, an all-girls boarding school in the town of Cold Ash. Even though Downe House was just a ten-minute drive from Oak Acre, Catherine quickly grew homesick. For whatever reason, she was also being systematically bullied by several of the "mean girls" in the school.

The bullying continued despite the Middletons' complaints, so in April 1996 Catherine transferred to Marlborough College. The coed atmosphere was evident from the moment she walked into the school's dining hall and her looks were judged a "2" on a scale of 1 to 10 by a group of tittering adolescent boys.

Kate was about to be joined by her sister, Pippa, at Marlborough when, on August 31, 1997, Princess Diana was killed along with her boyfriend Dodi and their driver in a horrific Paris car crash. For the next week, the Middletons, along with hundreds of millions of people around the world, sat glued to their television screens, transfixed by the unfolding royal drama. From Rome, Berlin, Tokyo, and Beijing to Moscow, New York, and Washington, D.C., thousands of mourners stood in line for hours to sign books of condolence and leave floral tributes at British consulates and embassies.

Nowhere, certainly, was there a more palpable sense of loss than in London. The images would be indelibly etched in everyone's minds—waves of cards and flowers lapping at the iron gates of Kensington Palace, candlelight vigils, weeping in the streets.

What the Middletons did not see was the heavy drama being played out away from the cameras. From that moment in the early morning hours of August 31, 1997, when Sir Robert Fellowes called Balmoral with news that Diana had died, Elizabeth II faced a crisis like none she had ever faced before—a crushing personal loss for the young princes and for untold millions around the world who loved Diana, but also a public relations calamity that quickly proved to be the monarchy's worst nightmare.

....

CHARLES INSTINCTIVELY KNEW HOW DEEPLY Diana's death would be felt by the British people, and that the Royal Family must acknowledge the loss if it had any hope of surviving. But the Queen had other things on her mind. Her first call to the British Embassy in Paris was not to seek details about Diana's injuries or the crash itself, but to ask if the major pieces of state jewelry Diana sometimes traveled with—tiaras, bracelets, rings, or necklaces that actually belonged to the crown—were anywhere in evidence.

Beatrice Humbert, chief nurse at Paris's Pitié-Salpêtrière Hospital, was standing by the bed where Diana's body lay naked beneath a plain white sheet when the British Consul General burst into the room. "The Queen! The Queen," he said. "Madame, the Queen is worried about the jewelry. We must find the jewelry, quickly. The Queen wants to know, *'Where are the jewels?!'* "

"But there *isn't* any jewelry," replied Humbert, who was taken aback by the question. "No wedding band, of course. No rings, no necklace." (The Queen had an encyclopedic knowledge of the jewels in the royal collection and guarded them jealously. Once, when told that the avant-garde artist Damien Hirst was using diamonds to make a jeweled skull, she smiled. "I prefer diamonds," the Queen said, "around my neck.")

Charles, meanwhile, had his hands full just convincing his mother to let him accompany Diana's body home from Paris. "She is no longer a member of this family," the Queen told him. "She gave that up when she divorced you." It was inappropriate, she said, for the Windsors to step in at this point. "The Spencers are her family, Charles," she said. "They should be the ones to bring Diana back." She went so far as to say that it was not even acceptable for Charles to be at RAF Northhold to meet the plane bearing Diana's body, much less be on it.

The Prince of Wales, a battle-scarred veteran of the media wars waged with Diana over the course of seventeen years, knew better. So did Prime Minister Tony Blair, who believed there would be an enormous public outcry if no member of the Royal Family made the trip to Paris. Charles overruled the Queen and took off with Diana's sisters, Lady Sarah McCorquedale and Lady Jane Fellowes, aboard an RAF transport with its distinctive red tail and the Union Jack emblazoned on the fuselage.

Charles spent much of the flight from London to Paris conferring with Camilla over the phone. At this point, Camilla had never officially met the Queen or, for that matter, William and Harry. Yet, in times like these, she was nothing less than a pillar of emotional support for Charles. Badly shaken by news of Diana's death, he wept over the phone to the only woman he ever really loved. He was also weeping for what lay in store for Camilla. They both knew that, in an instant, any progress that had been made in selling Camilla to the public as a possible wife for Charles had gone up in smoke.

Only three months earlier, in late May 1997, Camilla had taken matters into her own hands. She approached Charles's deputy private secretary and principal media advisor, Mark Bolland, and asked for his help. Specifically, she informed Bolland that she wanted to brainstorm with Peter Mandelson, Tony Blair's media spinmaster, about ways to win over the hearts and minds of the people. Over lunch at Highgrove, Charles, Camilla, Bolland, and Mandelson hammered out a top-secret scheme to make the Prince of Wales's scorned mistress acceptable as Diana's successor. The plan was to be called "Operation PB"—shorthand for Operation Parker Bowles.

....

EVEN BEFORE A CAR CRASH in Paris changed the trajectory of British history, Camilla made it clear that she was no longer content to someday simply be the King's mistress. Following the divorce of Charles and Diana, "Camilla started plotting to become the next queen," Lady Bowker said. "She thought the most she could hope for was to someday be the King's mistress, but now Diana was out of the way and Camilla wanted more." The media summit at Highgrove kicked off what became, according to Diana's private secretary Patrick Jephson, "a sustained political-style spin that hijacked Charles's reputation to serve the needs of his true love's ambition."

Incredibly, less than two weeks after that critical meeting with Mark Bolland and Peter Mandelson—and only two months before Diana's death—Camilla caused a car crash that left her injured and nearly killed another woman, then fled the scene. A notoriously fast and not necessarily cautious driver, Camilla was speeding toward Highgrove one evening when she plowed into a car driven by fifty-three-year-old interior designer Carolyn

Melville-Smith. "That car was going hellish fast," Melville-Smith recalled. "The next thing I knew the other car was flying through the air and I was in a ditch." Trapped inside, Melville-Smith cried for help, but to no avail.

Camilla called Prince Charles on her cellphone, then walked over to look at the other vehicle. From the road, she could make out that the car was tipped on its side and that someone was behind the wheel. Rather than doing anything to help, Camilla screamed, panicked, and ran away. The Royal Protection officers Charles dispatched to the scene found the Prince of Wales's mistress sitting by her car at the side of the road, rocking back and forth, smoking a cigarette, and sobbing. Other passing motorists, meanwhile, stopped to help Melville-Smith and summoned police and an ambulance, which took her to a local hospital to be treated for minor scrapes and bruises. Camilla was given a breathalyzer test on the spot, which she passed, and was taken to Highgrove to be treated for a minor concussion and a badly twisted wrist. In the meantime, no one bothered to tell Melville-Smith who the other driver was.

St. James's Palace was pleased to see the next day's newspaper articles headlined CAMILLA THE HEROINE telling the story of how Mrs. Parker Bowles came upon a crash victim and pulled her to safety. Once Melville-Smith realized that the other driver was none other than Mrs. Parker Bowles, she hurried to set the record straight. Camilla was no hero, she angrily insisted. "I was trapped in my car, yelling for help, and she did not come," Melville-Smith said. "I could have been badly hurt and she just left me there." Authorities were still looking into the possibility of filing criminal reckless driving charges against Camilla when Diana was killed.

Out of deference to the Prince of Wales, prosecutors decided not to pursue legal action against his mistress in the immediate aftermath of the crash that took his ex-wife's life.

....

ON LEARNING OF DIANA'S TRAGIC death, Charles and Camilla could only believe that their dreams of marriage had been dashed forever. Yet the emotion of the moment—and the heartbreaking realization that William and Harry had lost the mother they loved so deeply—trumped all else. Walking into the Paris hospital room where Diana's body had already been placed in an open coffin, Charles turned sheet-white and stumbled back, his head snapping "in one involuntary motion," Humbert said, "as if he had actually been stricken. It was just too much to take in, too much, too much . . ." Another nurse, Jeanne Lecorcher, had always thought of all the Royals as "very cold and unfeeling, and like everyone else I knew that the Prince really loved Camilla." She changed her mind about Charles on the spot. "I was very impressed by how emotional the Prince became."

On the flight back to London, Charles took a call from Tony Blair, who warned the Prince that it would be a "fatal mistake" for Diana's Spencer relatives to proceed with their original plans for a private funeral. The Princess's funeral would have to be a national event unlike any other—the people, Blair told Charles, demanded it.

Once the Spencers agreed to a public funeral for Diana, the Prince and the Prime Minister turned their attention to convincing the one person who had the last word on the matter. Enlisting the help of Sir Robert Fellowes, Blair and Prince Charles tried but failed to persuade the Queen that a large public funeral was in order. Anything less, they reasoned, would leave Her Majesty's subjects feeling resentful of the monarchy.

Only monarchs were entitled to a full state funeral, although by order of the crown and a vote in Parliament this honor could be extended to someone like Winston Churchill. There was also the possibility of a private royal funeral attended only by members of the Royal Family, or perhaps a larger ceremonial funeral of the sort reserved for the heir to the throne or the consort of the monarch. Finally, Lord Airlie, who as Lord Chamberlain would handle the details of any public funeral, weighed in. He agreed with Charles and Tony Blair that what was needed was a "unique funeral for a unique person—a mixture of the traditional and modern."

While Charles, Blair, Lord Airlie, and others grappled with the question of how best to pay tribute to Diana, the Queen and Prince Philip remained at Balmoral with their devastated grandsons. The night Diana died, William and Harry were not awakened to be told the news; the Queen felt that nothing would be gained by robbing them of these last few precious hours of sleep before their world collapsed around them. To spare them any further upset after they were told, she ordered a news blackout at Balmoral. No newspapers were to be brought inside the castle, and all television sets and radios were turned off.

Had the televisions at Balmoral been on, William and Harry would have seen one world leader after another expressing shock and sympathy. "A beacon of light has been extinguished," declared former British Prime Minister Margaret Thatcher. French President Jacques Chirac described Diana as "a woman of our times, warm, full of life and generosity. Her tragic death will be deeply felt." Vacationing on Martha's Vineyard, a solemn President Bill Clinton praised her for embracing AIDS patients and working to "end the scourge of land mines in the world."

Standing outside the church he attended in his parliamentary district, Tony Blair struggled to maintain his composure as he talked to reporters. "I feel like everyone else in this country today, utterly devastated. . . . Our thoughts and prayers are with Princess Diana's family and in particular her two sons, the two boys. Our hearts go out to them. We are today a nation in a state of shock and in grief that is so deeply painful for us. . . . Princess Diana was the people's Princess, and that's how she will remain, in our hearts and in our memories forever."

The Palace, however, felt a simple, fifteen-word statement would suffice: "*The Queen and Prince of Wales are deeply shocked and distressed by this terrible news.*"

The Queen also saw no reason to disrupt the Windsors' summer routine at Balmoral. Just a few hours after learning their mother had been killed, the boys joined other members of the Royal Family at Crathie Church, just across the River Dee from the castle grounds. Asked earlier that morning if she wanted any change in the service to reflect what had happened, the Queen made it abundantly clear that she did not. Elizabeth was also asked if—just this once—Diana's name might be included in the morning prayer for the Royal Family. Again, Her Majesty felt that, since Diana had been stripped of her royal status, there was no need. The entire service, then, was conducted without any mention of Diana being made. Confused, Harry turned to his father at one point and asked, "Are you sure Mummy is dead?"

Some 550 miles away in London, grief-stricken Britons demanded to know why the flag over Buckingham Palace was not flying at half-mast when every other flag in the United Kingdom was. In keeping with royal protocol, the flag flew only when the monarch was in residence—and never at half-mast. The Queen, as with all matters, did not feel Diana's death rose to the level of requiring any break in precedent.

If the flag over Buckingham Palace flew only when the Queen was in residence, then why *wasn't* she there? And why, when tributes were pouring in from all over the world, had not only the Queen but the entire Royal Family remained totally silent on the subject of Diana's death?

LET THE FLAG FLY AT HALF MAST, insisted the *Daily Mail*. The *Mirror* pleaded SPEAK TO US MA'AM—YOUR PEOPLE ARE SUFFERING. WHERE IS OUR QUEEN? The *Sun* asked, WHERE IS HER FLAG? Polls now showed that 66 percent of all Britons were convinced Diana's death signaled the end of Britain's monarchy.

"A stunning reversal has taken place," observed constitutional expert Anthony Barrett. "The monarchy must bow its head, or it will be broken. We, the people, will henceforth define how they should represent us. . . . It's as if the country is crying, 'Diana is dead! Long live democracy!'" Agreed Harold Brooks-Baker of *Burke's Peerage*: "They have blood on their hands. . . . Here was a victim of the monarchy. Diana died a martyr. We can only hope her death brings about another kind of palace rebellion. The House of Windsor is in desperate need of a major overhaul, and if it doesn't get one soon, I fear for the very existence of the monarchy in Britain."

Tony Blair, caught in "that storm, unpredictable and unnerving," also saw a revolution in the making. "The outpouring of grief was turning into a mass movement for change," he recalled. "It was a moment of supreme national articulation and it was menacing for the royal family. . . . Public anger was turning towards the Queen."

It was left to Charles, who had the full backing of the Prime Minister, to stand up to his mother. Grudgingly, she agreed to a public funeral that would turn out to be quite unlike any the world had ever seen. Charles also urged the Queen to return to London immediately, fly the flag over Buckingham Palace at half-staff, and address her people. Either that, or the Prince of Wales would take to the airwaves himself to apologize to the nation on behalf of the Royal Family.

The Queen, finally beginning to grasp the gravity of the situation, yielded on all points. The next day, she departed for London. As soon as she arrived at Buckingham Palace, the royal standard went up—and when it stopped halfway up the flagpole, the massive crowd that had gathered at the palace gates began to cheer.

On the eve of Diana's funeral, Elizabeth gave what would be the most important speech of her reign—the speech on which hinged the very existence of Britain's thousand-year-old monarchy. She did it sitting in the opulently appointed Chinese Dining Room, the crowds milling in front of Buckingham Palace clearly visible in the background. "We have seen, throughout Britain and around the world, an overwhelming expression of sadness at Diana's death," Elizabeth II said. "We have all been trying in our different ways to cope. It is not easy to express a sense of loss, since the initial shock is often succeeded by a mixture of other feelings: disbelief, incomprehension, anger—and concern for those who remain.

"So what I say to you now as your Queen and as a grandmother, I say from my heart," Her Majesty continued. "First, I want to pay tribute to Diana, myself. She was an exceptional and gifted human being. In good times and bad, she never lost her capacity to smile and laugh, to inspire others with her warmth and kindness. I admired and respected her for her energy and commitment to others, especially her devotion to her two boys."

The Queen went on to explain that she had remained at Balmoral only to help William and Harry "come to terms with the devastating loss," and that she believed "there are lessons to be drawn from her life and from the extraordinary and moving reaction to her death." Taking into account the public's mounting anger over her absence and her silence, Elizabeth II had learned her lesson the hard way. "I share in your determination," she pledged, "to cherish her memory."

At St. James's Palace, Charles prepared for the possibility that he might be shot down in the streets the next day. He had already done all he could to protect Camilla, ordering that the usual security detail guarding her at Ray Mill House be beefed up with an additional four Royal Protection officers. The "Close Protection Team," as Prince Charles's security detail was sometimes called, usually consisted of four plainclothes bodyguards armed with Glock 9-mm pistols. It was doubled to eight.

That night before Diana's funeral, facing the prospect of his own imminent assassination, Charles sat down in his study and scribbled four brief letters in his distinctive, spidery script—to William, to Harry, to Camilla, and to the people of Great Britain. Each, according to an intimate friend with whom he shared the letters' contents, was signed, then placed in a small red envelope bearing the three-plumed seal of the Prince of Wales.

In his note to William, Charles lauded his elder son for his maturity and predicted he would make a great king. He praised Harry for supporting his brother, but at the same time urged him to live his own life and not be overshadowed by William. He told Camilla that she was the only woman he had ever loved, and that, had he lived, he would have fulfilled his promise to make her queen. Writing to his countrymen, Charles noted that, despite making some serious mistakes, he had done his best as Prince of Wales. Charles was now sorry that he would not have the chance to serve his country as its king. The four red envelopes were left on Prince Charles's desk with instructions to deliver them only "in the event of my death."

....

ALONG WITH 2.5 BILLION OTHERS around the world—the largest audience for a live event in television history—Kate's family watched the Windsor men walk behind Diana's casket as it was pulled on a horse-drawn caisson through eerily silent streets lined with an estimated 1.5 million people. "It was the most harrowing experience of my life," said Diana's brother, Earl Spencer, who walked between William and Harry. "There was a clear feeling of high emotion around you of the most sad and confused sort, all hammering in on you. It was a tunnel of grief."

What no one knew at the time was that, from the beginning, Diana's brother opposed putting fifteen-year-old William and Harry, twelve, through such punishing stress. Spencer later claimed that the Palace's string-pulling Men in Gray had orchestrated the grim procession from Kensington Palace to Westminster Abbey, and then "tricked" him into believing that the boys had asked to walk behind their mother's coffin. "I genuinely felt that Diana would not have wanted them to have done it," Spencer said. But by the time he learned the truth, it was too late.

The most historically significant moment during the procession occurred just as Diana's coffin passed in front of Buckingham Palace. Queen Elizabeth, standing outside with her family, bowed her head—a seemingly spontaneous tribute to the young woman who had breathed new life into the monarchy while at the same time pushing it to the brink of extinction.

Of course, there was nothing spontaneous about the Queen's bow. It was a gesture that had been discussed with Charles, Philip, and the Queen's cadre of advisors now pushing for some dramatic gesture on Her Majesty's part—a sign that she truly cared. Elizabeth II was moved to consider bowing to Diana's coffin only after Charles bluntly cautioned her that, despite whatever concessions she had already made, the Queen might be jeered at the funeral. Scotland Yard, monitoring a flood of threats against the Crown, now feared the Queen might even be attacked.

For Earl Spencer, Her Majesty's history-making bow in tribute to Diana was all too little, too late. He was especially outraged by the Palace's duplicity in forcing William and Harry to walk behind their mother's coffin—a scheme in which he was an unwitting accomplice. It was this final act of deception, Spencer later said, that led him to deliver a scathing attack on the Royal Family during his history-making eulogy inside the Abbey.

It would have been impossible to find a more appropriate setting for Diana's final, official exit from the Game of Crowns. The tombs of some of history's most formidable queens—"Bloody Mary" Tudor, Elizabeth I, and Mary, Queen of Scots—were all located in the thousand-year-old Abbey, the site of every coronation since William the Conqueror in 1066.

The Queen sat, expressionless, among two thousand mourners inside the Abbey while Elton John sang "Candle in the Wind 1997," a moving tribute to his old friend that would become the number-one best-selling single of all time. Even at this late date, the Palace objected to inviting a rock star—albeit a rock star who would be knighted the following year—to perform at such a solemn occasion.

With the sovereign and the rest of the Royals seated just a few yards away, Earl Spencer praised Diana as "someone with a natural nobility who proved in that last year that she needed no royal title to continue to generate her particular brand of magic." In the name of Diana's "blood family," Spencer then pledged to his sister that he "would not allow" William and Harry to "suffer the anguish that used regularly to drive you to tearful despair." He added that the Spencers would "continue the imaginative way in which you were steering these two exceptional young men so that their souls are not simply immersed by duty and tradition but can sing openly as you planned."

Prince Charles, who despite his own efforts to pay proper tribute to Diana could still become enraged by such impudence, pounded his knee with his fist. The Queen Mother looked aghast, and First Lady Hillary Clinton, seated not far from the Royal Family, gasped at Spencer's unexpectedly frank remarks. The Queen, an expert at concealing her emotions, continued to sit sphinx-like, Queen Victoria's hundred-carat diamond bow brooch glistening on the left shoulder of her black wool suit.

There was little doubt where public sentiment still stood at that moment. The tens of thousands of people who watched the service on jumbo television screens outside the Abbey reacted to Earl Spencer's attack on the Royal Family with thunderous applause. The reaction was similar inside, and while William and Harry joined in the applause, the Queen and Queen Mother, Prince Philip, Charles, and the rest of the Royal Family managed to maintain their customary air of benign indifference.

....

THE FIRM HAD STUMBLED BADLY, but no member of the Royal Family was as universally despised as Camilla Parker Bowles. It had been only a month since Charles threw his highly touted fiftieth birthday party for Camilla—a pivotal event that signaled widespread public approval of Camilla as Charles's future bride. In less than two weeks, she was to host a celebrity-packed charity ball that would mark their first appearance together at a public event. Now that event was canceled, and Charles's long-postponed dream of marrying his mistress was put on hold—perhaps forever.

That would have been perfectly fine with the Middletons, who were planted firmly in Diana's camp. Kate's grandmother spoke for the family when she told a neighbor they were "pretty fed up with the way the Royal Family was acting." Like nearly all of her schoolmates, Kate bemoaned the heartlessness of the Royal Family and cooed over the two young princes who showed such bravery in the face of crushing personal loss.

A familiar face was brought in to help the boys cope. Tiggy Legge-Bourke, who unbeknownst to Diana had been spending time with the boys at Balmoral while Diana was out of the country, rushed in to fill the void. At times, she even cradled Harry to sleep. Everyone agreed that Diana would have approved. "At least Tiggy," a friend said, "was there to give William and Harry the hugs and kisses the Princess could not."

Fleet Street also did its part to help the princes get over their mother's death. In the immediate aftermath of the crash, paparazzi were blamed for literally hounding Diana to death—until it was determined that Dodi's driver, who was killed along with Dodi and Diana, was drunk and under the influence of painkillers. Hewing to guidelines imposed by Britain's watchdog Press Complaints Commission, press photographers agreed to keep a respectful distance from the boys, and not photograph them in private situations until they turned eighteen.

The Men in Gray, no longer burdened by the Princess of Wales's inconvenient notions of humanizing the monarchy, also took steps to eradicate whatever remained of Diana's influence in her sons' lives. Overnight, family and friends, some of whom had known the boys all their lives, were barred from seeing or speaking with William and Harry. Diana's longtime friend Roberto Devorik tried repeatedly and without success to contact the boys, as did Lady Elsa Bowker, Annabel Goldsmith, Rosa Monckton, and many others. Always the answer was the same: Prince William and Prince Harry were simply "unavailable."

Regardless of Earl Spencer's vow that the young princes' "blood family" would continue to guide them as Diana had done, the Queen and Prince Charles were determined to Windsorize William and Harry. "Blood family?" the Queen had indignantly asked her private secretary. "Are we not 'blood family' as well?"

At Eton, Housemaster Andrew Gailey and his wife, Shauna, made certain that William and Harry were completely insulated from any outside influences—and that there would be no calls or visitors not vetted by the Palace. Weekends and holidays were usually devoted to the traditional pursuits of Britain's upper classes: shooting, polo, and foxhunting.

On December 15, facing their first Christmas without their

mother, William and Harry arrived unannounced at a foxhunt outside London. Although Charles felt it unwise to introduce them to his mistress so soon after Diana's death, the boys got their first look in person at Camilla, astride a horse and wearing the usual foxhunting getup, known as "ratcatcher": buff (never white) breeches, shirt and tie, tattersall vest, hacking jacket, black field boots, and hunt cap.

Camilla would not actually meet the future king for another six months—and then only because William felt it was time to get it over with. On June 12, 1998, William was driven by his Royal Protection officers from Eton to London, where he was going to the movies with friends. William called from the car to say he planned to stop by his flat in York House to change, but was warned by his father that Mrs. Parker Bowles happened to be there.

"Fine, I'd love to meet her," William replied. Camilla wasn't so sure. For months she had essentially been holed up at her house in Wiltshire, away from the prying eyes of the media. Only recently had she screwed up her courage enough to spend time with Charles at St. James's Palace and Sandringham.

Camilla was about to bolt, but Charles stopped her. "No, stay," he said. "This is ridiculous." Camilla was in the drawing room going over her schedule with her personal assistant, Amanda McManus, when William arrived at 4:00 p.m. and went straight to his rooms upstairs. Charles took her by the arm. "He's here. Let's get on with it," he insisted. "I'm taking you to meet him now." Understandably flustered when the big moment finally came, Mrs. Parker Bowles curtsied awkwardly, then reached out to accept William's extended hand.

Charles left Camilla and William alone to chat. It would have been understandable if both young princes blamed her for their mother's unhappiness and, at the very least, destroying their parents' marriage. But William, ever the peacemaker, tried to put Camilla at ease with talk of polo and foxhunting.

Thirty minutes later, William was off to the movies and Camilla was still, as she put it, "trembling like a leaf." As soon as William was out the door, Camilla plopped into a chair and sighed.

"Charles," she said, "I *really* need a vodka and tonic."

Several weeks later, Charles arranged for Harry to meet Camilla at Highgrove. Both boys, apparently remembering that their mother had come to a kind of understanding with their father toward the end, quickly grew fond of Camilla. The frumpy, disheveled, self-deprecating Mrs. PB was miles away from their mother in looks, style, and temperament—which made it much easier for them to like her. "Camilla was more like a colorful aunt to them," a Highgrove neighbor said. "She was loud and fun, and most important of all, she obviously made their papa very happy."

The Queen was not quite so amenable. Like Diana's friends, who complained loudly that the introduction to Camilla was an affront to the Princess's memory, Her Majesty had not changed her mind about Charles's mistress. Neither, it turned out, had the Queen Mother. "I cannot bear that woman," she told the sovereign in the presence of their ladies-in-waiting. "The sheer *gall*." Not only did the Queen Mother liken Camilla to the late Duchess of Windsor—ironically, the very personification of evil in the eyes of the family that actually bore the name—but she blamed Camilla for steering her favorite grandson away from his princely destiny, threatening to wreck the monarchy in the process.

Mrs. PB was "Satan incarnate as far as the Queen Mother was

concerned," Brooks-Baker said. "She was deeply troubled by their affair from the very beginning." In the presence of Charles, however, William's great-grandmother said nothing. "The one tricky thing between them was that the Queen Mother never mentioned Camilla to Charles at all," said royal historian Hugo Vickers. "It was almost as if she didn't exist." Charles adored his grandmother, as she adored him, and over the years they shared their deepest thoughts with each other. "Charles is a great love of mine," she once wrote to Elizabeth. To Charles, his grandmother's complete silence on the subject of Camilla spoke volumes.

The Queen Mother made her daughter promise that she would not give her consent to a marriage between Charles and Camilla—an easy promise to keep, or so it seemed, since Camilla remained wildly unpopular. According to one Palace advisor, the Queen suspected that Charles might use his sons to hasten Camilla's rehabilitation in the eyes of the public. If Diana's own sons approved of Camilla, then how could the average Briton reject her? But Elizabeth worried that the public's love of Diana and corresponding resentment of Camilla ran too deep. The woman Diana called the Rottweiler was still toxic. If he were to be seen with her in public, William might do irreparable damage to his own reputation—a heretofore pristine image upon which the future of the monarchy rested.

The Queen had little influence over Charles, but William and Harry were another matter. She ordered that the young princes were not to appear in public together with Camilla, and that under no circumstances were they to be photographed together.

While Camilla tried to forge a relationship with William and Harry behind closed doors, the Queen was busy trying to regain the trust of her subjects. She had woefully underestimated the spell Diana cast over not only the British people, but the world at large. The Palace's first move was to hire an outside public relations firm to tell the tone-deaf monarch how best to proceed.

In the course of twenty-four months, Elizabeth II listened to her new team of image consultants and then took unprecedented steps to win back her subjects. The Queen visited a pub for the first time, as well as a McDonald's, and took her maiden ride in one of London's iconic taxicabs. She commanded that henceforth all curtsying and bowing to Royals should be strictly voluntary (the crown presumably would not take offense if one didn't), and agreed to major changes in the laws of succession—namely, ending primogeniture so that the monarch's eldest child, not just the eldest son, would become heir to the throne. Although the Royal Family had been voluntarily paying taxes since 1993, the Queen also agreed to release financial records that previously had been considered top secret.

William and Harry got some sobering financial news of their own. Diana had bequeathed the bulk of her $35 million estate to her sons, but Inland Revenue informed them that 40 percent of that was to be paid in taxes—a whopping $14 million. In the end, they divided the remaining $21 million, with $10.5 million being place in trust for each.

....

EVEN AS THE ROYALS TRIED to adjust to what would become the new normal, sixteen-year-old Kate Middleton was making some big changes of her own. Over the summer of 1998, she underwent a transformation from mousy bookworm to chestnut-maned beauty. Not that Kate was ever considered glamorous, or a clothes horse. Unlike most of the other female students who, said fellow student and friend Gemma Williamson, dressed "quite tartily to attract the boys," Kate's look was casual, subdued, conservative. "Sweaters and jeans and almost no makeup—just totally natural," Williamson added. "Everything looked good on her, because she had such a perfect body."

Now determined to take risks and be noticed, she even started flashing her naked derriere at boys from her second-story dormitory window. Unfortunately, her passion for mooning became something of an obsession; over the course of the year she exposed her nude posterior to exceedingly grateful male students no fewer than ninety times. "She kind of got addicted to it," said her schoolmate and close friend, Jessica Hay. Soon, she was known across the campus as "Kate Middlebum"—a moniker that, according to her friends, Kate took considerable pride in.

With the exception of a few relatively innocent "snogging" (necking) sessions here and there, Kate never had a serious boyfriend at Marlborough. "She never," Hay said bluntly, "lost her virginity at school." She did, however, eagerly devour every morsel she could find in the tabloids about the Heir. Hay, who wound up dating William's cousin and fellow Etonian Nicholas Knatchbull for three years, was also a valuable source of information. Kate "wanted to know everything I could find out about William," she said. "When I told him how shy he was, and that he had a wonderful sense of humor, she just sighed."

Kate paid less attention to what was going on in the lives of the older Royals, but most of her countrymen were still riveted by the continuing saga of Charles and Camilla. In January 1999, they made their first public appearance together on the steps of the Ritz Hotel in London's swank Mayfair district.

It was no accident that they chose this moment and this particular event—a fiftieth birthday bash for Camilla's sister Annabel—to make what amounted to a public proclamation of their love. It was exactly ten years earlier, at Annabel's fortieth birthday party, that Diana had pushed past Charles and his friends to confront a shaken Camilla for the very first time.

As 150 cameramen snapped away, Charles walked Camilla to their waiting car and then stopped to put his arm around her. Camilla's children, Tom and Laura Parker Bowles, stood behind them at the top of the hotel's stairs, beaming with pride. Noticeably absent were William and Harry, who, in accordance with the Queen's wishes that they not be seen in public with Camilla, were not invited.

Operation PB continued apace into the spring, with Camilla returning to the London Ritz that May to host a dinner for the National Osteoporosis Society. This time she was intent on flaunting her status as the future monarch's official mistress; on her right collar glittered a diamond brooch bearing the Prince of Wales's distinctive emblem of three plumed feathers. Later, when she and Charles made what was only their third public appearance together, Camilla wore a spectacular $200,000 necklace that had been a favorite of Diana's. "It's simply heartbreaking," said the late Princess's friend Vivienne Parry, "to see someone else wearing Diana's things."

The Queen was not amused. Ignoring Charles's protests, she barred Camilla from attending the June 19, 1999, wedding of her youngest son, Prince Edward, to Sophie Rhys-Jones. If there was any doubt that Elizabeth still resented Camilla, it vanished when reporters asked if this obvious snub meant that Her Majesty was still a long way from welcoming Charles's notorious mistress into the bosom of the Royal Family. The Queen, a Palace spokesman answered succinctly, "made it clear that any rapprochement is out of the question."

The Queen's express order that Camilla's children keep their distance from William sat well with Kate. She worried that Tom Parker Bowles might be a bad influence, along with William's other club-hopping, drug-abusing aristo pals. Tom, who frequented London's trendiest nightspots with William, had been convicted of possessing marijuana and the drug ecstasy in 1995. Now he admitted to snorting cocaine in clubs William frequented, along with Nicky Knatchbull and another of William's cousins, Lord Frederick Windsor.

The Queen's own fondness for gin made her somewhat tolerant of other people's alcohol consumption, and she usually looked the other way when she heard stories about drug abuse among members of the aristocracy. But it was all very different where William was concerned. The Queen paid very close attention to the people William consorted with, routinely asking her advisors to weigh in on the young women and men he invited to join his inner circle.

"The stories of drug use by William's friends shocked and upset the Queen," said a longtime staff member at St. James's Palace. "She was especially angry about Tom Parker Bowles, and she told Prince Charles to do something about it."

Unlike the very hands-on Diana, Camilla had always been a laissez-faire parent, reluctant to discipline her children. With Camilla's blessing, Charles came down hard on Tom, scolding him for embarrassing his mother and barring him from contact with William until he cleaned up his act. The Prince of Wales sent similarly stern warnings to Nicky Knatchbull's parents, Lord and Lady Brabourne, and to Lord Freddie Windsor's father and mother, Prince and Princess Michael of Kent.

"When you're in the Firm, and the Queen and the Prince of Wales come down hard on you," a friend of Prince Michael said, "you feel it."

Not that Kate doubted for a moment that William had, as she put it, "the good sense to stay away from drugs." She was less sanguine about his choices in the romance department. Now that William and Harry had their own digs at York House, the northwestern wing of St. James's Palace where, ironically, a nineteenth-century Duke and Duchess of Cambridge once lived, they occasionally entertained female visitors—albeit always ostensibly for "tea."

Even as Kate wound down her final year at Marlborough without a boyfriend, the tabloids were filled with stories about the highborn young ladies circling around the future king. The most notable of these were Emilia (Mili) d'Erlanger, the niece of Viscount Exmouth as well as a schoolmate of Kate's; Diana's distant cousin Davina Duckworth-Chad, dubbed "the Deb on the Web" after donning a rubber dress to promote a website; and Alexandra Knatchbull, William's stunningly beautiful third cousin.

Equally eyebrow-raising were the torrid emails William exchanged with two Americans: model Lauren Bush, the niece of soon-to-be President George W. Bush and granddaughter of President George H. W. Bush, and Britney Spears. The playful correspondence with Spears began after William, who actually had her photo taped to his bedroom wall at Eton, invited the pop star to a party he was throwing to celebrate the arrival of the new millennium.

Sadly, the planned "Willennium," as he took to calling it, never got off the ground. Instead, he wound up bingeing with friends at the Norfolk home of Diana's sister, Lady Jane Fellowes. The next day, Lady Jane's husband, Sir Robert Fellowes, reported to his boss the Queen that her grandson had survived the dawn of 2000—but not without consequences. On his first official trip to Wales with his father two days later, the future Prince of Wales told British Airways flight attendant Claire Owens that he was "still hung over from the Millennium—I think everyone is."

The Queen, meanwhile, embarked on a daunting two-week tour of Australia—her thirteenth visit Down Under as monarch—in March 2000. Just a few months before, Australia had voted by a slim margin to keep the Queen as their head of state even though polls showed a strong majority in favor of leaving the Commonwealth and becoming a republic. Experts believed the vote would have gone the other way had it not been for the fact that the proposed changes did not provide for the direct election of a president.

In a speech at the Sydney Opera House, Elizabeth told her hosts that "the future of the monarchy is an issue for you, the Australian people, and you alone to decide." But she also reminded them that, whatever their choice, her "deep affection will remain as strong as ever."

Along with the rise in Scottish nationalism, polls showing that two-thirds of Canadians wanted to get rid of the Queen as their head of state, and similar rumblings throughout the Commonwealth, Australia's referendum left Elizabeth badly shaken. If the monarchy was to survive, Lord Charteris had told her immediately after the Australian vote, everything would depend on the personal popularity of the next sovereign.

The Queen had regained much of her standing since the public relations debacle that followed Diana's death, and she had no illusions about why. Britons were fast in the thrall of the late Princess of Wales's handsome, athletic, dynamic, and engaging young sons. Harry, whose paternity grew increasingly in doubt as he grew more and more to strongly resemble James Hewitt, was cast as the likable, mischievous scamp. William was also fun-loving and charismatic, but possessed an air of maturity and seriousness befitting the heir. He also looked the part of a king; at six feet three inches he would be the tallest monarch since Henry VIII.

Conversely, Charles had always seemed aloof, supercilious, and, to the average Briton, deadly dull. Then there was the matter of Camilla; while she was no longer pelted with bread and booed in the streets, the Prince of Wales's slatternly mistress still represented the biggest threat to the future of the monarchy. "The Queen began to understand what Diana meant," said a former deputy private secretary, "when she said she was putting all her hopes on William."

Needless to say, William and Harry were not the only Royals who commanded the public's affection. The Queen threw a grand ball for more than eight hundred guests at Windsor Castle on June 21 to celebrate the seventieth birthday of Princess Margaret, Princess Anne's fiftieth, and Prince Andrew's fortieth. Two weeks later, on the Queen Mother's hundredth birthday, Prince Charles rode with his grandmother in a horse-drawn carriage from St. James's Palace up the Mall to Buckingham Palace. As she stepped out onto the balcony, a throng of well-wishers applauded and cheered. Coming just three years after Diana's death brought the monarchy to its knees, the public outpouring of devotion was reassuring. The Queen Mother, however, took it in stride. "It's all very nice, dear," she joked as she prepared to down her second gin and tonic of the evening. "But I won't be around forever."

While she *was* around, the Queen Mother let it be known that she still disapproved of her grandson's mistress. Elizabeth included Andrew Parker Bowles—a longtime Royal Family favorite—on the guest list for the Queen Mother's hundredth birthday dinner at Windsor Castle, but given the birthday girl's lingering resentment, Camilla was pointedly excluded. Thus far, Camilla had been an overnight guest at Balmoral and Holyrood in Scotland, Sandringham, and even Buckingham Palace when the sovereign was not in residence. Windsor was the only royal residence where Camilla hadn't spent the night, and apparently the Queen Mum meant to keep it that way.

Charles understood that the Queen could not counter her mother's wishes. At the same time, if there was any hope of perhaps someday marrying the woman he loved, the Queen would have to meet her. The Prince of Wales had, in fact, made securing his mother's tolerance (if not approval) of Camilla the number-one priority for his staff.

No one was more dismayed and irritated by the Queen's two-decade-long snub than the Prince of Wales's mistress, who concocted a plan to end it. Charles and Camilla were both longtime friends of King Constantine of Greece, who was about to turn sixty and happened to also be the Queen's third cousin. If Charles hosted a birthday party at Highgrove for the King, Charles's mother would be hesitant to insult her fellow monarch by not attending.

"For royal watchers," said the *New York Times*'s Warren Hoge, "birthday party attendance has become an important measure of whether the sovereign's thumb is up or down." On June 3, 2000, the Queen showed up with one hundred other guests at the Highgrove party for King Constantine, and met Camilla for the first time since her affair with Charles began. Camilla made a low, formal curtsy, and then she and the Queen engaged in small talk, apparently about their shared love of horses, before heading off to different tables for what was described as a "barbecue lunch."

It was a significant gesture. "The Queen is cool in her judgment and would have assessed the whole issue," said constitutional expert Lord St. John of Fawsley. "It is a very good thing that this potential rift between Her Majesty and the Prince of Wales has been healed." St. James's Palace was quick to assert that the meeting, although significant, did not mean Charles had any intention of marrying Camilla. They pointed, in fact, to his pledge at the time of his divorce that he would never remarry. Pressed on the point, Charles's staff insisted yet again that Camilla had "no interest in becoming queen."

Privately, it was an entirely different matter.

"Prince Charles and Camilla were walking on air," said one guest at the party. With good reason. Over the past two years, Charles had stepped up the campaign to make Camilla palatable to the public. He and Camilla were even photographed enjoying each other's company on a ten-day Greek island cruise, and, although photos of Camilla with William and Harry were strictly forbidden, Charles's staff fed numerous stories to the press about her warm relationship with Diana's young sons.

To underscore Camilla's potential as a representative of the monarchy, Charles dispatched her on a high-profile solo trip to New York. With the Prince's media spinmeister Mark Bolland at her elbow, Camilla was photographed with the likes of philanthropy queen Brooke Astor, designer Oscar de la Renta, *Vogue* editor Anna Wintour, media tycoon Michael Bloomberg, and UN Secretary General Kofi Annan. Astor, then ninety-seven, had actually met Camilla's great-grandmother Alice Keppel in the 1930s, more than two decades after Edward VII's death. By then the late King's mistress, who had never actually been considered a beauty, was shunned by society and had begun her descent into alcoholism. "Mrs. Parker Bowles wanted to know everything, but at the time most people believed Mrs. Keppel to be a wanton woman and a schemer," Astor later said. "She ended up a rather pathetic figure. I thought it best to change the subject, considering."

....

THE FATE OF THE HOUSE of Windsor would have to wait as Prince William sorted out his academic future. After he aced his A-levels—the British equivalent of finals and the SATs combined—and graduated with honors, William had his pick of any institution of higher learning in the world. (The notion that any university would turn down the future King of England even if he were a mediocre student seemed, in the words of one British journalist, "laughable.")

The pressure on William to attend Oxford (the Spencers' alma mater) or Cambridge (Charles's) was such that he decided to choose neither. Instead, he took Granny's advice and began considering Scottish universities. Nationalism was on the rise in Scotland, and the Queen's advisors were warning her that a referendum to break away from the United Kingdom seemed likely at some point. It could only help matters for the Crown, she suggested over tea, if for the very first time an heir to the throne attended a Scottish university.

At first unaware that William was considering breaking with tradition to attend a college in Scotland, Kate Middleton was also weighing her options. Carole Middleton, in particular, wanted all her of children to attend one of three elite British universities—the kinds of institutions where, Dorothy Goldsmith told her cousin, "you meet the sons of all the right people."

As had been the case for William, Oxford and Cambridge were the default choices. But Kate had her eye on a career curating contemporary art and photography shows, and the University of Edinburgh in Scotland was known for having a particularly strong arts curriculum. After visiting the Edinburgh campus together, Kate and her mother agreed that it was the best place for her to pursue a degree in art history. Another deciding factor: By late spring of 2000, newspapers were reporting that Prince William would be attending Edinburgh once he completely his "gap year" doing volunteer work abroad.

Like many of their art student peers, Kate headed for Florence, where she divided her time among museums and galleries and sidewalk cafés. William's gap year, however, was meticulously crafted by the Palace to plump up the resume of a monarch-in-training.

First stop: the jungles of Belize in Central America, where William encountered poisonous snakes, wild boars, mosquitoes, and scorpions while training with a unit of the Welsh Guards. Then came a three-week expedition with the Royal Geographical Society's marine observation program, scuba diving and snorkeling off Rodrigues Island in the Indian Ocean.

Before embarking on his next adventure, William returned to London, only to face another, wholly unexpected challenge. Diana's former private secretary, Patrick Jephson, had published *Shadows of a Princess*, a scathing indictment of the Princess that portrayed her as shrewd, unstable, and manipulative.

With permission from both Charles and the Queen, William gave his first-ever press conference to defend his mother's memory. Incredibly, the Press Complaints Commission had done such a splendid job of keeping journalists at bay that this marked the first time the public had actually heard William's voice. The Heir allowed that both he and Harry were "quite upset" about Jephson's book—that "our mother's trust has been betrayed and that even now she is still being exploited."

One person in particular delighted in anything that portrayed Diana as an emotionally unbalanced Machiavellian schemer. The implications for Camilla's own standing in terms of public opinion were glaringly obvious. At one of their small Highgrove gatherings, Charles railed against Jephson, only to have Camilla blurt out, "Well, yes, darling, but it is all *true*, isn't it?"

In October 2000, William headed out on his own again—this time to a remote village in southern Chile where for three months the heir to the British throne chopped wood, scoured latrines, and taught English to local schoolchildren.

Once back home in February 2001, William milked cows as a minimum-wage worker on a dairy farm in southwest England—his favorite gap year experience, he would later conclude. More important, it was during this time that he also made his first official public appearance as a senior member of the Royal Family—and his first appearance alongside his father at a public event. The occasion was the tenth anniversary of the Press Complaints

Commission. To insure continued cordial relations with Fleet Street, this was William's way of thanking the press for keeping a respectful distance while he was at Eton and during the first part of his gap year.

The Queen knew she was powerless to prevent her headstrong son from being seen publicly with his mistress, but she warned Charles that under no circumstances was Camilla to be seen in the same photograph as William—not even in the background. (Harry stayed away, submerged in his studies at Eton.)

Arriving at the Press Complaints Commission party fifteen minutes after the princes, Camilla remained stationary while father and son worked the opposite end of the room for ninety minutes. Charles and William then left together, without ever having been within fifty feet of Camilla. "It was brilliant, the manner in which they pulled that off," allowed one London *Sunday Times* reporter. "Particularly when you consider there were more than five hundred journalists milling about."

One more gap year adventure was to come. Six weeks after making his first official public appearance and deftly avoiding Camilla, William was hard at work at the Lewa Conservancy, a fifty-five-thousand-acre wildlife preserve in northern Kenya. For the next four months, he coped with snakes, wild dogs, and every conceivable sort of giant insect when he wasn't walking fence lines, digging ditches, or tracking wildlife. There was no electricity and no plumbing, and the Heir showered like everyone else, beneath a canvas bucket.

For a young man spending time in what one writer called a "secret Eden," there were other compensations—namely, working closely with the sanctuary owner's strikingly attractive nineteen-year-old daughter, Jessica "Jecca" Craig, under the hot African sun. Soon, they were swept up in a breathless romance. At one point, William went so far as to stage a mock wedding proposal, getting down on one knee at the foot of Mount Kenya to jokingly ask Jecca if she would marry him.

Back home in England, meanwhile, a series of new scandals were brewing that would rock the monarchy to its foundations. With Charles and William away from Highgrove, the Spare was left to his own devices. Prince Harry was still two years below Britain's legal drinking age of eighteen, but that didn't stop him from tossing back pints of ale with gin and vodka chasers in the bar at the local Rattlebone Inn. On at least one occasion, he became so drunk that—royalty or not—Harry and his friends were unceremoniously thrown out, as one patron put it, "on their aristo arses."

Public drunkenness was one thing, but when Charles learned that Harry had been smoking marijuana in a toolshed behind the Rattlebone Inn, he took immediate action. Harry was sent to spend a day with recovering heroin and cocaine addicts at the Featherstone Lodge Rehabilitation Center in South London. The prince was "completely shocked," said Featherstone staff member Wilma Graham. "It was quite an eye-opener for Harry."

It was certainly an eye-opener for the country. It would be months before the press got wind of Harry's pot smoking, but when it did the headlines were scathing. PRINCE HARRY: I TOOK DRUGS, blared the *Daily Mail* headline, while the *News of the World* went with melodramatic HARRY'S DRUG SHAME.

The "Harry Pothead Affair," as it soon came to be called, was only the tip of the iceberg. On August 16, 2001, former royal butler Paul Burrell, the man Diana called "My Rock" and a longtime personal favorite of the Queen, was charged with stealing 342 items worth an estimated $7.7 million from the late Princess's Kensington Palace apartments.

No one in the Royal Family believed it was possible. Burrell was the man who dressed Diana's body for burial, and who took William and Harry by the hand and gently led them from room to room in Kensington Palace when they selected their mother's keepsakes. But Scotland Yard insisted they had substantial evidence that Burrell was selling some of Diana's most prized possessions in the United States—a claim that later turned out to be patently untrue.

Burrell insisted that all the items uncovered by the authorities in his home were either gifts from the Princess or items he had been entrusted with for safekeeping. William and Harry implored their father to come to Burrell's defense, but to no avail. As long as investigators insisted they had a strong case, Prince Charles was reluctant to get involved. Why, then, didn't William step up to defend his mother's confidant? Insisting that William knew Burrell "better than anyone else," Richard Kay said "everyone wondered why he wasn't coming forward early on to say, 'This is crazy. Paul Burrell would never steal anything from Mother.' "

Certainly the Queen knew that to be true. Not long after Diana's death, the butler had asked for a private meeting with the Queen. During their chat, Burrell informed Her Majesty that he was holding on to some of Diana's things temporarily for safekeeping, and she nodded in approval. Elizabeth later recalled that nothing about what Burrell said seemed "the least bit extraordinary."

It was at this point in the conversation, however, that the

Queen spoke up, warning Burrell to "be careful" of the mysterious "powers at work" in the country. Burrell remembered that she was "deadly serious" and "clearly warning me to be vigilant."

Her Majesty knew all too well that, whatever other psychological problems Diana may have had, the Princess of Wales was not being irrational when she complained of being spied on by the government. Diana "was not being paranoid at all," said her longtime Royal Protection officer, Ken Wharfe. "Her every move was being watched," Wharfe said. "They routinely taped the Princess's telephone calls. Princess Diana was under constant surveillance."

As it turned out, *every* member of the Royal Family was being spied on by Britain's intelligence agencies. "Their personal conversations, both on the phone and sometimes person to person, are monitored and recorded," said Glynn Jones, one of the British military surveillance experts placed in charge of spying on Diana. In addition, "many of their movements are captured on videotape. It's impossible for them to keep any secrets. The most personal things are recorded. Charles, Camilla, and William are always under surveillance by secret service personnel."

Nevertheless, Burrell, who incorrectly assumed the Queen was exempt from such incursions on her privacy, considered his conversations with the sovereign to be strictly confidential. The butler clung to the belief that his Queen, seeing that her trusted servant was being prosecuted for a crime she knew he did not commit, would come forward on her own. Yet no member of the Royal Family spoke up. "The silence was deafening," he said. "I thought I was being fed to the lions."

The case dragged on for two years, leaving Burrell's reputation in tatters. Facing bankruptcy and jail time, he contemplated taking his own life. Just days before Burrell was to testify, the Queen, Prince Philip, and Charles were on their way to a memorial service when Philip blithely mentioned the Queen's 1997 conversation with the butler. The Queen told her horrified son that she didn't think the talk was "significant." Once Charles passed this information along to the police, the entire case was finally dropped.

"It's all thanks to the Queen," Burrell sobbed on the courthouse steps. The butler was saved, but not the Royal Family. During the trial, investigators finally revealed what they were really looking for when they raided Burrell's house: a mahogany box marked with a "D." Among items contained in Diana's "Box of Secrets" was her taped interview with Kensington Palace valet and footman George Smith. On the tape, Smith told Diana he was raped by one of Charles's most trusted servants—and that he had witnessed this same servant and a member of the Royal Family in a position that could only be described as compromising.

Diana had taken the tape to Charles and demanded that the alleged rapist be fired. Not only did the Prince of Wales dismiss the charge as "staff tittle-tattle," but he went on to spend nearly $200,000 covering the purported rapist's legal bills. Eventually, Smith dropped the matter after departing the Palace with a $59,000 cash payment—all of which, understandably, gave rise to charges of a cover-up.

The *Daily Mail*'s full-page headline, I WAS RAPED BY CHARLES'S SERVANT, left little to the imagination, and it was hard to argue with the sentiment in the follow-up headline, PANIC GRIPS THE PALACE. "They've really kicked the hornet's nest, haven't they?" the Queen muttered while scanning the papers. She had always been aware of the X-rated goings on inside palace walls, and it was no secret that, like her mother, the Queen had a taste for gossip of even the most salacious variety.

Rape was another matter entirely. When the Queen summoned Charles to Balmoral to explain what he knew about the newest royal scandal, the Prince turned for advice to the woman he now called "My Touchstone"—Camilla.

From the grave, Diana had struck yet another blow to Charles's reputation. It was the sort of public relations fiasco both he and Camilla could ill afford—not if they had any hope of selling themselves as a royal couple. For a fleeting moment, it may well have occurred to Charles and Camilla that one of the infamous Men in Gray was behind this latest batch of humiliating revelations.

"Buckingham Palace and St. James's Palace have been at war with each other for a long, long time," said one courtier. "Charles's advisors are constantly pushing to give him more to do, to get him on the throne sooner rather than later." But, he added, "there are also people close to the Queen who strongly believe that Charles will be a total disaster as king." Operation PB, the Mark Bolland–engineered campaign to revamp Camilla's image, simply "poured gasoline on the fire."

....

LIKE NEARLY ALL OF HER countrymen, Carole Middleton watched the unfolding Burrell Affair with mounting incredulity. "One wonders," she asked a Bucklebury neighbor, "how all this makes William and Harry feel. It's pretty tawdry." Kate's mother was consumed with the details of running her flourishing party supply empire, but not so busy that she didn't notice that William had abandoned his original plan to attend the University of

Edinburgh. Instead, William would be attending the University of St. Andrews, alma mater of his Eton housemaster, Andrew Gailey.

Famous as the place where the sport of golf was invented in the fifteenth century, St. Andrews had a student body of six thousand—roughly half the size of Cambridge's undergraduate student body and a quarter the size of Oxford's. St. Andrews was Scotland's oldest university, and its most remote, jutting into the North Sea some 475 miles north of London. With its Gothic stone architecture, and narrow streets and alleyways with names like Gregory's Lane, Butts Wynd, and Mercat Gate, St. Andrews oozed history and charm. Since there was also little to do but study and drink, St. Andrews had a reputation as one of the United Kingdom's premier party schools. At one point, St. Andrews boasted more drinking establishments than any other town in Scotland—twenty-two pubs in the center of town alone.

The Queen was pleased that William was going to St. Andrews, and not merely because she needed to shore up the Crown's image in Scotland. Scotland Yard had briefed her on the growing number of credible threats to William's safety—from anti-foxhunting groups, violent elements in the Scottish nationalist movement, and, most disturbingly, a paramilitary splinter group of the Irish Republic Army called the Real IRA.

It had been only three years since the Real IRA set off a bomb in the town of Omagh in Northern Ireland, killing twenty-nine people. The Royal Protection Branch (also known as SO14) determined that it would be easier to protect William at St. Andrews than at the University of Edinburgh, which is located in the bustling center of Scotland's capital city.

Elizabeth was at Balmoral reviewing some of the security precautions being taken for William at St. Andrews when her new private secretary, Robin Janvrin, called with news that Islamic terrorists had carried out the 9/11 attacks on New York's World Trade Center and the Pentagon in Washington. After watching the collapse of the Twin Towers on television, she sat down at her desk and wrote to President George W. Bush that she was following events with "growing disbelief and total shock."

This time, the Queen did not hesitate to order that the Union Jack at Buckingham Palace and all royal residences be lowered to half-staff. She also wanted American music and the American national anthem to be added to the repertoire during the daily Changing of the Guard ceremonies in front of Buckingham Palace. (Compounding the sadness for the Queen that day was the sudden death of her racing manager and best friend since childhood, Lord Carnarvon.)

Three days later, the Queen, Prince Philip, Prince Charles, and other members of the Royal Family joined twenty-seven hundred people in St. Paul's Cathedral for a memorial service honoring the victims. After the crowd delivered a stirring rendition of "The Battle Hymn of the Republic," Her Majesty stood up to sing every word of "The Star-Spangled Banner"—loudly. It was the first time an English monarch, who never joins in on her own anthem ("God save . . . me?" she had tried to explain early in her reign to one of her sister's American friends), ever sang the national anthem of the United States.

It was an important show of sympathy and support for Britain's American cousins. From this point on, Tony Blair briefed the Queen on all the important details of the war on terror leading up to the invasion of Afghanistan by the United States, Britain, and their NATO allies. Blair also leaned heavily on the monarch for advice. "Obviously, there was a huge focus on the Arab world," he recalled, "and that is something she has immense experience of." After all, he continued, the Queen "knew the royal families over a long, long period of time—she has a lot of real insight into how they work, how they operate, how they think."

There were other ramifications for the Royal Family. Additional security precautions were initiated following the 9/11 attacks, including the construction of "panic rooms" at Buckingham Palace and Windsor Castle. In the event of an attack, the Queen and other senior Royals on the premises would be rushed to one of these chambers. Once inside, they would presumably be safe behind eighteen-inch-thick, flame-resistant steel walls designed to withstand a protracted artillery bombardment or a direct hit by a light aircraft.

It may have seemed as if the world was unraveling, but that didn't keep the British press from being there in force to cover the chaos that accompanied William's first day on campus. St. James's Palace gave unfettered access to the press the day of William's arrival at St. Andrews, provided they agreed to depart after twenty-four hours and never return. "It beggars belief," said St. Andrews's rector Andrew Neil, "when I think of the efforts we have gone to to allow William a normal undergraduate life."

Kate's mother was more concerned about incursions of a different sort. When she learned that former Marlborough student Mili d'Erlanger, whose name had been linked to William, was headed for St. Andrews, Carole Middleton began lobbying her own daughter to switch. Kate insisted on her original choice—Edinburgh's art history program was second to none—but Carole flew to Florence to persuade her in person that St. Andrews offered something no other university in the world offered: proximity to the future King of England.

At the beginning, proximity was all they had. No sooner had he moved into his fifteen-by-fifteen-foot room at St. Salvatore's residence hall than William fell hard for Kate's friend Carly Massy-Birch, the daughter of a Devon farmer ("They were lovers, yes," confirmed Mimi Massy-Birch, Carly's mum). But Carly soon grew tired of William's bodyguards, who always tailed them in a Land Rover with blacked-out windows and then lurked in the shadows whenever the couple ventured to a restaurant or a pub. After eight weeks of this, she abruptly broke off the relationship.

As it happened, William had not been entirely faithful to Carly. Before enrolling at St. Andrews, he had had a sizzling summer romance with Arabella Musgrave, a fixture at the Beaufort Polo Club near Highgrove. According to one of William's competitors on the polo field, he was "completely crushed" when Musgrave, rightly suspecting that William had a "roving eye," abruptly ended their affair. Determined to win "Bella" Musgrave back, the prince made frequent weekend trips to Highgrove even after he had already begun dating Carly Massy-Birch.

Musgrave continued to rebuff his advances, but William would have better luck with other young ladies he romanced while weekending at Highgrove. Rose Farquhar, daughter of the Master of the Beaufort Hunt, had known William since they were children, but things turned serious between them once he graduated from Eton. Then there was Beaufort Polo club employee Amanda Bush. Known as "Tigger" because of her bouncy personality, Bush reportedly did more than merely cheer the Prince on from the sidelines. Also drifting in and out of the Prince's orbit at this time was Isabella Anstruther-Gough-Calthorpe, a direct (albeit illegitimate) descendent of Charles II. (Isabella later acted under the name Isabella Calthorpe and eventually married Richard Branson's son Sam, heir to a $6 billion fortune.)

Kate was less frenetic in the romance department. Within weeks of arriving at the university, she fell for a senior named Rupert Finch, the burly, tall, dark-haired star of St. Andrews's cricket team. Finch was also among those cheering in the audience when Kate loped down the fashion runway in a see-through negligee, but after a year together it was becoming increasingly clear that the clock was about to run out on their romance. He would soon be taking the cricket team on a tour of South Africa, and after that had plans to start work at one of the most prestigious law firms in London.

As alluring as she was that fateful day of the charity fashion show, William already knew there was far more to Kate than met the eye. Even while she was dating Rupert Finch and he was juggling relationships with several young women, the heir to the throne and the flight attendant's daughter were forging a solid friendship. Soon, Kate was a member in good standing of the Sally's Boys—the small group of St. Salvatore's residents who made up the Prince's inner circle at St. Andrews: Graham Booth, Ali Coutts-Wood, Charlie Nelson, Oli Baker, and William's Eton pal Fergus Boyd.

Both "sporty" types, Kate and William cycled up and down the beach on weekends and swam laps together almost daily at the Old Course Hotel pool. If the Prince missed a class (she never did), Kate shared her notes with him. There was also the occasional drink at the West Port Bar or Broons, or even a late-night karaoke session at Ma Bells, a loud, knotty pine–paneled student hangout in the lobby of the St. Andrews Golf Hotel.

None of this had been enough, however, to keep both William and Kate from wondering if St. Andrews was the right place for them. During the Christmas break months earlier, they both announced to their respective families that they felt overworked and isolated—and that they wanted to transfer to Edinburgh immediately.

Mark Bolland considered this to be "nothing more than a wobble—a touch of homesickness, entirely normal." But Prince Charles and the Queen both knew the situation was far from normal. It would not do for William to appear pampered and weak by leaving after a single semester. "He would have been seen as a quitter," a royal aide told journalist Robert Jobson, "and it would have been an even bigger disaster for the monarchy."

A deal was quickly hammered out with St. Andrews. Acknowledging that it would also have been a public relations catastrophe for St. Andrews if William left after only one semester, Rector Andrew Neil added that the administration "worked very hard to keep him." William received counseling and switched his major from art history to geography. "I don't think I was homesick," William later conceded. "I was more daunted." Neil understood completely: "He got the blues, which happens." Charles sweetened the arrangement by rewarding his son with a $32,000 gold-inlaid hunting rifle.

In truth, Kate was the most important factor in William's decision to stick it out at St. Andrews. When she expressed doubts to her parents about returning—and explained that William shared those doubts—Carole pointed out how damaging such a departure would be to William's reputation. Now more than ever, Kate's mother continued, the Prince needed the support of his friends.

Kate went a step further. She told William that she would join him in trying to make a go of it in dreary, fog-shrouded St. Andrews. If, in the end, he still wanted to leave, Kate promised to follow William out the door. After all, she informed him coyly, "Edinburgh was my first choice."

The Queen breathed a sigh of relief. For the moment, at least, William did not look like a "whinger" (whiner), and a Scottish crisis of confidence had been averted. Soon, however, Her Majesty's world would be shaken yet again—this time by the loss of the two women who were closest to her.

At 6:30 p.m. on February 9, 2002, Princess Margaret died at King Edward VII Hospital after suffering the last in a series of strokes. Instead of consoling his mother at Windsor Castle, Charles rushed to the side of the Queen Mother at Sandringham. The indomitable Windsor matriarch managed to put a positive spin on her youngest child's death. Earlier strokes and heart problems had rendered the once hard-living Margaret Rose blind and bedridden. The Princess's death at age seventy-one, the Queen Mother said, was nothing less than "a merciful release."

Six weeks later, on the afternoon of March 30, 2002, the Queen Mother was at Windsor for the Easter weekend when she suddenly grew tired. Elizabeth, who had been out horseback riding, was summoned to her mother's side. When she arrived, the Queen Mother was dressed in a lounging robe, sitting upright in a chair by the fireplace in her bedroom. The Queen, still wearing her riding clothes and muddy riding boots, knelt by her mother's side and exchanged a few words. Within minutes the Queen Mother lost consciousness. At 3:15 p.m., with Elizabeth weeping at her bedside, the Queen Mother slipped peacefully away.

The back-to-back losses of the Queen's only sibling and her

mother were, her cousin Margaret Rhodes said, a "terrible wallop of grief." The two family members she often spoke with several times a day—"gone. It doesn't matter how old someone is," Tony Blair said, "or how long you've had to prepare. It was a terrible shock."

It was also another opportunity to show what a powerful unifying force the monarchy could be. The Prince of Wales took to the airwaves to praise his grandmother as "magical" and "fun—we laughed until we cried." In a separate address to the nation, the Queen thanked her people for the "outpouring of affection" that was "overwhelming . . . I thank you also from my heart for the love you gave her during her life and the honor you now give her in death."

More than a million people lined the funeral route from St. James's Palace to Westminster Abbey. Inside, three present and future British monarchs—the Queen, Charles, and William—were among twenty-two hundred world leaders, crowned heads, titled aristocrats, and other dignitaries who had come to pay their respects.

Kate Middleton, now arguably William's closest friend if not yet his lover, could only watch the funeral service on the television in her common room at St. Andrews. Camilla was another matter. At first it was believed Charles's mistress, whom the Queen Mother detested, would not be invited to the funeral. But Charles lobbied his mother through their respective private secretaries, Stephen Lamport and Robin Janvrin, and the Queen grudgingly agreed. Sitting at a discreet distance from the Windsors, Camilla watched as the world formally bade farewell to the one person who for years had stood in the way of her marriage to Charles.

Throughout the service, the eyes of the Royal Family were

trained on the casket, draped with the Queen Mother's personal blue, red, white, and gold standard. Resting atop the standard was the Queen Mother's coronation crown. For all the pomp and circumstance, nothing was more moving in its heartfelt sentiment than the hand-lettered card affixed to a wreath of white camellias atop the coffin. It read, simply:

IN LOVING MEMORY—LILIBET

She was marginalized for so long that she believes she has every right to be Queen.

—JAMES WHITAKER

....

Of course. What else?

—CAMILLA, WHEN ASKED IF CHARLES GOT DOWN ON ONE KNEE TO PROPOSE

....

Thank you for taking on the task of being married to me.

—CHARLES TO CAMILLA ON THEIR WEDDING DAY

6

"THE KATE EFFECT"

BUCKINGHAM PALACE

JANUARY 2005

The royal jeweler opened the red velvet box, and the Queen peered eagerly inside. He pointed to the Plasticine bag containing a small chunk of twenty-one-carat gold. This was all that remained of the Welsh nugget that had been used to make the rings of royal brides starting with the Queen Mother's ring in 1923—Elizabeth's in 1947, Princess Margaret's in 1960, Princess Anne's in 1973, and Diana's in 1981. This was the nugget, taken from the Clogau St. David's mine at Bontddu in North Wales, that Her Majesty reserved only for those she deemed worthy: members of her immediate family, or—as was the case of Elizabeth and Diana, Princess of Wales—future queens. She put on her reading glasses and took a closer look. "Oh, dear," sighed the Queen as she shook her head. "There is very little of it left."

With a white-gloved hand, the royal jeweler then pointed to another bag containing a larger nugget, this one made from gold taken from the River Mawdach as well as St. David's mine. Gold from this nugget was used in 1986 to make the wedding ring for the problematic and much-resented Sarah, Duchess of York. It seemed only fitting to the Queen that this bit of Welsh gold, and not the nugget that held such significance for the Windsors, be used for Camilla's wedding ring. "This," she told the royal jeweler, "will do."

Over the past few years, the Queen had come to regard as inevitable the marriage of her eldest son to his longtime mistress. Elizabeth had kept her promise to the Queen Mother not to permit it, but there had been mounting pressure from Charles and his St. James's team to make the Prince's relationship with Camilla official.

Camilla had certainly not been shy about staking her claim on royal territory—whether she was officially a Windsor or not. Even before the Queen Mother's death, Camilla had her eye on redecorating Clarence House, home to the "Old Queen" for nearly a half-century.

Immediately after the Queen Mother's death, Clarence House, the epitome of "English Shabby" with its frayed drapes and threadbare furnishings—and, on the brighter side, a staff of ninety—became the official residence of Charles, William, and Harry. But the person who would have the greatest impact on the four-story, 172-year-old royal palace was not royal at all.

Camilla, who had hired British interior designer Robert Kime to spruce up Ray Mill House and Highgrove, now assigned Kime the unenviable task of redoing Clarence House without entirely eradicating the memory of Charles's adored Granny. Toward that end the public spaces on the main floor—the imposing Main Hall, the book-lined Lancaster Room, the Horse Corridor lined with the Queen Mother's favorite equestrian paintings, the Garden Room—remained essentially the same in spirit.

The upper floors—Charles's and Camilla's adjoining suites on the second floor, the young princes' rooms on the floor above, and a separate suite for Camilla's father, Major Bruce Shand—were another matter entirely. By the time she was finished, Camilla had racked up a bill of $10 million.

Not surprisingly, there was an uproar over spending *any* money on rooms for the Prince of Wales's mistress—particularly since a special committee in the House of Commons determined that Charles spent $500,000 in taxpayer funds on Camilla every year. In the end, Charles reluctantly agreed to pony up a whopping $2 million to pay for the cost of redoing Camilla's room and that of her father.

By late 2004, Elizabeth's own advisors were warning her that Charles would proceed on his own with plans to marry Mrs. PB, thereby exposing his rift with the Queen and embarrassing the family. They also argued that the British people needed time to get used to the idea of Charles and Camilla as King and Consort.

Her Majesty dug in her heels. On November 6, the Queen and Prince Philip, along with William and Harry, attended the wedding of Lady Tamara Grosvenor and Charles's godson Edward van Cutsem. But Camilla and Charles, who been instructed to arrive in separate cars and sit in separate pews, boycotted the ceremony.

It was, in fact, Camilla—not Charles—who was throwing down the gauntlet. Pressured by his mistress, Charles now made it abundantly clear to his mother and the Men in Gray that he was going to go ahead and announce the couple's engagement—whether Her Majesty approved or not. "And whatever Mrs. Parker Bowles wants," Richard Kay remarked, "Mrs. Parker Bowles gets."

The Queen grudgingly gave her long-withheld consent during the Royal Family's Christmas holiday at Sandringham—with the proviso that Charles stick to his oft-stated promise not to make Camilla his queen after he inherited the crown. Charles's new wife had no interest in being Princess of Wales now or Queen later, Charles insisted. Both he and Camilla felt it appropriate that, once he became King, she would become Princess Consort. The Men in Gray, resistant to the idea of giving Camilla any title at all, suggested she simply be called "Camilla Windsor."

After going a step further and getting his sons' blessing, Charles got down on one knee at Highgrove shortly after New Year's 2005 and proposed. The couple hosted a reception at Windsor to announce the engagement and show off the ring—an emerald-cut diamond with three diamond baguettes on either side, all weighing a total of eight carats. Ironically, the ring had been left to Charles by the Queen Mother.

Wearing a scarlet dress and a Cheshire-cat grin, Camilla held up her engagement ring for the cameras. "I'm just coming down to earth," she said, giddily.

The official announcement from Buckingham Palace was, in a word, terse: "The Duke of Edinburgh and I are very happy that the Prince of Wales and Mrs. Parker Bowles are to marry. We have given them our warmest good wishes for their future together."

Good wishes aside, Crown lawyers were now insisting that Camilla sign a prenuptial agreement. Since Diana had never signed one, Charles had to reach deep into his pocket to pay her the agreed-upon $22.5 million divorce settlement. The Prince of

Wales was forced to "liquidate everything so he could give her cash," said lawyer Geoffrey Bignell, who oversaw the Prince's finances at the time. "Princess Diana took every penny he had."

Since Diana hadn't been required to sign a prenup, Charles could not bring himself to even broach the issue with Camilla. Quite the contrary, to protect her financial interests in the event something happened to him before the marriage, he established a generous $20 million trust fund that provided her with a guaranteed annual income of $700,000. The money, however, could not be passed on to her family; in the event of Camilla's death, the $20 million reverted to the royal estate—and, presumably, passed along to William and Harry.

However reticent the Queen may have been to give royal consent to her son's remarriage, it was a welcome change from having to deal with Harry's latest headline-making gaffe. This time, the hapless Prince attended a costume party wearing the khaki uniform of desert tank commander Erwin Rommel's Afrika Korps, complete with a swastika arm band.

The next day's *Sun* ran a full-page shot of Harry whooping it up in costume with the headline HARRY THE NAZI, igniting a firestorm of protest from members of Parliament, World War II veterans, the Israeli foreign minister, and the families of Holocaust survivors. Lord Levy, Britain's special envoy to the Middle East, called Harry "clueless about the reality of what happened in the Holocaust" and branded his behavior "appalling." By wearing a swastika, Lord Levy continued, the young prince had "sent shock waves through the international community."

Mortified that he had once again brought shame to the Royal Family, Harry, who was about to enter Britain's elite Sandhurst military academy, conceded his ignorance: The third in line to the throne had no idea what the swastika signified, or why it might be deemed monumentally offensive. Branding Harry "a complete thicko," and a "stupid young man who meant no harm," British commentator Tom Utley went on to ask, "What the hell did they teach him during his five years at Eton?"

Charles was, in the words of one friend, "apoplectic" about what Rabbi Marvin Hier of the Simon Wiesenthal Center denounced as Harry's "shameful act." Clarence House immediately issued an apology on Prince Harry's behalf. That was not sufficient for Conservative Party leader Michael Howard, who joined the growing chorus demanding that Prince Harry appear on television to deliver a personal apology. Prince Harry, Howard said, should "tell us himself just how contrite he is." Charles, convinced that his younger son was now being unfairly pilloried for an innocent if spectacularly stupid mistake, refused. Camilla agreed. "The poor boy," she said, "has been through quite enough. He made a mistake, he's said he's sorry. What is all the fuss about?"

Throughout Harry's Nazi ordeal, Buckingham Palace remained curiously silent. Of all senior Royals, the Queen was perhaps least judgmental. "He's young," she told Charles. "He didn't live through it like I did." The Queen would have her own explaining to do a full decade later, when photographs surfaced showing Elizabeth doing a Nazi salute as a young girl six years before the start of World War II. Joining in, enthusiastically, are the Queen Mother and Princess Margaret. At the time, the Queen's Nazi-sympathizing uncle Edward VIII, who would eventually give up the throne to marry Wallis Simpson, was actually at Balmoral teaching the entire Royal Family the proper way to Sieg Heil. "Both Queen Elizabeths, mother and daughter, have commanded such affection and respect for so long," observed British writer Max Hastings, "it is painful to see their images tarnished."

....

AS SERIOUS AS THE SCANDAL surrounding Harry's Nazi costume had been, it paled in comparison to the events that were rapidly unfolding in the House of Windsor. Now that she had publicly welcomed the woman she once repeatedly called "wicked" into the Royal Family, Elizabeth had no choice but to believe that Charles would keep his word not to make Camilla his queen. It certainly didn't help matters when, at a Highgrove party just before the impending nuptials, Charles insisted on calling Camilla "my queen."

"Yes, well," Camilla responded in her deep, Tallulah Bankhead chain smoker's voice, "let's not get carried away." She also claimed to be nonplussed by all the fuss in the press. "It's just," she cracked, "two old people getting hitched."

Two old people who, even after being given a green light by the Queen, remained the object of considerable public scorn. It was all taking a toll on Charles, who complained bitterly about being "tortured" over his relationship with Camilla. "I thought the British people were supposed to be compassionate—I don't see much of it. . . . All of my life, people have been telling me what to do. I'm tired of it."

The Queen could not disguise her true feelings as the April 9, 2005, wedding date for Prince Charles and "Mrs. PB" approached. There would also be several last-minute complications, most notably the death of Pope John Paul II; the wedding was hastily postponed one day so that Charles could represent his country at the pontiff's funeral in Rome.

Ironically, Charles, who was destined to replace his mother as head of the Church of England, was forced to abandon his hope of being married by the Archbishop of Canterbury. Despite changes in church policy that would technically have allowed the divorced future king to marry his divorced mistress in a religious ceremony, it would simply ruffle too many feathers. The solution, a brief civil wedding ceremony at Windsor Guildhall, obviously did not satisfy everyone; guests tried to disregard protesters who stood outside waving placards and booing.

Inside the Guildhall, William and Harry looked on as Charles placed the Welsh gold wedding band on his bride's finger. Then Camilla slipped a wedding ring on the pinky finger of their father's left hand, which Charles immediately covered up with the three-feathered Prince of Wales signet ring he wore at all times. At one point, Harry leaned into his brother. "Where's Granny?" he asked. The Queen, William whispered in reply, was not coming.

Having delivered an unmistakable message to the newlyweds by boycotting the marriage ceremony itself, the Queen did join 750 others at the carefully titled "Service of Prayer and Dedication Following the Marriage" that took place in St. George's Chapel. The fact that the newlyweds were required by the Archbishop of Canterbury to get on their knees and beg God's forgiveness for "provoking thy wrath and indignation" did little to cheer up the monarch. She stared straight ahead, and her expression conveyed a mood of sullen indifference.

Kate, by now the object of endless gossip and speculation, was conspicuously absent from both the civil ceremony and the prayer service at Windsor Castle—all thanks to the woman who would eventually become her mother-in-law. "This was, at long,

long last, Camilla's moment," observed a longtime friend of the Parker Bowles family. "She was not about to be upstaged by any other woman—and certainly not by someone as stunning as Kate Middleton who might someday be a court rival. Camilla is no fool." Her former roommate Jane Churchill claimed she had "never, ever seen Camilla look so happy as when she walked down the aisle. But, you know, when they walk past you must curtsy. And, I tell you, it's just sort of surreal to curtsy to your former flatmate."

After the ceremony at St. George's, Camilla, dressed in an elegant porcelain-blue shantung silk coat dress with gold embroidery and a flamboyant Philip Treacy "half-halo" hat festooned with baby ostrich feathers, exited arm-in-arm with her husband out the chapel's West Door. The Queen, right behind them, announced to Charles that she was leaving and abruptly took off, ignoring his plea that she stick around for at least one family photo on the chapel steps.

It was enough, the Queen reasoned, that she agreed to host a reception at the castle for eight hundred guests, including King Constantine and Queen Anne-Marie of Greece, King Hamad of Bahrain, Sir David Frost, Tony and Cherie Blair, rocker Phil Collins, and Charles's old friend, comedian and QVC jewelry designer Joan Rivers. "I'm going on *Larry King* tonight," Rivers told the Queen as she pointed to the magnificent yellow-and-blue-white diamond Australian Wattle Brooch glittering on Her Majesty's lapel, "and I'm going to tell him how beautiful your pin is!" The Queen appeared confused, but thanked Rivers anyway.

In her speech that afternoon, Britain's horse-obsessed Queen made sly reference to the Grand National steeplechase, which had just taken place. After telling her guests that Hedgehunter had won the legendary race, she went on to say that her son was "home and dry with the woman he loves. They have been over difficult jumps," she continued, "and all kinds of other terrible obstacles. And now they're in the winners enclosure."

At no time did Charles and Camilla kiss—not when the well-wishers were begging them to outside the chapel, and not now as they left the reception. Camilla's new stepsons, however, were not so shy. By way of making it abundantly clear that they approved of the woman who destroyed their parents' marriage, William and Harry each kissed Camilla on both cheeks—the first time they had done so publicly.

Even more significantly, as the newlyweds paused on the steps outside before leaving Windsor for their honeymoon in Scotland, the Queen and Camilla kissed good-bye. The choreographed gesture was designed to convey harmony in the House of Windsor, and left Camilla visibly shaking.

Then it was off to Balmoral and Birkhall on the banks of the River Muick, where the Queen Mother never had a kind word about either Diana or Camilla. "The Queen Mum loved Prince Charles more than anything," said a Balmoral groundskeeper who worked for the Royal Family for more than forty years. "But if the old girl hadn't died already, this would have killed her."

By any measure, it was a long-delayed victory for Camilla—if, as the Men in Gray argued, not necessarily for the monarchy. "There was a real sense of triumph," said Charles's goddaughter, Santa Sebag Montefiore. "Everybody was filled with this feeling that they're together at last, and without any doubt about Camilla's position, *finally*."

....

24

After deftly navigating the treacherous waters of the royal court for a full decade, Kate married Prince William on April 29, 2011. Conspiring behind the scenes to make it all happen was Kate's ambitious, self-made mother, Carole, who celebrated with the Queen and Camilla.

25

The "Kate Effect." In her first outing as a royal, the Duchess of Cambridge dazzled the crowd at a London gala that raised $28 million for charity. A month later, she watched William get ready to throw a barrel at the Calgary Stampede. Kate brought along a touch of Diana, delighting crowds and hugging a little girl battling cancer.

27

28

29

30

31

The Country Girl. Flanked by Philip, Charles, and Camilla in their royal tartans, the Queen cheers on Balmoral's tug-of-war team during the annual Braemar Games in Scotland. One of the rare times the Queen doesn't carry a purse: when she walks one of her beloved corgis.

32 

Kicking off Elizabeth's Diamond Jubilee, the three queens peer into gift baskets presented to them by London's Fortnum and Mason gourmet store.

33 

Royal flush. Making his debut on the Buckingham Palace balcony, George and his Windsor relatives gaze up at the RAF flyover celebrating Elizabeth's sixty years on the throne. This marked the first time in history that four generations of present and future monarchs appeared together on the royal balcony.

34

The three queens watched as a Jubilee flotilla sailed down the Thames on June 3, 2012. Kate, who wore red, was criticized for upstaging the other royals. Later, the Queen surprised everyone by inviting Camilla to take an ailing Philip's place next to her in the royal carriage. Philip was back to his charming self two weeks later, sharing a laugh with Carole Middleton at Ascot.

36 35

After six decades still a serious student of world affairs, the Queen met with then–secretary of state Hillary Clinton and French president Nicolas Sarkozy in 2009. The next year, she covered her head and took off her shoes to visit the Sheikh Zayed Grand Mosque in Abu Dhabi, and was all ears during a meeting of Prime Minister David Cameron's cabinet at 10 Downing Street.

37

38

39

40

For the first time in seventeen years, Charles attended the State Opening of Parliament in May 2013—another sign the Queen was turning more power over to her son. Elizabeth II visited Pope Francis I at the Vatican in May 2014. She was shocked, and influenced, by his predecessor Benedict XVI's decision to become the first pope to abdicate in six hundred years.

41

43

On his first trip abroad in the spring of 2014, Prince George met an Australian bilby at Sydney's Taronga Zoo. A windblown Camilla, meanwhile, joined Charles and her mother-in-law at ceremonies in Normandy marking the seventieth anniversary of D-day.

Aware that she will someday be seated beside King Charles III on such occasions, Camilla looked every inch the Queen at the State Opening of Parliament in May 2015.

45

While Daddy flies helicopters for the East Anglian Air Ambulance out of nearby Cambridge, two-year-old George prepares for takeoff with a little help from his mother, the duchess.

46

47

At ninety-four and wearing the seven-pound bearskin hat of the Grenadier Guards, the Duke of Edinburgh was back alongside his wife for the 2015 Trooping of the Colour. The Queen plans to move to Balmoral full-time after Philip's death.

Prince George seemed unimpressed as the Queen and Camilla peered in on his sister Charlotte after her christening at Sandringham in July 2015. Wearing her nanny's uniform, Maria Teresa Borrallo smiled at George and Great Granny sharing a heart-to-heart. With the end of primogeniture, Charlotte ranks fourth in line to the throne.

Wearing the Queen Mother's Lotus Flower tiara for her first state banquet at Buckingham Palace in October 2015, Kate was given a place of honor next to Chinese president Xi Jinping.

52

His country's queen looks on as newly elected Canadian prime minister Justin Trudeau meets the Prince of Wales at the Commonwealth summit meeting in Malta in November 2015. Poll numbers show that Canada, Australia, and other nations do not want Charles as their king. Nearing the end of her reign, eighty-nine-year-old Elizabeth plants a tree in Malta, where she lived the more simple life of a naval officer's wife before becoming queen.

53

KATE MIDDLETON, MEANWHILE, WAS HOLED up in the farmhouse she now shared with William on the outskirts of St. Andrews, dividing her time between studying for final exams and watching live coverage of the wedding on television. Kate knew William and Harry planned to decorate their father's Bentley, and laughed as she watched it pull away from Windsor Castle trailing Mylar balloons, the words PRINCE+DUCHESS scribbled across its windshield. When cameras showed the young Princes tossing confetti, then waving their arms wildly as they chased the car down the road, Kate doubled over laughing.

It had been three years since Kate, at her mother Carole's insistence, agreed to share a four-bedroom ground-floor flat in St. Andrews's Old Town district with William and their friend Fergus Boyd. As was to be expected, this move sparked the usual over-the-top headlines, including the *Sun*'s WILLIAM SHACKS UP WITH STUNNING UNDIES MODEL and WILLIAM AND HIS UNDIE-GRADUATE FRIEND KATE TO SHARE A STUDENT FLAT in the *Mail on Sunday*.

Within days of moving in together, William and Kate were lovers—a fact that, due to the Palace's special hands-off arrangement with the press, went unconfirmed for two years. During that time, the coeds essentially lived like any young married couple, shopping at the local Tesco supermarket (William called himself an "enthusiastic food shopper—I get very carried away"), renting videos, dining on take-out from Ruby's Chinese and Pizza Express, playing chess.

When they did go shopping, William and Kate often debated about whether to pay using a credit card or "grannys." Since the Queen's face was on Britain's brightly colored currency, William and Harry called five-pound notes "green grannys," ten-pound notes "brown grannys," twenty-pound notes "purple grannys," and fifty-pound notes "pink grannys." When they did opt to pay with a credit card, they used Kate's. "If you're working as a clerk at a gas station," their friend Jules Knight said, "looking down and seeing 'William Windsor' on the credit card can be quite a shock.

"We were all in a safe bubble at St. Andrews," Knight added. "There was no intrusion. Kate and Will could go for a drink and hold hands and no one batted an eyelid." William was the first to agree that it was all "quite a cozy setup." For the most part, Knight added, "it was a carefree existence."

There were times, of course, when they all climbed into Land Rovers and escaped to Edinburgh and London for a little club-hopping with William's old pals. In sharp contrast to some of the other girls William had been involved with, Kate easily adjusted to the constant presence of royal bodyguards and the cloak-and-dagger climate surrounding William's comings and goings. In an effort to remain beneath the radar, they arrived at restaurants and dinner parties separately, and agreed to no public displays of affection—not even hand-holding.

Kate went the extra step of getting to know the men and women assigned to protect the man she loved. "Kate knew all their names, asked about their families, wanted to make sure they got enough to eat and drink," Knight said. "She's a very kind, very caring, very down-to-earth person." According to one Royal Protection officer, "She insisted we call her Kate and treated us like human beings, which isn't always the case with members of the Royal Family and their posh friends."

Months into the relationship, the Middletons weren't exactly sure how serious things were between the Prince and their Kate. Fearing that Pippa would let the secret slip, Kate insisted to her parents that she and William were merely roomies and friends.

Nevertheless, Carole decided that, if William was going to be spending many weekends at Windsor, Highgrove, and Sandringham, then Kate would need a toehold in London. Toward that end, the Middletons plunked down $2 million for a two-bedroom pied-à-terre in Chelsea.

Kate got her first real taste of what it's like to be royal in December 2002, when she was invited to a shooting party at Sandringham. To throw off the press, fourteen friends bunked with them at Wood Farm, a six-bedroom guest house on the grounds of the estate. William hoped to introduce Kate to his father, but Prince Charles was too busy playing host to the Queen of Denmark at the main residence on the estate, Sandringham House.

Still, it gave Kate a chance to show off her marksmanship skills. Unlike the Queen, Camilla, and most of William's friends, Kate was not schooled in what British aristocracy referred to as "country pursuits" or familiar with firearms of any kind. Before meeting William, she, like most of her contemporaries, was actually sharply critical of foxhunting, deer hunting, game bird shoots, and other blood sports. "The Middletons didn't go in for that sort of thing at all," said a Marlborough classmate. "They knew absolutely nothing about firearms. Kate agreed with Princess Diana. She thought killing animals was disgusting."

Until William, that is. When he offered to give her some pointers in shooting at St. Andrews, Kate balked at first. But Carole, who understood how important such things were to all the Royals, quickly convinced her daughter that it would be rude to refuse the Prince's offer. By the time she set foot on the grounds of Sandringham, Kate was, in the words of one of the beaters whose job was to flush out game, "not a bad shot—not at all bad for a beginner."

It was not long before Kate scored another major coup by becoming the first girl William had ever felt worthy of being invited to Balmoral. Kate no longer needed coaching from her mother on this score; at Sandringham she had seen firsthand what a key role outdoor pursuits played in the lives of the Windsors—a part of royal life Diana had rejected outright.

With William as her guide, Kate nimbly negotiated the rocky banks of the River Dee, then watched carefully as he showed her the proper way to cast a fishing line. Soon she was angling for fish and trout "as if she'd been doing it her whole life," the Prince remarked.

It was not William Kate had come to impress, however. It was at Balmoral that she met the Prince of Wales for the first time. Charles was instantly charmed by the fact that Kate "is clearly a country girl," a senior aide said. That alone was "a huge advantage." William's father even forgave her when she tried to sit in Queen Victoria's chair, kept vacant since the monarch's death out of respect—usually considered a major, if common, faux pas. During predinner drinks, Kate had begun to lower herself into the chair when William, Charles, and the other guests yelled for her to stop. "Every new person goes for it," said Jean Carnarvon, whose husband, the seventh Earl of Carnarvon, owned Highclere Castle of *Downton Abbey* fame, "and everyone screams."

Later in the spring of 2003, William made a surprise visit to Kate's delayed twenty-first birthday party at the Middleton home in Bucklebury. It marked the first time he met Kate's parents, who stopped asking their daughter if the Prince was coming only when his Land Rover pulled up to their front door.

Once the press got wind of William's visit to Oak Acre, the Middletons decided to issue a flat denial that their daughter and the Prince were anything more than "good friends . . . the best of pals. We are very amused at the thought of being in-laws to Prince William," Michael Middleton added disingenuously, "but I don't think it's going to happen."

Unfortunately, at his *Out of Africa*–themed twenty-first birthday party at Windsor Castle, it seemed that William had turned his attention away from Kate and toward an old flame. The $800,000 bash, which featured elephant rides and monkeys swinging overhead on vines, was most memorable for the guests who showed up in costume. William and Kate wore Tarzan-and-Jane costumes—a loincloth for him, a skimpy animal-print dress for her—while Charles donned a dashiki, Camilla wore a multicolored caftan with a red-feathered headdress, and Elizabeth, as the Queen of Swaziland, opted for a white headdress, a white shift dress gown, and a white fur cape.

But it was Jecca Craig, William's old gap-year love, who stole the show. With Kate's blessing, William had invited Jecca, and stuck by her side the entire evening. Not surprisingly, the press promptly shifted its attention away from Kate and toward Jecca. Since she was dating his old Etonian buddy Henry Ropner at the time, William asked his father to issue a public statement denying that he had ever had a serious relationship with Jecca—or, for that matter, with anyone. "If and when Prince William gets his first serious girlfriend," a St. James's Palace spokesman said, "we will work out something to say."

Incredibly, the ruse worked. Leaving Fergus Boyd behind, Babykins and Big Willy—their pet names for each other—moved into Balgove House, a four-bedroom farmhouse on a sprawling private estate about a quarter of a mile outside St. Andrews. Bombproof windows and doors were installed, along with surveillance cameras and alarms—all to the tune of 2.5 million taxpayer dollars. William's Close Protection detail, meanwhile, operated out of a separate building on the property.

Their life in St. Andrews was now more serene, private, and cosseted than ever. But William's bar-hopping, binge-drinking forays into London—where he usually joined forces with his hard-partying brother—were another matter. When British tabloids ran photos of the drunken princes openly groping women at bars in central London, Carole called her daughter to reassure her that the stories were probably blown out of proportion. But if Kate wanted to spend more time with William in London, Carole also made it clear that the Middletons' Chelsea flat was at her disposal. "Carole was afraid," said a Goldsmith cousin, "that he was losing interest and slipping right through Kate's fingers."

Heeding her mother's sage advice, Kate made sure that she accompanied William on trips to Edinburgh and especially into London. In the VIP rooms at places like Chinawhite, Boujis, or Purple, Kate was, in the words of a Boujis waitress, "positively glued to the Prince. If any girl even tried to flirt with him—well, if looks could kill . . ."

NO ONE APPRECIATED KATE'S GUMPTION more than Camilla, who became serious about staking her permanent claim on the Prince long before their nuptials. Starting back in 2002, when the Queen's trusted treasurer Sir Michael Peat became Prince Charles's private secretary, Camilla ramped up her efforts to be publicly seen and accepted as the next sovereign's rightful life companion.

Even as she promoted an image of herself in the media as a

guileless, garden-tending matron, Camilla furiously battled senior courtiers behind the scenes. According to former members of the Prince of Wales's staff, she spent hours strategizing with spin doctors, leaking self-aggrandizing stories to the press, sniping at perceived foes, and currying favor with the Crown. "Despite her carefully cultivated image as the comfortable countrywoman," Patrick Jephson said, "Mrs. PB operates a high-powered PR strategy."

As far as Camilla was concerned, the small slights added up. When Charles attended a community event in Derbyshire to mark Shrove Tuesday, he was pointedly informed the invitation did not extend to Camilla. Later, the Prince of Wales was asked to attend a Shakespeare tribute evening at London's Globe Theater for his charity, the Prince's Trust—and again, she was omitted. This time, she showed up anyway.

Before their marriage, at a celebrity-packed Fashion Rocks gala at London's Albert Hall honoring Charles, Camilla materialized at his side. Again, she had made the bold decision to defy the Prince's own senior staffers, who feared the unpopular Mrs. PB would be an unwelcome distraction at a time when Charles needed as much goodwill as he could muster.

Such bitter rows between Camilla and Charles's inner circle of seven top advisors (out of the Prince of Wales's total staff of 125) were common. Diana had called the St. James's crew who catered to her husband "The Enemy." Now that Camilla had essentially replaced Diana, she called her husband's advisors—yes, "The Enemy." (Camilla had a special nickname for her nemesis Sir Michael Peat: "The Bidet, because you know what it's called, you just don't know what it's for.")

Camilla kept a close eye on those farther down the food chain as well. Secretaries and clerks, housekeepers and bodyguards—anyone employed in the service of the Prince of Wales was subject to Camilla's whim. Women she felt threatened by were, for obvious reasons, particularly vulnerable. Sarah Goodhall had been answering Prince Charles's correspondence for more than a decade when Camilla arranged for her to be invited for a week's vacation at Birkhall. Camilla was careful to sit next to the thirty-four-year-old secretary at dinner and engage her in conversation about everything from their shared love of horses to their cancer-stricken mothers.

Once Goodhall returned to the office, however, things were very different. Camilla had complained to Goodhall's superior, Mark Bolland, that the staffer had been too flirtatious with Prince Charles. "Camilla had made it clear she did not want me working there," Goodhall said.

Similarly, Camilla eased Tiggy Legge-Bourke out of the picture, as well as several other female employees she felt might pose a threat to her relationship with the Prince. As in every other area, when it came hiring and firing staff Camilla had the upper hand. "Prince Charles," Goodhall said, "is not strong enough to say no to Camilla."

"The ambition that has brought Camilla this far has not died," observed Jephson, who accused Camilla of routinely "trampling on underlings" and continually leaking stories to the press to serve her own purposes. "Camilla is deliberately orchestrating events and setting the media agenda."

Now that the Prince of Wales was well into his fifties, it seemed to everyone who knew him that he needed Camilla more than ever. "Every sinew of his organization and every shred of royal dignity," Jephson said, had been "subordinated to the task of getting her into his life." Now that she was, "the whole apparatus, instead of being dismantled, is being refueled and rearmed to get her on to the throne." In the meantime, Camilla's modus operandi was, Jephson went on, "drawn from every shelf of the spin doctor's medicine cupboard, and from some pretty dark corners, too."

Camilla reached into those dark corners, according to Jephson, Richard Kay, and others, principally to defame Diana's memory. "Many of the friends who conspired in Charles's and Camilla's extramarital affairs," Jephson said, "who conceived and executed their mission plan for public acceptability, would happily wish away Diana's achievements." Agreed Diana's friend Vivienne Parry: "It feels like there's a conspiracy to forget Diana."

Polls taken just before the wedding of Charles and Camilla showed that 74 percent of all Britons believed that the Queen and other members of the Royal Family had "deliberately avoided" mentioning Diana's name since her death. Earl Spencer believed that his sister's memory was being "marginalized" by the Royal Family, and that there was an orchestrated effort to "tell people she never mattered, that in the first week of September 1997 they were all suffering from mass hysteria." Certainly the Queen and her husband came in for more than their share of criticism on this score. When it was proposed that Heathrow be renamed in Diana's honor, Elizabeth promptly vetoed the idea. The Queen also nixed a proposal to commission a large statue of Diana to be placed outside Kensington Palace. What the public did not know was that, in both cases, Camilla convinced Charles to lobby his mother against these ideas on the grounds that they were "tasteless." In determining what was an appropriate memorial for Diana, the Queen relied heavily on Charles's opinion.

....

YET THERE WAS A GROWING feeling that all the damaging stories about Diana's emotional instability, her manipulative behavior, and her sordid affairs were part of a larger orchestrated effort to slander the late Princess. The Queen and Prince Philip in particular, said writer Nicholas Davies, were guilty of trying to "besmirch the name and memory of the People's Princess by leaking and spreading disturbing innuendos that she was mentally ill."

Camilla was careful to express heartfelt concern for William and Harry every time a once-trusted employee or confidant of Diana's unleashed another book or tabloid series on the reading public.

Yet in private she gleefully devoured Paul Burrell's revelations—sold to the *Daily Mirror* for $468,000—about Diana's obsession with Hasnet Khan (at one point she considering tricking him into marriage by becoming pregnant) and books like *Diana: Closely Guarded Secret*, in which Royal Protection officer Ken Wharfe revealed that Diana always kept a vibrator in her handbag. At home, she called it "le gadget"; packed away in a suitcase whenever she traveled, the vibrator was Diana's "secret mascot."

More than once, servants came upon Camilla reading the more titillating passages aloud to friends and then "howling" with laughter. "Every time there was another scandalous story about Diana it was horribly painful for William and Harry," said one. "They felt terribly betrayed, as you can imagine. But for Camilla, any nasty thing anyone could say or write about Diana was pure gold."

James Hewitt gave Charles's mistress plenty to work with when he tried to sell sixty-four steamy love letters from Diana to the now-defunct *News of the World* for more than $16 million. In several of the letters, Diana referred to Hewitt's penis as "my friend."

Indeed, each juicy new tell-all memoir or leaked tidbit "peeled away the layers of the myth until nothing was left," said a former aide to Prince Charles. "That was the objective—to allow Diana's memory to be debased to such an extent that Camilla looked good by comparison."

"People often say that Camilla is such a sweet and uncomplicated woman, but all you have to do is look at how she plots, schemes—the deception," Lady Elsa Bowker remarked. "She despised Diana in life, and I think even more so in death, because Diana was even more beloved for her kindness in death."

With Charles's help—and the benign acquiescence of the Queen—a number of figures in the sovereign's inner circle were enlisted to join in the Diana-bashing. The Queen's friend Lady Kennard branded Diana "very damaged" and "impossible to understand." Another of Her Majesty's pals and a former lady-in-waiting to the Queen Mother, Lady Penn, mentioned that Diana may have suffered some "mental instability." One of Charles's closest allies, Countess Mountbatten, chimed in that Diana "had a side the public never saw," while her sister Lady Pamela Hicks called Diana "spiteful" and "truly unkind." With a nod to Camilla, Lady Hicks later said Prince Charles had "blossomed" in the years since Diana's death.

Airbrushing Diana from history entirely would nonetheless prove to be an impossible task. Whatever she said or did behind closed doors, the Queen, who still suffered flashbacks to the days when Diana's death imperiled the monarchy, was careful to never utter a negative word about her late daughter-in-law in public. At the dedication of the modest Diana Fountain in Hyde Park in July

2004, the Princess's boys struggled to contain their emotions as the Queen spoke of an England "coming to terms with the loss, united by an extraordinary sense of shock, grief, and sadness." She went on to praise Diana "especially for the happiness she gave my two grandsons. I cannot forget . . . the Diana who made such an impact on our lives."

Camilla, of course, had been told not to come. So had Kate, whose romance with William had been out of the bag ever since they were caught just a few months earlier embracing on the slopes at the Swiss ski resort of Klosters.

Shared slights aside, Charles's wife eyed Kate warily. Even before she married the Prince of Wales, Camilla felt it was perfectly appropriate for her to weigh in on the suitability of William's women. Now that she was the Duchess of Cornwall (and, although no one dared say it, technically the new Princess of Wales), Charles's bride had a lofty perspective from her new perch as the second-ranking female in the kingdom.

For his part, Charles harbored no qualms about Kate. Just by shoring up William's self-confidence during those uncertain early days at St. Andrews, Kate had earned the Prince of Wales's gratitude and respect. The beautiful young commoner's eager embrace of the Windsor lifestyle at Sandringham and Balmoral, her ability to withstand the twin pressures of being guarded around the clock and pursued by the press, her wit, style, natural grace, sense of discretion, and seemingly innate unflappability—these were the attributes that set Kate apart.

At Charles's insistence, Kate was among a small group invited to Highgrove to celebrate the Prince of Wales's fifty-sixth birthday. Ever the charming hostess, Camilla paid special attention to Kate that evening, doing her best to make William's girlfriend feel comfortable and welcome. "Mrs. Parker Bowles," Kate later told her parents, "couldn't have been nicer. She's very warm—a kind of earth mother type, really."

Appearances were deceiving. Camilla had been closely monitoring William's love life since his final year at Eton, and actively campaigning for William to marry an aristocrat—ideally someone from one of the royal houses of Europe. Camilla had also used the resources available to her through St. James's Palace to find out all she could about Kate's working-class background—from her family's roots in the coal fields of County Durham through to Kate's flight attendant mother and the mail-order empire she built as a supplier of children's party favors.

Camilla was profoundly unimpressed. Based on reports she was getting from mutual friends in Berkshire, Carole Middleton sounded gauche and pushy, lacking in background and breeding. To top it off, Kate's self-made mother was an unrepentant chain smoker who chewed gum furiously whenever she wasn't permitted to light up. Since having to give up cigarettes cold turkey to please Charles and the Queen, Camilla had come to view smoking as the nastiest of habits. "Like a lot of ex-smokers," said a former Highgrove staffer, "she couldn't stand to see anyone else smoke. She said the smell made her sick. It was rather funny, since she blew smoke in other people's faces for fifty years." (Further complicating the issue was the fact that both William and Harry smoked whenever they were out of camera range. Camilla, unwilling to appear as if she were trying to take Diana's place as a mother figure, refused Charles's repeated request to talk with the boys about quitting.)

Putting Kate's up-by-the-bootstraps family background aside, what did Mrs. Parker Bowles think of William's girlfriend as a person? To Camilla, Kate seemed "pretty, but rather dim."

"Beneath it all," says a friend of the Parker Bowleses, "Camilla is a snob. Her family has always moved in royal circles. It's simply second nature to her. She simply felt Kate and the Middletons were too lowly to marry into the Royal Family." After waiting more than thirty years to be openly accepted by the Queen, the friend went on, "she wasn't going to have someone just march in and sort of drag the whole thing down. Like I said, Camilla is really an awful snob."

She was also someone who had learned to love the limelight. Now that the press had fallen in love with Kate and was pursuing her everywhere, Camilla was apparently jealous of the attention she was getting. "Members of the Royal Family simply cannot stand being upstaged," Richard Kay said. "Charles hated it when the press trampled over him to get to Diana, and it only makes sense that Camilla resented being eclipsed by a beautiful young woman like Kate Middleton."

Yet there was nothing Camilla could do to keep Kate from sharing the spotlight with William when they graduated from St. Andrews on June 23, 2005. The Queen had been sick for a week with the flu, but she showed up anyway along with Prince Philip. It was a first for the Duke of Edinburgh, who had never attended the graduation ceremonies for any of his own children.

This year as every year, Vice Chancellor Bryan Lang told members of the graduating class of 2005 that "you may have met your husband or wife." After joking that St. Andrews was the "Top Matchmaking University in Britain," Lang ended by telling graduates to "go forth and multiply."

The Queen laughed, but she had already made clear her feelings about people who marry too young. After brief courtships, Charles, Anne, and Andrew all saw their marriages go up in flames. Elizabeth now decreed that all royal courtships should last at least five years "so people can really get to know each other."

That was perfectly fine with William, who told a reporter that he was not marching to the altar anytime soon. "I'm too young to marry," he declared. "I don't want to get married until I'm at least twenty-eight or maybe thirty."

As it happened, Kate and William had already been together for four years, much of that time spent under the radar. There had been a flurry of speculation in the press about a possible engagement on the horizon, but the last thing Kate and the Middletons wanted at this point was to appear grasping.

After the ceremony, as families milled about and chatted effusively outside St. Andrews's Younger Hall, the Middletons—Carole, Michael, Pippa, and James—kept a discreet distance from the Royals at the edge of the crowd. Carole, dressed in a chic pink wool suit and craving a cigarette, could just make out the Queen in the distance—a tiny, white-gloved figure swathed in canary yellow, her wide hat tilting from one side to the next as William bent down to kiss his grandmother on both cheeks.

No sooner had he made eye contact with Kate over Camilla's shoulder than William made a beeline for the Middletons. Pulling Kate by the elbow, he whispered that he wanted to take the Middletons to meet the Queen. But Kate realized that such a group introduction in public might appear presumptuous, and wisely demurred. "Perhaps you're right," William agreed. "There's plenty of time for that."

William also felt there was plenty of time for him to assume a full schedule of tree plantings, plaque unveilings, and other ceremonial duties as a working member of the Royal Family. Right now, he wanted to embark on the military career he had always dreamed of having. For the next forty-four weeks, the Heir would be training at Sandhurst just as Harry had done before him. "That's why I put my brother in," William joked, "as a guinea pig."

....

THE HARSH REALITIES OF MILITARY training were nothing compared to the emotional torment of reliving his mother's violent and untimely death. Operation Paget, Scotland Yard's long-delayed investigation into Mohamed Al Fayed's accusation that Prince Philip ordered British intelligence to murder Diana and Dodi, was finally in full swing, and William (along with Harry, Charles, and Philip) were among hundreds of witnesses grilled by investigators.

Among other things, William told investigators that his mother had no intention of marrying Dodi, as Mohamed Al Fayed claimed. Lord Stevens, who ran the investigation, was especially blunt with Charles. At the end of a punishing three-hour-long interrogation at Clarence House, the Prince of Wales was shocked by Lord Stevens's final question: "Did you, Your Highness, plot to murder the Princess or have anything to do with her death?"

"No," Charles replied curtly. "I did *not.*"

The Duke of Edinburgh was even more incensed at the tone of Lord Stevens's questions, although Diana's repeated comments in the final year of her life made it easy to see why Stevens had to ask them. "Prince Philip wants to see me dead," she told Lord Mishcon. "I am sure Prince Philip is involved with the security services," she insisted on another occasion. "They are going to get rid of me." Not long after the divorce, Diana was in the VIP lounge at Heathrow waiting to board a flight to Italy when she looked up at a portrait of Prince Philip. "He really hates me and would like to see me disappear," she told her friend Roberto Devorik. Then, as she was about to be escorted to her flight, the Princess took a deep breath and shook her head. "Well, cross your fingers," Diana said. "Any minute they will blow me up. . . . They, the machinery, are going to blow me up."

Ultimately, the provocatively-titled, 832-page *Operation Paget Inquiry Report into the Allegation of Conspiracy to Murder* would confirm the findings of the original 1999 accident investigation. Diana's undeniably eerie premonitions aside, the man behind the wheel of the Mercedes sedan in which she and Dodi Fayed were riding that night had a blood alcohol content more than three times the legal limit. As mundane as it sounded, the Princess of Wales and her Egyptian lover, neither of whom were wearing seat belts that night, were the victims of a drunk-driving accident.

By dredging up memories of how William's mother was relentlessly pursued by the press, Operation Paget did give a new sense of urgency to a more immediate problem. Now that William was at Sandhurst—where a close-cropped military haircut revealed the famous Windsor bald spot—and Kate on her own in London, Fleet Street no longer felt obliged to abide by the hands-off policy that had been in force at St. Andrews. Now, whenever Kate left her family's stucco-walled Chelsea pied-à-terre, photographers leaped out at her from behind trees and parked vehicles, then pursued their hapless prey on foot.

Through it all, Kate displayed the sort of calm under fire that would impress a queen. She smiled convincingly for the cameras, never voiced a word of complaint to the paparazzi, and certainly never showed a flash of temper—something several members of the Royal Family were famously prone to do.

However, just two weeks after William and Kate graduated from St. Andrews, bombs planted by Islamist terrorists went off on the buses and subways of London, killing fifty-two people and injuring more than seven hundred others. Once again, the Queen immediately ordered the Union Jack over Buckingham Palace to be flown at half-staff. Less than twenty-fours after the attack, she was touring the wreckage and making the rounds of hospitals to comfort the injured.

A moment of silence in memory of the victims was observed the following week throughout Europe. As Big Ben tolled, members of the Royal Family gathered, heads bowed, in the forecourt of Buckingham Palace. The image of the Queen, standing in an archway with her handbag dangling from her elbow, was, said former Prime Minister John Major, "a powerful reminder of the unifying power of the monarchy—and, more specifically, the bond between the Queen and her people."

Just ten days later, William swept Kate and a dozen of their closest friend off to his favorite place on the planet—the foothills of Mount Kenya. But no sooner did they return than Kate was once again darting down streets with packs of paparazzi in hot pursuit.

Kate had no official standing and therefore was not technically entitled to government protection of any sort. But when a German magazine published a photograph pinpointing Kate's Chelsea flat with a big red arrow, William asked the Palace to do something about it. Prince Charles was happy to oblige. At his personal request, the Queen's law firm of Harbottle & Lewis fired off letters to newspaper and magazine publishers threatening legal action if they didn't back off.

This time, however, the Palace's threats fell on deaf ears. "Kate Middleton wants the privacy of a nun," said the *Sun*'s Fergus Shanahan, "yet she chooses to go out with Prince William. She can't have it both ways."

....

IF ANYONE KNEW WHAT IT was like to exist unprotected on the fringes of Royal Family life, it was Camilla. Now that she was the Duchess of Cornwall, Camilla was finding that things weren't much easier. When she made her all-important first official walkabout just a few days after her wedding, the press pointed out that she had worn the same tartan wrap and coat for the third time in less than a week.

Determined not to embarrass her husband, Camilla packed fifty dresses for their six-day tour of the United States in November 2005. "We're going to be going into Diana territory," she told Charles, referring to the fact that Americans admired the late princess as much as if not more than her own countrymen did. "I at least want a fighting chance."

After a stop at Ground Zero and a celebrity-crammed champagne reception at the Museum of Modern Art, the couple awoke the next morning to a front-page photo of Camilla wearing an ill-fitting blue velvet dress and the headline QUEEN CAMILLA IS NEW YORK'S FRUMP TOWER. "If it was Diana they were looking for, forget it," New York columnist Cindy Adams remarked. "Glamorous Camilla definitely ain't."

Still, as Charles and his bride wended their way from Washington to New Orleans (where they seemed genuinely horrified by the devastation wrought by Hurricane Katrina) and then on to San Francisco, the American press and public began to warm to the charmingly stodgy older couple.

From Camilla's standpoint, it was just as important that she not repeat Diana's mistake by competing with her husband for attention. With that in mind, Camilla adhered to the Four Steps Back Rule, always careful to walk at least four paces behind a ranking Royal—in this case Charles—after arriving at an event.

The American press had occasionally been less than kind, but the opposite was true back home in England. The entire trip had basically been designed as a public relations juggernaut for the woman Charles was intent on someday making his queen, and in that sense it seemed to have succeeded brilliantly. The British media declared the tour to be nothing less than a triumph, and gave much of the credit to Camilla. As a seasoned veteran of court intrigue, the Duchess realized that praise was a good thing—but not too much praise. "Charles never likes to share the limelight," said Richard Kay. "He was jealous of Diana and at times he is jealous of Camilla."

Conversely, Charles became livid whenever he felt his second wife's reputation was being impugned. Their debut as a married couple abroad may have gone exceedingly well, but not well enough to keep the Queen from specifically excluding the newly minted Duchess of Cornwall from the state prayers for the Royal Family recited at all Church of England Sunday services.

With prodding from Camilla, Charles pointed out to his mother that Diana's name had been included in the prayers before their divorce. This latest slight, he argued, hampered his efforts to win over that sizable portion of the public that still found Camilla objectionable.

Her Majesty refused to budge. The Men in Gray had shown her new polls indicating that three out of four Britons still strongly opposed the idea of a future "Queen Camilla." The Queen told her son that there were simply "too many people who are still unhappy about the marriage." She was not about to offend them.

Camilla took solace in the fact that, for the first time as a member of the Royal Family, she had been invited to the Windsors' lavish Christmas festivities at Sandringham. More important for the Duchess of Cornwall, who had been relegated to the shadows for so long, this was the first time in decades that she could spend Christmas with the man she loved.

It also marked the first time that Camilla pitched in to help the Queen and the rest of the Royal Family finish decorating the twenty-foot tree that had been cut down on the grounds of the estate. Presents were opened on Christmas Eve, following the German custom adhered to by the Royals since the reign of Queen Victoria. The family that truly had everything restricted themselves to exchanging gag gifts—a white leather toilet seat for Charles one year, a shower cap from Prince Harry with "Ain't life a bitch" embroidered on it for the Queen the next. The Duchess of Cornwall, whose earthy sense of humor was agonizingly evident in the notorious "Camillagate" tapes, had for years picked out the gag gifts that Charles handed out to his relatives. "It's such wonderful fun," she told her Wiltshire neighbor, "to finally see the looks on their faces when they open them—especially the Queen's."

Afterward, there was an extravagant black-tie banquet where Camilla's high rank now meant she was seated next to Prince

Philip and directly opposite the monarch. At church services the next day, Camilla was visibly moved when two thousand people turned out to greet the newest member of the Royal Family. However, none of this kept Charles from wincing and shaking his head when, during the service, the Duchess of Cornwall's name was not read aloud during prayers for the Royal Family.

Once again, Carole Middleton asked her daughter repeatedly if she had received the coveted invitation to spend Christmas with the Royal Family at Sandringham. And, for the fourth year in a row, Kate would have to disappoint her mother. While Charles and the Queen clearly approved of William's girlfriend, Christmas at Sandringham was reserved exclusively for Royal Family members or those who were officially about to become one.

What Kate could not know at the time was that William had pleaded with his father to ask the Queen if she would make an exception in Kate's case. According to one Clarence House staff member, Charles was about to broach the subject with Buckingham Palace but abruptly changed his mind. "She has waited so much longer for this moment," Prince Charles said of Camilla. "I don't think it's fair to ask her to share it with someone else. Perhaps next year."

Over the coming weeks, Kate and William would savor the occasional romantic interlude—toasting the New Year at Wood Farm, a ski holiday in Switzerland (where they were photographed kissing for the first time), cozy weekends at Highgrove or at Kate's Chelsea flat. Yet by keeping such a low profile, the couple inadvertently fueled speculation that their affair had fizzled.

In the meantime, Charles saw to it that his bride was given every possible opportunity to be seen in the presence of the monarch. During ceremonies unveiling the new home of the Welsh

Assembly in early March 2006, the Queen actually planted a kiss on Camilla's cheek—a royal seal of approval, or as close as one could get to it.

With no defined role within the Royal Family and no invitations forthcoming from Clarence House, Kate would have to act if she was going to keep her place at the royal table. After a full month of virtual invisibility, Kate took her mother's advice and showed up with a girlfriend, uninvited and unannounced, at one of the most important thoroughbred racing events of the season—the Cheltenham Gold Cup. It was no coincidence that the Prince of Wales and his wife were also in attendance.

Determined that her daughter not be overlooked in the crowd, Carole lent Kate her tall, Russian-style fur hat. Not surprisingly, reporters swarmed around Kate from the moment she set foot on the racecourse grounds. Moments later, she was whisked away to join Charles and Camilla in the royal box.

Ironically, Camilla was especially glad to see Kate. After years of skulking in the background as Charles's mistress, the Duchess was still uncomfortable in her new role as a full-fledged member of the Royal Family. As she prepared to present the trophy to the winning horse and jockey, Camilla was clearly relieved to have William's beautiful girlfriend on hand to soak up some of the attention.

The next day, Kate got an added boost when William was sprung from Sandhurst for a weekend to compete in alumni games at Eton. This time, they were openly amorous in a way they had never been before, hugging and kissing in full view of spectators and the press.

If Carole worried that her daughter had somehow fallen off the royal radar, she shouldn't have. At William's behest, Charles paid out of his own pocket to provide Kate with round-the-clock armed protection. Meanwhile the Queen, who had yet to meet Kate, had read and heard enough about her to form what her private secretary called "a highly favorable opinion" of William's "young lady." By way of giving her grandson a slight nudge, she handed him the keys to a completely renovated, three-bedroom cottage in a pine-forested corner of Balmoral known as Brochdhu, not far from Birkhall.

Kate would have to wait to learn her fate, but Camilla was already living hers. Just days after nervously presenting the Cheltenham Cup, she and Charles set off on a two-week tour of Egypt, Saudi Arabia, and India. Contending with flies, sand, wind, and temperatures that hovered around 108 degrees ("It almost did me in," Camilla later allowed), the Prince and the Duchess never complained. As she prepared to sign the guest book at a Sikh shrine in Punjab, someone accidentally pulled the chair out from under Camilla, sending her crashing to the floor. All the way down, a reporter observed, the Duchess "managed to keep smiling."

Apparently she had good reason to smile. In their zeal to impress the future Charles III, the Saudi royal family showered Camilla with, well, a king's ransom in precious jewels—including two blinding ruby-and-diamond necklaces valued at $1.8 million each. Rubies, the Saudis had learned, were the Duchess of Cornwall's favorite gem.

APRIL 21, 2006

SHE EMERGED FROM WINDSOR CASTLE into the April sunshine, a familiar figure in a pink wool coat and matching hat, the ever-present handbag dangling from the crook of her arm. On cue, the band of the Irish Guards struck up "Happy Birthday" as the Queen waded into a crowd of twenty-five thousand Union Jack–waving well-wishers. She later hosted a tea at Buckingham Palace for ninety-nine people who also happened to be turning eighty on that same day, and clapped with delight when she was shown an aerial photograph of five hundred crew members spelling out "Happy 80th " on the deck of the aircraft carrier HMS *Illustrious.*

That evening she stood on the front steps of the newly refurbished Kew Palace, once home to George III, and gazed up in childlike wonder at a fireworks display while the Royal Marine Band played a selection of Beatles songs and show tunes. Then, along with twenty-five members of her family, she dined in front of a fire in the white-paneled dining room on smoked salmon, Morecambe Bay shrimp, and juniper-roast loin of Sandringham venison.

Seated to the Queen's right was Charles. To her left, William. The Duchess of Cornwall, seated directly opposite the Queen, appeared subdued throughout the evening. Not so the birthday girl. "That day," said Countess Mountbatten, the Queen was "as happy as I have ever seen her."

With reason. Flanked by her son and her grandson, she could be reasonably assured that the monarchy would last at least two more generations. She would have been happier still, of course, if Kate had been sitting at the table. Always careful not to push William—or for that matter any of her children or grandchildren—on the subject of matrimony, the Queen gently inquired about Miss Middleton and left it at that.

After a brief (and much-photographed) frolic with her Prince on the exclusive island enclave of Mustique in the Grenadines,

Kate cleared another hurdle when she was invited to attend the wedding of Camilla's daughter Laura Parker Bowles to Harry Lopes, grandson of the late Lord Astor of Hever and a former Calvin Klein underwear model. It was Kate's first Royal Family wedding, and, noted the *Sunday Telegraph*, a "significant step forward" in her relationship with the Heir.

That step was taken in spite of Camilla; the mother of the bride was determined that neither she nor her only daughter be eclipsed by Kate, and initially included neither her nor Harry's stunning steady girlfriend, Chelsy Davy, on the guest list. It was only after Kate argued that her absence would set tongues wagging that William forced the issue. "Kate and I will be there, Papa," he told the Prince of Wales. "Please tell Camilla that we are both looking forward to it."

With a royal engagement seemingly just over the horizon, Kate's ferociously ambitious, social-climbing grandmother succumbed to lung cancer on July 21, 2006. "Lady Dorothy" Goldsmith, a lifelong chain smoker, was seventy-one. According to a Goldsmith cousin, the matriarch "came from nothing, but she always behaved like a queen. She was completely thrilled that her own granddaughter might become one."

At this point, William was spending almost as much time in the company of Kate's family as his own. When he and Kate weren't ordering take-out and watching videos at the Middletons' Chelsea flat, he got behind the wheel of a royal Land Rover and, with four bodyguards in tow, drove the thirty-three miles from Sandhurst to Oak Acre.

Charles had already given permission for William and Kate to have their own room at Highgrove—rather than go through the charade of being assigned separate bedrooms. Things were the same at Oak Acre, where William fell into an easy rhythm with the comparatively unstuffy, affable Middleton clan. Since Carole had not yet managed to kick her pack-a-day habit, it was also one of the few places where the Prince felt free to smoke. Soon William, who always called his own father "Papa," was referring to Michael Middleton as "Dad." William refrained at first from calling Carole "Mom," presumably out of deference to Diana.

Over the next several months, William and Kate popped up everywhere together—sunning themselves on the Mediterranean resort island of Ibiza off the coast of Spain, popping in and out of London nightspots, turning heads at the high-profile weddings of their blue-blooded friends. But when she heard through the Clarence House grapevine that Britain's hard-working monarch was asking why William's girlfriend didn't have a job, Kate rushed to land one.

....

IN THE MEANTIME, THE QUEEN found herself under the microscope when the Stephen Frears–directed film *The Queen* was released that fall. The movie, in which Dame Helen Mirren delivered a nuanced and ultimately sympathetic portrayal of Elizabeth as both benighted monarch and loving grandmother, imagined what it was like for the Queen during those precarious days following Diana's death.

Asssured by those closest to her that *The Queen* was good for the Royal Family and the institution of the monarchy because it humanized the sovereign, Elizabeth nevertheless refused to see the movie on the grounds that to see someone else portray her on screen would be "irritating." During one of their weekly audiences, she even mentioned the movie to Prime Minister Tony

Blair. "I'd just like you to know," she said, "that I'm not going to watch it. Are you?"

Blair gave Her Majesty the response she wanted. "No," he said. "Of course not." Of course, he did, and so did Charles, Camilla, William, Kate, Kate's parents, and virtually all the other members of the Queen's family. None mentioned this to Elizabeth, and for one principal reason. While the Queen, Charles, and Blair were depicted favorably, the Duke of Edinburgh was not.

The Queen garnered great critical acclaim and was a worldwide box office success, earning Mirren an Academy Award as Best Actress. Ironically, the actress had always been an outspoken antimonarchist republican and in 1996 even turned down an appointment as CBE (Commander of the Most Excellent Order of the British Empire); still no fan of the Royal Family in 2003, Mirren had to be persuaded that year to accept a damehood. Now, Dame Helen described herself as a dedicated "Queenist."

During her Oscar acceptance speech, Mirren praised "Elizabeth Windsor" for maintaining "her dignity, her sense of duty, and her hairstyle" for more than a half-century. "She's had her feet planted firmly on the ground, her hat on her head, her handbag on her arm, and she's weathered many, many storms, and I salute her courage and her consistency. Ladies and gentleman," she concluded, holding her Oscar high, "I give you the Queen!"

A year later at Ascot, the Queen asked Mirren to join her for tea in the royal box. "Hello," the Queen said as Mirren curtsied. "It's lovely to meet you." The two women talked about the horses running that day, and Mirren, who was never quite sure how the monarch felt about her portrayal, left feeling "very touched to be invited. I wouldn't have been invited to tea," Mirren told *Vanity*

Fair's Sally Bedell Smith, "if she had hated the film." (In 2015, Mirren won a Best Actress Tony Award for portraying Elizabeth II yet again in *The Audience*, a fictional account of the Queen's private weekly meetings with twelve prime ministers over sixty-three years.)

Elizabeth recognized that *The Queen* had given a huge boost to her image. Even the notoriously taciturn Men in Gray were pleased, informing the woman Diana called "The Boss" that the film's release had even had a positive impact on British tourism. More specifically, she was also told that *The Queen*, set predominantly at Balmoral, had spurred travel to the region and ignited a sudden explosion of tartan plaids on fashion runways and in magazine spreads.

While audiences around the world sought insight into the iconic Elizabeth's personality on the silver screen, Kate searched for gainful employment. "The Queen doesn't expect the people around her to work as hard as she does," said Lady Joseph, wife of the noted British statesman Keith Joseph. "But she does expect them to work."

....

IN LATE NOVEMBER, KATE WAS hired by Jigsaw, the British clothing store chain, as an assistant buyer for the company's junior accessories line. According to Jigsaw founder Belle Robinson, the part-time position gave Kate the flexibility she needed so that she could "drop everything at a moment's notice" if that's what her prince required. At the end of Kate's first day at work, Robinson suggested she duck out the back to avoid the press. Instead, Kate obliged photographers by marching out the front entrance and smiling for a moment before sliding behind the wheel of her car.

The next morning, Her Majesty saw the front-page photos of William's girlfriend leaving after a hard day on the job—precisely as Kate had intended. Just a few days later, those same tabloids were filled with pictures of Kate at Sandringham, carrying several bloody game birds that had just been shot by the Heir. Around her neck were the binoculars William had given her the previous year for Christmas. "How sad," observed the legendary French movie bombshell-turned-animal-rights-advocate Brigitte Bardot. "She was trying to win William and his family. But this is not the way to get a man. And I do know one or two things about it, you know."

Bardot's remarks only pushed the Queen more squarely into Kate's corner. Elizabeth had come in for plenty of criticism from animal rights activists before, especially after she was caught on video clubbing a pheasant to death with her walking stick after it was brought to her, still thrashing, by one of Philip's hunting dogs. Her Majesty, a Palace spokesman explained at the time, was only acting quickly to put the bird out of its misery—something she was rather expert at, since she'd been required to beat not-quite-dead animals to death several times before. "Miss Bardot," the Queen told her former private secretary, "is a silly woman who has absolutely no idea what she's talking about. She wasn't a terribly good actress either, as I recall."

Kate ramped things up even more when she showed up at William's graduation from Sandhurst wearing a scarlet coat, high leather boots, and black hat. She had not been invited to sit with the Queen, Philip, Charles, and Camilla in the royal box (no-show Second Lieutenant Harry was on duty), but Kate and her parents had scarcely been banished to the hinterlands. Sitting alongside them in the front row of the general stand were two of

William's three godfathers, King Constantine of Greece and Norton Knatchbull, the eighth Baron Brabourne.

Just as his brother had done eight months before, William, wearing the red sash of the sovereign's banner holder, tried not to break up when the Queen passed before him while reviewing the troops. From here, William would join Harry with the Household Cavalry's hard-drinking Blue and Royals (nicknamed the Booze and Royals). While Harry was destined for an army career that included combat duty in Iraq and Afghanistan, the future king would also do stints in the Royal Navy and the Royal Air Force to acquaint himself with all branches of the British military.

At one point during the proceedings, everyone repaired to Sandhurst's Grand Entrance Hall for the unveiling of a new group portrait of the Windsors. Camilla held her breath—it was the first official portrait of the Royal Family to include her. The painting by Sergei Pavlenko depicted the Queen dressed in a pale yellow, fur-trimmed coat and the Windsor men in all their gold-braided, medaled glory. Looking sadly out of place in a funereal black dress, the Duchess of Cornwall was shoved into the background, her face and body almost completely obscured by Sandhurst's Commandant, Major General Andrew Ritchie. The Queen pronounced the work—practically invisible Camilla and all—to be nothing less than "splendid."

Kate beamed as Sandhurst's brass band broke into an upbeat rendition of Abba's "Dancing Queen." As William marched by, she cooed to Carole, "I love the uniform. It's so, so sexy."

The next day's papers made it abundantly clear that neither the Queen nor even William (and certainly not Charles or Camilla) were the stars at Sandhurst that day. The front-page headline in the *Telegraph* said it all: KATE REIGNS AT WILLIAM'S PARADE.

More to the point, the Middletons' presence at one of the most important milestones in William's life seemed to sweep away any lingering doubts about where this was all heading. Overnight, British bookmakers cut the odds of a royal engagement from five to one to two to one, and then stopped taking bets completely. For all practical intents and purposes, William and Kate's future was, or at least so it seemed, a fait accompli.

No one, least of all Kate, was prepared for what Fleet Street had up its collective sleeve. The next day's papers were filled with photos of Carole Middleton madly chewing gum—albeit nicotine, to help her quit smoking—as well as reports of her crassly asking for directions to the "toilet" when she should have said "lavatory."

Soon Kate's mother was being called "Carole Meddleton," and the instructions given to British cabin crews once a plane has landed—"doors to manual"—were now used to mock her past as a flight attendant. "A whispering campaign was launched to make Kate's mother look uncouth and scheming," said a courtier who believed the Palace's Men in Gray were behind it. "There was nothing subtle about it."

The ploy backfired. After years of waiting, Kate was finally invited by the Queen to join the Royal Family for Christmas lunch at Sandringham—the first time any girlfriend had received such an invitation. Carole later said she wept when she heard the news.

"Waity Katie," as the tabloid press now derisively referred to her, was markedly less enthusiastic. Rather than instantly accepting the coveted invitation, she used it to try to force William's hand. Kate politely declined, reminding her prince that the Queen always insisted Christmas was for close family only, and that as long as there was no engagement ring on her finger, she could not bring herself to intrude.

Instead, Miss Middleton opted to spend Christmas with her family just as she always did—only this time at Jordanstone House, an eighteenth-century estate the family was renting just outside the sleepy Scottish hamlet of Alyth. William promised to join the Middletons for New Year' Eve, but called at the last minute to cancel. Kate, who like the rest of the world was convinced a marriage proposal was imminent, ended the phone conversation in tears.

To the outside world, it was only a question of when. "The time is ripe for the announcement of an engagement," wrote the *Sunday Times*'s Deirdre Fernand, who argued that Kate's "elegance, dignity, and beauty" made her "the People's Choice." Engagement rumors gathered further momentum when, in a *Spectator* story headlined "The Next People's Princess," Patrick Jephson went so far as to predict William would pop the question on Kate's twenty-fifth birthday. Scores of photographers were camped outside Oak Acre to snap the "engagement picture" on January 9, but when nothing happened it hardly mattered. Souvenir shops throughout the United Kingdom continued to do a brisk business selling cups, plates, mouse pads, pens, pencils, and cellphone covers bearing the happy couple's likeness.

Over the next few months, when he wasn't undergoing tank commander training at a base in Dorset, William partied hard with his army buddies. Kate, left alone in London to fend off the paparazzi, grew more humiliated with each new snapshot of William dancing the night away with some random girl in a smoky London club.

By the time they showed up together at the annual Cheltenham horse race at the end of March 2007, their body language said it all. The normally ebullient Kate scowled behind dark glasses as William walked several steps ahead of her, eyes downcast.

If no one else took notice of this sea change in the couple's relationship, the Queen certainly did. In fact, there was ample anecdotal evidence that very little that went on in and around the Royal Family escaped her eagle eye. On one occasion, for example, the Queen glanced out the window of her Buckingham Palace study and spotted something strange. "Do the Welsh Guards have new uniform requirements?" she asked her equerry. "That soldier setting up the bandstand is wearing red socks instead of the regulation green."

After Trooping the Colour ceremonies or at other times when she was called upon to inspect soldiers, commanding officers could expect quick critiques from Her Majesty. "Why was that soldier in the second row slightly out of step?" she asked one year, while another time she wanted to know if a soldier in the back row who had nicked his hand on his bayonet required medical attention. The senior officer couldn't answer the Queen; no one else had noticed that the soldier was bleeding.

So it came as no surprise when the Queen noticed that, public sentiment to the contrary, there had been a decided shift in William's attitude toward Miss Middleton. When she inquired, Prince Philip, who had been discussing the matter with Charles, filled his wife in on the latest developments in their grandson's romantic life. It seemed William had gone to his father, seeking advice. Before he gave any, the Prince of Wales asked about William's long-term intentions. Did he plan to marry Kate "in the end?" William replied that his relationship with Kate now felt "claustrophobic." He was only twenty-five, he asserted, and not ready to settle down with anyone.

Charles went on to tell his son that it was cruel to keep stringing Kate along. It was, said the man who had essentially kept the love of his life waiting for forty years, "better that you break it off now."

Before counseling William, Charles had, of course, asked Camilla for her opinion. The Duchess of Cornwall had always liked and even admired Kate, but that was not the issue. Camilla still harbored misgivings about Kate's working-class roots, and believed that the best match for William was to be found among the daughters of their aristocratic friends. She was also "disgusted with William and Kate sucking up all the attention," a former Clarence House staffer said. "Camilla knew the Prince of Wales suffered this as much as she did. Charles and Camilla needed the love of the people and they figured there is only so much love to go around."

At first, Charles was reluctant to tell William to break it off with Kate. After all, among the senior Royals, the Prince of Wales had always been Kate's biggest booster. But Camilla argued convincingly that, out of deference to Kate, this was the wisest course.

Kate became suspicious when William, who had spent at least part of every Easter holiday with the Middletons for the past five years, declined their invitation. Then, on April 11, 2007, Kate sought privacy in a back conference room at Jigsaw—and listened as William ended their six-year romance in a cellphone call.

It’s not a question of wanting to be King. It’s something that I was born into and it’s my duty.

—WILLIAM

....

From the pit to the palace in three generations!

—MALCOLM ROSS, LONGTIME COURTIER, ON THE RISE OF THE MIDDLETONS

7

THE MAGNIFICENT SEVEN

WESTMINSTER ABBEY

APRIL 29, 2011

This time, the Queen was nothing short of ecstatic—so much so that she declared a national holiday to mark the historic event. It was "not just about the beautiful Princess and the handsome Prince," said Prime Minister David Cameron, who as a teenager had slept in the streets to catch a glimpse of Charles and Diana on their wedding day. "It's a day we celebrate the monarchy itself." It was also a day, Cameron added, that the world got its first look at "the team of the future" that would take the monarchy—"the incredible, extraordinary institution that binds us all together"—deep into the twenty-first century.

Less than five months earlier, antimonarchist mobs screaming "Off with their heads!" had attacked the classic 1977 Rolls-Royce Phantom VI carrying Charles and Camilla. Kate had her pick of any car in the royal fleet to use on her wedding day, but insisted instead that the same heavily battered car be repaired. This way, when she and her father arrived at Westminster Abbey, there could be no doubt: The monarchy was as strong as ever.

The ceremony itself was flawless, right down to the bride's wedding band made of Welsh gold—the final precious fragment from the original Clogau St. David's mine nugget that the Queen had denied to Camilla but happily reserved for Kate. (Unlike his father, William decided not to wear a wedding ring.)

After the world's most famous newlyweds exchanged vows—like Diana before her, Kate omitted the word "obey"—a roar of approval went up outside the Abbey when the Archbishop of Canterbury pronounced them "man and wife." Once outside, William and Kate climbed into the same horse-drawn open carriage that had carried Charles and Diana from St. Paul's Cathedral three decades earlier. Just as the 1902 State Landau began its trip past one million well-wishers lining the wedding route to Buckingham Palace, Kate turned to her new husband and smiled. "I'm so happy," she said.

The Wedding of the Century had cost an estimated $34 million—$500,000 of that graciously contributed by the parents of the bride. Easily the biggest media event of the twenty-first century thus far, the royal wedding of William and Kate was covered by ten thousand journalists and watched on television and via the internet by an estimated 3 billion people in 180 countries—the largest global audience since Diana's funeral.

Understandably, much of the commentary centered on the dazzling bride, who wore a dress of ivory silk overlaid with lace by Alexander McQueen's Sarah Burton, diamond chandelier earrings, and the Cartier Halo tiara, loaned to her by the Queen. This particular tiara, given to the Queen Mother just before her husband became king, had been passed along to Elizabeth II on her eighteenth birthday. William wore the scarlet and braided ceremonial uniform of a colonel in the Irish Guards, and the wings of the RAF on his light-blue garter sash.

Less showy, but equally powerful for the message they conveyed, were the blooms that made up Kate's bridal bouquet: sweet william and lily of the valley, Diana's favorite. To leave no doubt that the late Princess of Wales's presence was still very much felt here, Kate had large planters overflowing with lilies of the valley placed along the nave. The effect was, said wedding guest Barbie Allbritton, "very English country garden."

With forty television cameras inside the Abbey trained on their every expression and whispered confidence, William and Kate exuded remarkable confidence, dignity, and poise. "It was an image of vitality and strength mixed with sheer joy," said Paddy Harverson, communications secretary to the Prince of Wales and official spokesman for the newlyweds. "They were the perfect couple enjoying a perfect moment, and it gave a lift to the whole country. It was an historic moment for the monarchy, everyone could see that." Her Majesty was clearly thrilled with the result, leaning over to tell Prince Philip that the ceremony was simply "amazing!"

That morning, the Queen had bestowed upon them the titles Duke and Duchess of Cambridge—but with a difference. Tossing protocol out the window, it would also now be considered perfectly proper to call Kate "Princess Catherine." In the past, only a blood princess—someone born a princess—could have that title used in front of their Christian name. So technically, she was Catherine, Princess William of Wales. But the Queen was willing to make an exception in this one case. "It is absolutely natural that the public want to call them 'Prince William and Princess

Catherine,'" said Harverson. "No one is going to have any argument with that."

The same courtesy was not shown Camilla, who at the very least had the perfect right to be called Camilla, Princess of Wales—a right she wisely chose not to exercise for fear of offending fans of Diana. While Kate could now be called "Princess Catherine," Camilla was stuck for the time being with "Duchess."

By way of establishing Kate as a bona fide royal personage, her father was called upon weeks earlier to submit a Middleton coat of arms that could be "impaled" (merged) with William's. The bride selected three acorns and sprigs to represent herself, Pippa, and their brother, James—an allusion to Oak Acres, the family home in Berkshire. A gold chevron running across the center symbolized both Carole's place at the heart of the family and her maiden name, Goldsmith.

Stepping out onto the Buckingham Palace balcony with the rest of the royal wedding party, the bride and groom waved, smiled, and then quickly kissed for the euphoric throng gathered around Victoria fountain. Instantly aware that they had disappointed the crowd, they kissed again—this time passionately—and the multitude responded with a thunderous cheer.

Camilla, who had looked nervous and distracted throughout the ceremony, spent much of her time on the balcony trying to corral her squirming three-year-old granddaughter Eliza Lopes, youngest of the three bridesmaids. The Queen stood to one side to allow William and Kate their moment in the sun, then briskly took charge and herded everyone back inside for formal portraits of the wedding party followed by an intimate "Queen's Breakfast" for 650 guests. There were no tables piled high with wedding presents; the bride and groom, who had also invited representatives of organizations that Diana had supported to the wedding, asked that donations be made to twenty-six of their favorite charities in lieu of gifts.

That night, a glittering black-tie banquet for three hundred began in the Ballroom and wound up taking over the Music Room, the State Dining Room, and both the White and Blue drawing rooms. There were the requisite toasts and speeches: Harry apologized to his new sister-in-law for "having to marry a bald man," while Michael Middleton recalled how, during helicopter pilot training, William landed on his front lawn and nearly blew the roof off his house. Charles said he hoped his elder son would care for him in his old age, but now worried that instead he'd "push my wheelchair off a cliff."

No one laughed harder—or less convincingly—than Camilla.

FOR KATE, WHO JUST FIVE years earlier had been dumped by William, it had all been a remarkable reversal of fortune. It had also been no accident. Rather than wallow in the immediate aftermath of the sudden and shocking breakup, Kate—once again leaning heavily on her mother for advice and support—had taken matters into her own hands, vowing to win William back simply by making him jealous.

Looking anything but defeated, Kate donned thigh-skimming skirts and hit the London social scene with a vengeance—often with Pippa. Kate's fun-loving sister had also been linked to a number of wealthy, powerful young men—one or two with titles. Before long, Carole and Michael Middleton's daughters were being snidely referred to as the "Wisteria Sisters" because of their "ferocious ability to climb."

Soon the tabloids were filled with tales of Kate's exploits with and without Pippa. Most involved Kate showing up at William's favorite London hangouts, where she openly flirted and dirty-danced with a succession of men.

Kate also joined an all-female rowing crew called the Sisterhood, which was pitted against the all-male Brotherhood in a twenty-one-mile race across the English Channel. Training consisted of rowing up and down the Thames three times a week, which generated more alluring photos—this time of Kate standing in her body-hugging racing outfit, skillfully manning the tiller at the stern of the boat.

Soon Kate, now down to a size four from all the additional exercise, chucked her tastefully conservative Windsor-in-waiting wardrobe for miniskirts and skin-tight designer jeans. "Far from appearing shattered," Laura Collins and Louise Hannah wrote in the *Daily Mail*, "Kate sans William is cutting a frankly far sexier figure." Their friend Jules Knight believed Will, who now spent his evenings drowning his sorrows at clubs like Bougis and Purple, "suddenly felt that he had made a huge mistake."

On May 26, 2007—precisely six weeks after William broke off the relationship—William invited Kate to Clarence House and apologized. The public would learn they were back together only in July, when Kate reappeared with her Prince at the pop star–studded Concert for Diana marking the tenth anniversary of Diana's death.

At one of their teas at Windsor—a ritual that took place less frequently but that both Her Majesty and the Heir still found valuable—William confirmed to the Queen that he and Kate were back together. Granny was thrilled ("I'm glad to hear it. She's a nice girl"), but not merely for the sake of Prince William's happiness. She had long been concerned that William's drinking might get him into serious trouble and plunge the monarchy into yet another scandal. Monitoring Kate's "Keep Calm and Carry On" response to the breakup in the tabloids, the Queen was impressed. She instructed her private secretary to keep an eye out for a suitable occasion where she might finally meet the girl who stole her grandson's heart. "I think," Her Majesty reportedly conceded, "it's time."

In late April 2008 the Queen, fully appreciating the fact that her grandson was the sort of battlefield prize Al-Qaeda and the Taliban could only dream about, granted William his wish to serve with British forces in Afghanistan—but only for thirty hours. His top-secret assignment: Fly a C-17 Globemaster troop transport to the front lines in Afghanistan and pick up the body of a fallen British soldier.

Three weeks later, Kate was given a daunting assignment of her own—to fill in for William at the royal wedding of his cousin Peter Phillips and Autumn Kelly (the bride converted from Catholicism so Peter wouldn't have to give up being eleventh in line for the throne). For Kate, the wedding proved that the Royal Family considered her an appropriate stand-in for Prince William at important functions. It also offered a proper setting for Kate's first face-to-face meeting with the Queen. "It was in amongst a lot of other guests," Kate said of her first conversation with William's grandmother. Her Majesty was, she said, "very friendly and welcoming."

As William's military training—with the Household Cavalry, the RAF, and the Royal Navy—drew to a close at the end of 2008, it appeared as if the Prince was ready to become a full-time Royal. Instead, he surprised the Queen by opting to sign up for five years with the Royal Air Force as a search-and-rescue helicopter pilot.

He was still available to periodically meet and greet members of what the Royal Family called "the Chain Gang"—the mayors and other local officials who invariably showed up for walkabouts dripping with all manner of medals and ceremonial gold chains.

William knew, of course, that his destiny involved more than wreath layings and ribbon cuttings. The fate of a thousand-year-old institution—not only one of the world's oldest but one of its greatest—rested on his shoulders.

Since 2006, William had been permitted to attend the twice-yearly sessions of the Way Ahead Group at Buckingham Palace. In late 1992, then Lord Chamberlain David Airlie set up the Way Ahead Group to steer a future course for the monarchy. In addition to William and the Queen, its members included Prince Philip, Princes Charles, Andrew, and Edward, and Princess Anne. They were joined by a handful of trusted senior advisors whose identities remained a closely guarded secret.

Free from any outside influences—not even the Prime Minister knew what was said during these closed-door deliberations—the Queen and those closest to her discussed a number of key issues confronting the monarchy. Should the Queen pay income taxes? The Way Ahead Group decided she should, voluntarily. Should the royal yacht *Britannia* be scrapped? The Queen grudgingly agreed that it was the sort of unnecessary indulgence that made the monarchy look bad, particularly in times of economic hardship. Should primogeniture, the ancient rule giving precedence to males over females in the line of succession, come to an end? Although he was by far the junior member of the group, William argued convincingly that such a rule was unacceptably sexist—and the rest of the group agreed. (On April 25, 2013, the Succession to the Crown Bill received the Royal Assent, and primogeniture officially became a thing of the past. Under the new law, females now had equal footing with males when it came to determining who would inherit the crown.)

Camilla was not included in the Way Ahead Group meetings, but she wielded a great deal of influence with Prince Charles. "Her opinion," said longtime royal press secretary Dickie Arbiter, "matters more to him than anyone's."

Although Charles was clearly fond of Kate, her family was another matter. The jury was still out on whether they would make suitable in-laws, and on that subject Camilla's opinion carried considerable weight. "There was always a sense," said a St. James's Palace staffer, "that she was looking down her nose at the Middletons, and stirring up gossip about them. Maybe she felt threatened by Kate, or perhaps more by William and Kate as a team."

There were more bumps on the road to the royal wedding. Just a few months after William and Kate got back together, images of Kate's brother in a variety of sexually suggestive poses and situations surfaced online. Not long after, Carole came in for even more criticism than usual for appearing to use her daughter's royal connection to sell princess-themed dolls, dresses, tiaras, place mats, cups, dishes, and tricycles on the Party Pieces website.

For three years, Camilla and the Men in Gray—most of whom still doubted that commoner Kate was a suitable mate for a future king—had been hearing stories about Kate's wild Uncle Gary Goldsmith, the tattooed, profanity-spewing, cocaine-loving tech industry mogul who hosted William and Kate at "Le Maison de Bang Bang," his crudely named estate on Ibiza. Camilla relayed the stories to Charles, but once again, the Prince of Wales had no stomach for blowing the whistle on the Middletons.

It was not until July 2009 that security officials who were concerned about William's safety leaked the information to *News of the World,* which promptly launched an undercover sting operation of its own. The headlines were scathing: KATE MIDDLETON DRUG AND VICE SHOCK: TYCOON WHO BOASTS OF HOSTING WILLS VILLA HOLIDAY SUPPLIES COCAINE AND FIXES HOOKERS. Worst of all, Goldsmith boasted about his royal connections to the undercover tabloid reporters, saying that he planned to give the bride away at Kate's wedding to William, that he was looking forward to being the "Queen's uncle," and that he planned to be made a duke and have his own suite at Buckingham Palace, called "The Goldsmith Wing."

Whether it was someone in Camilla's camp or the Men in Gray who urged security officials to leak the story to the *News of the World,* the obvious intention was to derail William and Kate's relationship. Yet the Queen, rather than turning her back on Kate, expressed sympathy for a young woman who found herself perpetually in the crosshairs of the tabloid press. "We *all* have relatives," she muttered to an equerry as she perused her newspapers, "that we'd sometimes rather not think about."

Indeed, in a matter of months an in-law would drop another bombshell on the Palace, once again courtesy of a *News of the World* sting operation. This time, the tabloid released an undercover videotape showing Sarah Ferguson, the Duchess of York, soliciting a bribe of £500,000 (at the time the equivalent of more than $710,000) for access to her ex-husband, Prince Andrew. The enterprising undercover reporter, posing as an Arab sheik wanting to do business with the British government, had already snagged Prince Edward's wife, Sophie, for influence peddling using similar tactics. Despite her wayward uncle and exhibitionistic brother, Kate, observed well-known British publicist Max

Clifford, "must have seemed like a dream to the Queen, certainly compared to the other daughters-in-law."

Just as they had at St. Andrews, William and Kate fell back into the easy rhythm of living together as a young couple—this time in a rented five-bedroom farmhouse on the Welsh island of Anglesey, not far from the RAF Valley airbase. Given the remote location, an additional fifteen Royal Protection officers were assigned to protect the couple at a cost of $2 million. While she tended their garden and shopped for groceries at the local Waitrose supermarket, 22 Squadron C Flight's newly minted helicopter pilot was at the controls of his Sea King Mk 3, rescuing hikers stranded in the nearby Snowdonia Mountains and plucking heart attack victims off oil rigs in the Irish Sea.

There was still time for some on-the-job training of an entirely different sort. In early 2010, Kate stayed home in Wales while William journeyed to Australia and New Zealand on his first overseas tour. By choosing William to make the trip instead of Charles, the Queen gave rise to talk that her grandson was now her "Shadow King"—the person she was actively grooming for the top job.

William was distressed by any suggestion that he was trying to supplant the Prince of Wales as rightful heir to the throne. "My father works tremendously hard," protested William, pointing to the hundreds of millions of dollars Charles's Prince's Trust had raised for charity since its inception in 1976. The Trust, in alliance with The Prince's Charities, included sixteen separate organizations, all of which were presided over by Charles. "He is a marvelous, generous man who has really made an enormous impact on the world," William said. "My father is a great man in his own right, but unfortunately not everyone sees that."

Prince Charles's accomplishments aside, the Queen was determined to give her grandson the grounding in matters of state that a sovereign requires. Toward that end, she personally recruited Sir David Manning, the Court of St. James's former ambassador to the United States and Israel, to serve as William's guide and mentor. Just to make sure all went well in Australia and New Zealand, she also asked her trusted private secretary, Sir Christopher Geidt, to tag along.

It quickly became evident that, if there was any hope of retaining the monarchy Down Under, William was it. Polls that routinely showed 60 percent of Australians favoring a republic plunged to 44 percent after William's triumphant visit. Things weren't much different back home. In late 2010, polls showed that 64 percent of Britons wanted William as their next king—and only 19 percent wanted Charles.

It would take several months after William's Australian trip for the Heir to finally pop the question to Kate. But when he finally did ask Kate to marry him in October 2010, the setting was pure William: 12,500 above sea level, by a glistening lake nestled on the slopes of a snow-capped Mount Kenya. To get there, the Prince commandeered a helicopter and gave Kate an aerial tour of the Edenlike Rift Valley before setting down near a stand of East African junipers. Getting down on bended knee, he finally proposed to "Waity Katie" with his mother's famous eighteen-carat sapphire and diamond engagement ring—"my way of making sure my mother didn't miss out on today."

A month later, the news was announced over Twitter and the Queen's Facebook page. The Queen called it "brilliant news" and Charles professed to be "thrilled. They have been practicing long enough!" When asked what she thought of the engagement,

Camilla gave a two-word answer that hovered somewhere between sarcasm and Dr. Freud. "It's wicked," she said.

....

THE WEDDING OF THE CENTURY had indeed surpassed all expectations, but no sooner was it over than the newlyweds were pressed into service. Postponing their ten-day honeymoon in the Seychelles for several weeks, the Duke and Duchess of Cambridge stayed in England at the special request of the Queen. In mid-May, Charles and Camilla joined Elizabeth II and Prince Philip in welcoming Michelle and Barack Obama to the White House. Before the ceremonial luncheon and banquet, America's First Couple was ushered into the 1844 Drawing Room for a private twenty-minute chat with William and Kate, their first official appearance since the royal wedding. At Camilla's urging, Charles suggested that the newlyweds—about whom the world was still clamoring—not be invited to either the luncheon or the banquet, so as not to outshine the guests of honor.

The Duke and Duchess of Cambridge returned to their modest farmhouse in the Welsh countryside and tried to pick up where they left off. To give William and his bride a chance to enjoy their lives as young marrieds, the Queen promised them a two-year grace period of exemption from public duties. Kate's introduction to official engagements and charitable patronages, then, would be gradual—or at least gradual by Her Majesty's standards.

William and Kate had been back from their honeymoon just a matter of days when they attended the Queen's private party at Windsor to celebrate Philip's ninetieth birthday. Kate, Camilla, Charles, and Her Majesty then watched as William rode in the

Trooping the Colour parade for the first time. In July 2011, the newlyweds embarked on their first official trip overseas, to Canada and the United States. In Calgary they donned cowboy outfits for the Calgary Stampede, and later shook hands with star-struck cinematic icons like Charles's old flame Barbra Streisand and Tom Hanks at a British Academy of Film and Television Arts (BAFTA) gala held in the Cambridges' honor.

Notwithstanding the inevitable tide of pregnancy rumors that would ebb and flow over the coming two years, Kate divided her time between their cozy house in Anglesey and Kensington Palace. The first monarch to occupy "KP," as it was affectionately called by Kate's late mother-in-law, was William III, who bought it from the Earl of Nottingham in 1689. More than 322 years later, the impressive Georgian brick manor house with its manicured gardens and Christopher Wren–designed orangery seemed the perfect official residence for a future king named William.

For the time being Kate and William bunked at "Nott Cott," KP's two-bedroom Nottingham Cottage, while their permanent quarters underwent a staggering $7.6 million renovation. The royal couple would eventually be occupying Apartment 1A, formerly the home of Princess Margaret. The name was more than merely misleading. Apartment 1A was in fact a four-story, twenty-one-room house with several large reception rooms, six bedrooms, seven bathrooms, its own walled garden, and private tennis courts.

The newlyweds were now also free to spend holidays and week-ends at Anmer Hall, a ten-bedroom, Georgian brick-and-stone manor house on the grounds of Sandringham that was once the home of first Baron Rugby, who was appointed by Winston Churchill to be the United Kingdom's first official representative to the Republic of Ireland. More important, Diana had been born at nearby Park House, a mansion also situated on the Sandringham estate, and lived there until the Spencers took up residence at Althorp when she was fourteen.

Ultimately, the Queen would authorize extensive upgrades to Anmer Hall, including a conservatory, a new roof, and an updated, more family-friendly kitchen. Total cost: $3 million. Not to be outdone, the Middletons—with an assist from their son-in-law—plunked down $7.8 million for an even statelier home than the one they already had in Bucklebury.

Now that she was a full-fledged Royal Family member, Kate finally experienced her first Christmas at Sandringham—only to learn that her RAF search-and-rescue pilot husband was to depart February 1 on a six-week tour of duty in the Falkland Islands. As it happened, she would have her hands full taking care of their new, black English cocker spaniel puppy, Lupo, a Christmas gift from Michael and Carole Middleton. Back in London, Lupo and his mistress were soon a familiar sight walking to and from the Starbucks just two blocks from the palace on Kensington Church Street—Kate picking up after her dog with one hand while clutching a grande decaf soy latte in the other.

Not everyone was amused by the charming photos of Kate frolicking with her adorable puppy—nor the apparent confusion about who sat precisely where in the royal pecking order. After Charles married Camilla, Prince Edward's wife, Sophie, Countess of Wessex, objected when she was told she was now required to curtsy to the Duchess of Cornwall. However, at the time the Queen did change the all-important "Order of Precedence of the Royal Family To Be Observed at Court" on "blood principles" so that neither Princess Anne nor Princess Alexandra, the granddaughter of George V, would have to curtsy to Camilla when Charles was not present. (Anne, the "Princess Royal," had refused to curtsy to Diana in spite of the rules, and made it clear she had no intention of ever curtsying to Camilla.)

Given Kate's induction into The Firm, the Queen circulated a new document in the Royal Household clarifying the Duchess of Cambridge's status. According to the new rules, Kate, when not accompanied by her husband, was required to curtsy to the "blood princesses"—Anne (the Princess Royal), Alexandra, and Prince Andrew's daughters, Beatrice and Eugenie. When William was with her, Kate curtsied only to Charles, Camilla, Prince Philip, and of course the Queen.

There were other aspects of royal protocol affected by the new Order of Precedence, including who arrived first at a public event. Because she was not accompanied by the Prince of Wales to a memorial service at Windsor, Camilla had to wait outside in a downpour until Anne arrived so she could walk in behind the Princess Royal.

Like it or not, members of court quickly found themselves scrambling to abide by the Queen's complicated new lineup for royal women—a lineup that, regardless of the new law striking down primogeniture, changed dramatically when a female Royal was in the company of her spouse. The rankings: 1, the Queen; 2, the Dowager Queen (the late Queen Mother); 3, the Duchess of Cornwall; 4, wives of the sovereign's younger sons; 5, the sovereign's daughters; 6, wives of the sovereign's grandsons; 7, the sovereign's granddaughters; 8, wives of the sovereign's brothers; 9, the sovereign's sisters; 10, wives of the sovereign's uncles; 11, the sovereign's aunts; 12, wives of the sovereign's nephews; 13, the sovereign's nieces; 14, the sovereign's cousins.

It was significant that, even though her beloved mother had died years earlier, Elizabeth still placed the Queen Mother—Camilla's bitter enemy—above her. "The Queen has subtle ways of keeping those around her a little off-balance," said a senior diplomat who is close to the Royal Family. "She's a marvelous woman, but you can't be in her position without learning how to toy with people a bit. I'm sure she rather enjoys it at times, making Camilla squirm."

Camilla was conscious of more than her vaunted second-place rank at court. She was feeling overworked, and she placed part of the blame on Kate. The Duchess of Cornwall racked up 230 royal appearances in her first year of marriage alone, compared to Kate's meager 34 appearances in that same period of time—statistics she shared with friends who in turn leaked them to the press. (William, who in fairness was pulling ten-hour shifts as a search-and-rescue pilot, managed only 90 official engagements in 2011.)

It was not long before the unflattering articles had their desired effect. Elizabeth, as Camilla knew well, was extremely sensitive to any suggestion that members of the Royal Family weren't earning their keep. Well into her eighties, the Queen made 370 official appearances in 2011—a figure that would soar to 425 in 2012.

Soon Kate was under pressure to come up with her own list of charities and start supporting them. She did not have to look far for a role model. "Obviously I would love to have met her," Kate said of Diana. "She is an inspirational woman to look up to." Borrowing a page from her late mother-in-law, Kate made her first official speech as royal patron of the East Anglia Children's Hospices. She soon added the Art Room, an organization that uses art to treat abused children; the children's mental health support group Place2Be; the Girl Guides (the UK equivalent of the Girl Scouts); SportsAid, benefiting disabled athletes; the substance abuse group Action on Addiction; and two museums: the National History Museum and the National Portrait Gallery.

Kate also told the Queen directly that she wanted to keep busy while her husband was serving in the Falklands. Thrilled to hear it, Her Majesty put the Duchess of Cambridge down for several events kicking off the Diamond Jubilee celebrations of her sixtieth year on the throne.

....

IN MARCH 2012, KATE VISITED the legendary specialty shop Fortnum & Mason on Piccadilly with the Queen and her stepmother-in-law—a rare opportunity for the press and public to see the current and future queens shop for delicacies and share a cup of tea in the store's restaurant. Then she accompanied her grandparents-in-law on a two-hour train trip to the East Midlands city of Leicester. Elizabeth and Philip, aware that Kate had admitted to still being quite "jittery" at the prospect of meeting large crowds of people, spent the entire trip soothing her nerves and boosting her morale.

They needn't have worried. In the manner of Diana, Kate effortlessly connected with children, seniors, the disabled, her peers—whatever bouquet-bearing group confronted her along the rope line. Most important, never once did she seem condescending, miffed, brusque, uninterested, or simply stiff—criticisms that at one time or another had been leveled at virtually every senior member of the Royal Family, including the Queen.

The Leicester trip included a De Montfort University alumni fashion show, during which Kate, dressed in gray, and the Queen, clad head to toe in shocking pink, schmoozed and laughed for half an hour. Kate "looked amazing, and they were smiling and talking," said Leicester MP Liz Kendall. "They obviously have great affection for each other."

It was also evident that the newest member of the royal team was bringing along a touch of enchantment all her own. "It's a real coup to have the Queen," designer Karen Millen said, "but also to have Kate, who is a style icon and a great ambassador for British fashion and fashion everywhere." Kate Bostock, an executive with the British retailer Marks & Spencer, summed up what it was like having Kate and the Queen sitting together in the front row: "It was so . . . tingly."

The "Kate Effect," as the Men in Gray insiders now referred to it, was undeniable. It was also a powerful tool that the Queen intended to employ in her continuing efforts to keep the monarchy alive. By way of gauging just how useful Kate could be, all Elizabeth needed to do was look at the Duchess of Cambridge's startling poll numbers. A survey commissioned by the *Sunday Times* showed that 73 percent of Britons believed Kate was breathing new life into the Royal Family.

Two weeks after the triumphant inaugural tour of Leicester, Elizabeth II addressed both houses of Parliament for the sixth time in her sixty-year reign. Prince Philip sat next to her on his own, slightly smaller but nonetheless similarly gilded throne. Elizabeth II praised her husband for being her "constant strength and guide," but also pointed out that he was "well-known for declining compliments of any kind."

Flanked by Beefeaters and gold-helmeted officers of the Household Cavalry, the Queen also spoke of Britain's close ties to the Commonwealth—ties that, she was being told by her advisor, now seemed to hinge more than ever on her personal popularity. While acknowledging that most Australians had "deep affection" for the Queen, former Australian Prime Minister Julia Gillard predicted that Elizabeth's death would bring about a major change Down Under. "I think the appropriate time for this nation to move to be a republic," Gillard said, echoing the sentiments of several other Commonwealth nations, "is when we see the monarch change."

There was a mind-spinning stream of banquets, concerts, luncheons, receptions, garden parties, and teas both inside and outside London over the months leading up to the Queen's four-day Diamond Jubilee celebration in June. Following the three-day-long Royal Windsor Horse Show, the Queen hosted the largest assembly of crowned heads since she assumed the throne: twenty-four kings and queens, an emperor and an empress, a grand duke, an emir, and a sultan.

Camilla and Kate stood silently on the sidelines while their husbands paid effusive tribute to the Queen in a special hour-long television documentary. The program showed Charles sitting in the library at Balmoral, sometimes chortling, sometimes teary-eyed as he offered commentary on home movies that flickered on the screen before him. In one, eight-year-old Charles and his little sister, Anne, are at Holkham Beach near Sandringham, buried up to their necks in sand with one of "Mama's" corgis lording it over them. Praising her "amazing record of devotion, dedication, and commitment," all carried out with "amazing poise and natural grace," the Prince of Wales went a long way toward erasing the damage he had done eighteen years earlier when he described his mother as cold and distant.

In his own televised interview, William admitted that for a long time he found "Granny" intimidating. "Being a small boy, it's very daunting," he said, "seeing the Queen around and not really quite knowing what to talk about." Now, he added, "we are definitely a lot closer than we used to be." Close enough, it turned out, for William and Kate to ask her what to do when they were given a wedding guest list with the names of 777 people on it—none of whom the couple knew. The Queen's advice: "Tear it up and start with your friends. We'll add those we need to in due course. It's your day." In the end, William said he wanted to "take all of her experiences, all of her knowledge and put it in a small box and be able to constantly refer to it."

On Sunday, June 3, the Queen and Prince Philip boarded the *Spirit of Chartwell*, a 210-foot luxury cruiser that had been transformed into an opulently appointed, flower-festooned royal barge reminiscent of the royal barges in use during the reign of the first English sovereign named Elizabeth. More than 1.2 million Britons lined the banks of the Thames in a driving rain to watch as a flotilla of more than a thousand vessels passed in review. Representing every corner of the Commonwealth, the fleet included tall ships, tugboats, cutters, fishing boats, fireboats, kayaks, launches, cruisers, gondolas, skiffs, Viking longships, dragon boats, trawlers, a "jolly boat" carrying pirates, a torpedo boat that once carried Winston Churchill and Dwight Eisenhower to view the D-day fleet, a motorboat steered by the last survivor of Dunkirk (ninety-five-year-old Vic Viner), and a Maori war canoe.

The Queen, who wore a white, Swarovski crystal-studded coat and hat by her personal designer and assistant, Angela Kelly, waved and gestured at the vessels that passed, clearly delighted despite the heavy downpour. But neither she nor Camilla, who was also wearing white, could be easily spotted at a distance by the crowds. Kate was another matter. Since her husband was wearing his dashing flight lieutenant's blue dress uniform, the Duchess of

Cambridge saw no reason to tone down her look. After talking it over with her mother, Kate selected a scarlet dress by Alexander McQueen with an eye-catching hat to match.

Inevitably, there was grumbling in some quarters that Kate was trying to upstage the Queen. "Oh Kate, what were you thinking?" asked Amanda Platell in the *Daily Mail.* "While the rest of the royal party sensibly opted for a muted palette, determined not to outshine the woman at the center of it all, the Duchess of Cambridge opted for a scarlet dress so bold and bright it just screamed: 'Look at me!' " Across the pond, the *Washington Post* reported that the Diamond Jubilee Thames Pageant had "Brits seeing red over Kate Middleton's dress."

Kate's fashion choice was a calculated risk—Camilla and the other royal women on board had complied with Buckingham Palace's request that they wear white or beige. The risk, however, paid off. Echoing what appeared to be the majority sentiment, the *Telegraph* praised Kate for being the only Royal on board to "dazzle" the crowd. Even the once-critical *Daily Mail* changed its tune. The Duchess of Cambridge was "resplendent in red," the *Mail* declared in later editions, "cutting a swath through the gloomy weather. . . . Her dress was a vibrant choice which still allowed the Queen to shine on her big day."

In a family whose members "vie for attention every day," said one of Prince Charles's former advisors, Camilla "couldn't have been happy. Every time the spotlight is on William or Kate, for that matter, it undercuts the Prince of Wales just a little bit. He feels it, and she feels it."

The next day, the Queen had more important things on her mind. After standing on a boat in miserable weather for four hours and refusing to take a single bathroom break, Prince Philip was hospitalized with a severe bladder infection, just six days short of his ninety-first birthday. He would miss the three-hour jubilee concert in front of Buckingham Palace starring Sir Tom Jones, Grace Jones, Stevie Wonder, Ed Sheeran, Annie Lennox, Kylie Minogue, Dame Shirley Bassey, Sir Elton John, and Sir Paul McCartney, among others.

At the end of the concert, Charles pointed out that his father was too ill to attend. But, he added, "if we shout loud enough he might just hear us in hospital." A roar went up from the crowd of more than five hundred thousand people, who began chanting "Philip! Philip!" Camilla, standing next to Charles and the Queen, began to tear up. Elizabeth, whose stiff upper lip so rarely trembled, did, too. Moments later, all eyes, including the misty ones, turned skyward as a breathtaking fireworks display erupted over the palace.

The next day more than a million people lined the streets to wave the flag and cheer Elizabeth II as she rode in a horse-drawn carriage from a "Queen's Luncheon" with tradesmen at Westminster Hall back to Buckingham Palace. With Philip still recuperating in the hospital, Charles convinced his mother to ride with him and Camilla in the 1902 State Landau coach.

Camilla's new "place of pride" next to the monarch did not go unnoticed. "Once she was a pariah," said one of Princess Diana's close friends, journalist Richard Kay. Pointing out that the Queen once called Camilla "That Wicked Woman," Kay now agreed that Diana's replacement "is at the heart of the Royal Family. . . . Whichever way you look at it, hers has certainly been a remarkable transformation from scarlet woman to royal Duchess."

Still moved by the unprecedented outpouring of affection that had been going on unabated for days, the Queen seemed unprepared for the thunderous ovation that greeted her when she stepped out onto royal balcony. Although she had witnessed countless flyovers in her lifetime, Elizabeth also appeared more excited than ever to see World War II aircraft soar overhead, followed by the Red Arrows RAF aerobatic team painting the sky with their red, white, and blue contrails.

At one point, the Queen seemed genuinely overwhelmed. "Amazing," she said to Charles. "Oh, my goodness, how extraordinary." William leaned down, as if to reassure his flabbergasted grandmother. "Those cheers," he told her, "are for you." The Queen looked up at her grandson and gave him a wry smile.

Elizabeth was enough of a realist to know that, without the recent addition of William and Kate to the royal balcony tableau, the outpouring of love would have been markedly less effusive. What the world saw that day was what Palace officials now privately called "The Magnificent Seven": the Queen, Philip, Charles, Camilla, William, Kate, and Harry. Of these, there was no doubt that the youthful, energetic, gracious, and charismatic Duke and Duchess of Cambridge were the vital new face of the monarchy.

They proved it again later that summer during the London Olympics. As the "Official Ambassadors" of Team GB (Great Britain), they showed up in the stands to cheer for their countrymen, and whenever Team GB won a race or scored a point, leaped to their feet and hugged each other. It was impossible to top the Queen's performance at the opening ceremonies, however. Being picked up by Daniel Craig at Buckingham Palace and then "parachuted" into the stadium made Her Majesty "an awfully hard act to follow," cracked Prince Harry.

Somehow, Harry managed. Between army deployments in Afghanistan, the Spare decided to spend part of August living it up in Las Vegas. Unfortunately, what happened there didn't stay there. Photographs of Harry frolicking nude with a young woman during a game of strip billiards were leaked by the celebrity website TMZ and were soon splashed across the pages of tabloids everywhere.

No sooner had Harry issued one of his all-too-familiar profuse apologies than Kate suddenly found herself at the center of her own media firestorm. The Duke and Duchess of Cambridge were in the middle of a nine-day "Jubilee Tour" of Southeast Asia and the Pacific when topless images of the Duchess were published in French and Italian magazines. The photos, taken when William and Kate were sunbathing while on holiday at a private villa in Provence, were snapped from a distance of more than five hundred yards by a paparazzo using a telephoto lens.

Kate burst into tears when she saw the less-than-flattering pictures. Furious, William immediately ordered royal lawyers to obtain an injunction against the French magazine *Closer*, which ran the images, and to lodge a criminal invasion-of-privacy complaint with French authorities. The photographer who took the photos and the editor who decided to publish them were charged, but three years later the criminal case was still wending its way through France's notoriously slow court system.

Camilla, meanwhile, continued with the endless rounds of walkabouts, county fairs, dedications, memorials, horse races, flower shows, and charity events with and without her husband—a total of 276 official engagements in 2012. The Prince of Wales and his wife also embarked on their own Jubilee Tour that would take them to Australia, Canada, Scandinavia, and Germany.

Although that year Kate would ramp up her game somewhat, managing 111 appearances on behalf of the Crown, neither she nor Camilla came close to matching the indefatigable monarch (425 official engagements in her Jubilee year), her husband (325 engagements), or the hardest-working Royal in modern history, Charles. The Prince of Wales proved himself to be the Energizer Bunny of the Royal Family, making no fewer than 592 official appearances in 2012—nearly a dozen every single week.

Charles often boasted that there had never been a defined role for the Prince of Wales other than waiting for his predecessor to die. His was a job, the Prince of Wales liked to say, that he simply made up as he went along. In addition to raising more than $175 million annually for his personal charities, the Prince of Wales was the patron of another 350 charities and organizations, extending the reach of his influence across the globe.

Interested in everything from architecture, education, sustainable farming, climate change, and urban planning to meditation, Eastern philosophies, and alternative medicine, Charles expressed his opinions in countless speeches and long, rambling letters to government officials. These letters, known as the "Black Spider Memos" because they were written in Charles's distinctively spidery script, periodically drew criticism because the monarch—and by extension the heir apparent—was by tradition supposed to be politically neutral.

Unlike his mother, however, Charles did not hesitate to express his opinions to cabinet ministers and politicians in the strongest terms possible. "These letters were not merely routine and noncontroversial," Charles's senior press advisor Mark Bolland conceded, "but contained his views on political matters and political issues." According to Bolland, Charles frequently "denounced the elected leaders of other countries in extreme terms."

He did more than just write letters. In 1999, Charles infuriated Tony Blair's government by boycotting a banquet in honor of Chinese President Jiang Zemin in protest of China's occupation of Tibet. In a speech at Oxford in 2010, the Prince of Wales urged the world to follow Islamic "spiritual principles" in order to protect the environment. He based this, he said, on his own "extensive study" of the Koran, "which teaches there is no separation between man and nature." Needless to say, the comments—coming as they did from the head of the Church of England—raised eyebrows in Parliament, and at Buckingham Palace.

The Queen tried to rein her son in, but to no avail. Charles kept writing his Black Spider Memos at the rate of eighteen hundred or more a year, and pledged to break tradition by becoming a much more politically involved monarch once it was his turn on the throne. For now, he proudly called himself the Royal Family's "chief dissident" and, more poetically, "the Meddlesome Prince."

In the meantime, he would continue running in place, albeit at a frenetic pace. Taking on one massive social problem after another, Charles frantically searched for expert advice wherever he could find it, and then pitted these advisors against each other. Notoriously thin-skinned, he routinely lashed out over even the mildest criticism, leaving housemaids and senior officials quaking.

In addition to his epic flashes of temper, Charles was also given to long periods of sulking—usually in response to perceived slights or his own lingering feelings of inadequacy. "If you spent your entire life with people deferring to you just because of who your mother is," said a former aide, "you'd wonder if you truly deserved any praise at all. To this day, Prince Charles is a deeply insecure person."

As a result, wrote Royal watcher Catherine Mayer, "the court of the heir to the throne crackles with tension." Clarence House was so rife with intrigue, in fact, that insiders soon took to calling it "Wolf Hall"—a sly reference to Hilary Mantel's chilling account of duplicity and ambition run amok in the Court of Henry VIII.

A few of those closest to the Prince of Wales claimed to understand why he was so driven to succeed at so many things ("He only knows how to go full-tilt"), and why, when the Queen seemed so direct and uncomplicated, her son's personality was unsettlingly mercurial. "He's trying to save the world, dammit!" joked Elizabeth Buchanan, Charles's former private secretary. "If you can't stand the heat, get out of the kitchen!" As it happened, Buchanan had been through her own baptism by fire at Clarence House. At one point Camilla, apparently fearing that the Prince of Wales had become too dependent on Buchanan, demanded that Charles fire her. He not only refused, but later promoted her to the top spot on his staff.

That was a rare exception to the rule, for Camilla nearly always prevailed. As his chief advisor and biggest cheerleader, she could raise his spirits and bolster his confidence with a quip or a trenchant remark directed at his critics. "Camilla soothes things," said Anne Glenconner, a former lady-in-waiting to Princess Margaret and the widow of Colin Tennant, the flamboyant Scottish aristocrat who turned Mustique into a high society playground. Equally important in her relationship with Charles, Camilla does something he rarely does: She "anticipates what could go wrong."

So did the Queen, who for years had gradually, almost imperceptibly, shifted more and more responsibility to her son. Prince Charles was given more access to top-secret government papers (the Queen's dreaded boxes of state are red, Charles's green), presided at more investitures (the Queen never gave an honoree more than forty seconds; Charles could chat for up to a minute), and accepted more ambassadors' credentials. Most significantly, Charles began holding his own regular audiences with the Prime Minister and various Commonwealth leaders.

The Prince of Wales had also made a point of visiting thirty-three of the fifty-four Commonwealth countries, and attending the biennial meeting of the Commonwealth heads of government in his mother's place. He needed to. Contrary to popular belief, Charles will not automatically become head of the Commonwealth when he eventually becomes king. All fifty-four must vote him in, and a 2010 poll by the Royal Commonwealth Society showed that fewer than one in five citizens in the fifty-four member countries wanted Charles as the next Head of the Commonwealth.

Acknowledging that Elizabeth was greatly admired for uniting and guiding the Commonwealth, the Society stressed there was a "significant debate" about whether the job should be passed on to Charles "when the time comes. Many people are vehemently opposed to the idea." In a confidential U.S. London Embassy memo published on the WikiLeaks website, the Commonwealth's director of political affairs, Amitav Banerji, said the Prince of Wales simply did not "command the same respect" as the Queen.

The disclosure came as a blow to the Prince, who regarded heading the Commonwealth as a central part of the job. The Queen was more philosophical, going so far as to publicly reassure Australia, New Zealand, and Canada—three Commonwealth nations that were likely to ditch the British monarch as their head of state after Elizabeth departed—that, when the time came, it was strictly their decision to make.

....

CHARLES WAS NOT THE ONLY Royal forced to play a waiting game. By the summer of 2013, Waity Katie was at it again. This time, the entire world was right alongside her, anticipating with bated breath the arrival of the Cambridges' first child. From the outset, it had not been an easy pregnancy. Kate was barely six weeks along when she was hospitalized in early December with a severe form of morning sickness, forcing an early announcement that the Duchess was expecting. Joy turned to horror, however, after Jacintha Saldanha, a nurse at King Edward VII Hospital, put a prank call from two Australian radio shock jocks through to the nurse treating Kate. Upset over the call and the subsequent headlines, Saldanha, who had apparently suffered mental health problems, hanged herself at the hospital.

The bizarre incident of the nurse's suicide was a distant memory by the time Kate checked into the Lindo Wing of Paddington's St. Mary's Hospital—the same hospital wing where both William and Harry were born. She was a week overdue, and both the Windsors and the Middletons were on tenterhooks. "We're all," Camilla said, "waiting at the end of a telephone."

Finally, after twelve hours of labor with her husband at her side throughout, Kate gave birth to an eight-pound-six-ounce boy on the afternoon of July 22, 2013. Instead of following past practice and instantly proclaiming the news to the outside world, William insisted that the Palace wait four hours before making the official announcement. It was time they needed to spend alone as a family, he later explained—a few precious hours before their infant son became "public property."

That evening, the information was typed up and sent by a royal driver who sped it straight to Buckingham Palace. A notice was then placed on a wooden easel just outside the palace:

THE DUCHESS OF CAMBRIDGE

WAS SAFELY DELIVERED OF A SON

AT 4:24 P.M.

HER ROYAL HIGHNESS AND HER CHILD

ARE BOTH DOING WELL.

A sixty-two-round salute boomed from the Honorable Artillery Company at the Tower of London, while the King's Troop Royal Horse Artillery in Green Park next to Buckingham Palace fired off forty-one rounds. Church bells pealed, motorists honked their horns in celebration, and the fountain at Trafalgar Square was bathed in blue light.

The Queen was "delighted," of course, and Prince Charles declared that he and Camilla were both "overjoyed at the arrival of my first grandchild." Diana, had she lived, would have become a grandmother at fifty-two. It was left to her brother, Earl Spencer, to speak for the late Princess of Wales. "We're all so pleased—it's wonderful news," he said. "My father always told us how Diana was born on just such a blisteringly hot day, at Sandringham, in July 1961. It's another very happy summer's day, half a century on."

It would be a full twenty-seven hours before the world got its first look at the future king, and longer still before it learned the baby's name. In the meantime, the grandparents were in a breakneck race to see who could get to the hospital first. Camilla, according to a Clarence House staffer, was determined that she and Charles as senior Royals be the first to see and hold the little Prince. Unfortunately, they were two hours away doing yet another walkabout in the North Yorkshire village of Bugthorpe.

William saw no reason to stand on ceremony. Long ago he had fully embraced his in-laws; in fact, he was on leave from his search-and-rescue duties and staying at the Middletons' Bucklebury home as Kate waited out the final days of her pregnancy. By not holding off Kate's commoner parents to allow the baby's first visitors to be members of the Royal Family, he was making it clear that old class distinctions no longer applied.

There was no doubt that Carole Middleton intended to play a major role in the life of the future king. Arriving at the hospital by cab, the Middletons waved at reporters and ducked inside, emerging more than an hour later. When someone asked what the first "cuddle" with her new grandson was like, Carole replied, "Amazing. It's all coming back."

The Prince of Wales and Camilla were rushed to London by helicopter and arrived in a royal car. "Have you been there all along?" Charles asked reporters, many of whom had been camped outside the hospital for two weeks. The couple dashed in and, ten minutes later, reemerged. After proclaiming the baby "marvelous," he took off with Camilla. Neither royal grandparent had asked to hold the child, and the length of their visit—less than ten minutes versus an hour or more for the Middletons—spoke volumes. Perhaps even more important, Carole had taken part of the Middletons' visitation time to look over her son-in-law's shoulder while he changed his first diaper. Neither Charles nor Camilla, who had always maintained a sizable household staff, were known to have ever changed a "nappy."

A full day after the baby arrived, father, mother, and child finally emerged from the hospital to the accompaniment of reporters' shouts and a fusillade of camera flashes. "He's got a good pair of lungs, that's for sure," William told the press. "He's got her looks, thankfully." Kate, no less self-deprecating than her modest husband, interrupted. "No, no," she said. "I'm not sure about that." What color was the baby's hair? William wasn't sure as yet, but added, "He's got way more than me, thank God!" Moments later, they were driving off to Kensington Palace in their black Range Rover with the boy known only as "Baby Cambridge" strapped into his $160 Britax baby car seat.

It would be another full day before the world learned the baby's name. But before that could happen, the newest Windsor had to meet his great-grandmother. Arriving at Kensington Palace in a dark green Bentley, she went inside where the baby, William, Kate, and Prince Harry were waiting to greet her. It was the first time in 120 years that a reigning monarch had met her third-generation heir.

Before they announced the baby's name to the world, or even let Charles and Camilla in on their decision, they told the Queen. As she had done with all of her own children, Elizabeth, aware that any "suggestion" from her could be interpreted as a direct order, chose not to interfere in the naming process. William and Kate named their little prince George Alexander Louis—His Royal Highness Prince George of Cambridge. The Queen was thrilled, and Charles would be as well. George had been the name of six British kings, including the "Mad" King George who lost the American colonies, and of course Elizabeth's own father. Although his first name was actually Albert and he grew up as "Bertie," Elizabeth's predecessor on the throne chose to rule as George VI in honor of his own father, George V.

The couple took great care in choosing their baby boy's other names, as well. Alexander was a popular choice with the Scots, who regard Alexander III as one of their greatest kings. Louis honored Charles's mentor and father figure, his great-uncle Lord Mountbatten.

After half an hour, the Queen returned to Buckingham Palace and her dreaded boxes of state. She was determined to finish them all before heading off the next day for her traditional annual holiday at Balmoral. Ninety minutes later, the Cambridges drove off, too, bound for the Middleton family home in Berkshire with Boy George strapped in the backseat. For the next six weeks, Kate stayed with her parents while William shuttled between Bucklebury and his search-and-rescue duties in Wales. Carole, never one to let even the smallest detail slide, had gone to the trouble of setting up a nursery at the Middletons' mansion so that Kate could make an easy adjustment to motherhood and William could live out his stated wish to be a "hands-on dad."

From his christening at St. James's Palace, where the Archbishop of Canterbury baptized him using water from the River Jordan, to his first royal tour to Australia and New Zealand in April of 2014, the cherub-cheeked Prince evoked the same reaction throughout the realm that Diana's "William the Wombat" had three decades earlier.

Shortly after a platoon of reporters dutifully recorded images of the littlest Prince feeding baby kangaroos at Sydney's Taronga Zoo, tragedy struck when Camilla's brother, Mark Shand, died suddenly in New York. After attending a charity auction, the celebrated hedonist turned dedicated wildlife conservationist consumed five whiskies and a glass of champagne before joining friends at the Gramercy Park Hotel. Stepping outside for a smoke, Shand, sixty-two, tried to reenter the hotel through the revolving doors, slipped, and struck his head on the pavement. He died nine hours later. In addition to the fact that Shand's blood alcohol level was twice the legal limit, the coroner determined that Camilla's brother had an unusually thin skull—paper thin in places—and that anyone else "would have probably survived the fall."

Hearing the news at Birkhall, Camilla was, Prince Charles said, "utterly devastated." Recalling the moment, Camilla said "an anguished voice was on the other end telling me that something terrible had happened to my indestructible brother. My charismatic and sometimes infuriating brother, who had survived tsunamis, shipwrecks, poisoned arrows, and even the fearsome Komodo dragons, was no longer with us." At Shand's funeral, Camilla leaned on Charles's arm and wept as her brother's body was carried into the church in a biodegradable wicker coffin adorned with flower garlands.

William and Kate sent their condolences from Australia, where their squealing son was still charming the folks Down Under just the way his father had. But George represented something even more—something Great Britain and the Commonwealth had never seen. According to *Time* magazine's Andrew Ferguson, George embodied "almost American-style upward mobility, with a British twist: if you work hard and play by the rules, regardless of race, color or creed, you too can marry your daughter off to become the mother of a King. . . . The future King of England and Defender of the Faith has emerged from a mother who is without a drop of peerage blood. My guess is the boy, quite apart from his personal qualities, will prove an inconvenience to antiroyalists and monarchists alike."

Perhaps, but for now his parents were determined to shield their Little Prince from the unremitting glare of media scrutiny. Once George's first official overseas tour was over, he all but vanished from sight. William and Kate were determined to give him something akin to a normal toddlerhood, and toward that end they retreated to Bucklebury and Anmer House. It would be a full year before George made his next public appearance—and then only to join in as his country celebrated another blessed event.

On May 2, 2015, Kate gave birth to an eight-pound-three-ounce daughter, once again in the private maternity ward in the Lindo Wing of London's St. Mary's Hospital. As before, cannons boomed and church bells rang, but this time landmarks like the Trafalgar Square fountains, the Tower Bridge, and the London Eye were bathed in pink light instead of blue.

The birth of the Princess of Cambridge differed in other ways as well: She was taken outside to meet the press and public when she was less than ten hours old, and later that same day her name was announced: Charlotte Elizabeth Diana—Her Royal Highness, Princess Charlotte of Cambridge. Since Charlotte is the feminine form of Charles, the royal princess's name paid obvious tribute to three of the most important people in William's life.

Merely by being born, Charlotte made history. She was the first daughter of a future monarch born since the abolition of primogeniture, making her now fourth in line for the crown behind her big brother, George.

This time, Carole Middleton—who once again was the first grandparent to meet and hold the newest arrival—tagged along when the family repaired to Anmer Hall. Prince William's spokesmen explained that it was only logical for the maternal grandmother to be on hand to help with a newborn. However, this explanation for Carole's involvement in the Cambridges' lives made little sense to Royals and aristocrats who were cared for by nurses and nannies essentially from birth. There would be other differences in the way the Cambridges chose to bring up their children. In December 2015, Kate and William enrolled two-year-old George at Westacre Montessori nursery school in Norfolk. Although William was the first Royal Family member to attend preschool, his was located not far from Kensington Palace and cost upward of $20,000 annually. Westacre Montessori School, despite its comparatively modest cost of roughly $50 a day per pupil, nevertheless provided financial assistance to 85 percent of its students.

Before long, there were grumblings that Prince Charles, Camilla, and even the Queen were being denied access to the royal babies. "Spoil them, enjoy them—and give them back at the end of the day," Charles cracked when asked about the role of a grandparent. Yet, while the Middletons were a near-constant presence in the lives of George and Charlotte, Charles complained he "almost never" saw them.

For a second year in a row, William and Kate broke with holiday tradition by forsaking Christmas dinner at Sandringham to spend the holidays primarily with the Middletons. The Duke and Duchess of Cambridge attended church with the royal family sans George ("He's too noisy," Mummy explained), then headed back to Anmer House to host Kate's family. As much as this rankled the Duke and Duchess of Cornwall, the Queen waxed philosophical. "Deciding how to divide time between the two families," she said, "it's a difficult problem, especially when you have two small children."

The Queen realizes more than anyone that the current situation is unique, and is planning accordingly. That is all I will say.

—A SENIOR COURTIER, WHEN ASKED IF THE QUEEN HAD RULED OUT ABDICATING

8

A QUESTION OF ABDICATION

Prince George's arrival marked only the second time in history that three generations of direct royal heirs were alive while there was a reigning monarch on the throne. The last time this occurred was during the reign of Queen Victoria, when Edward VII, George V, and brothers Edward VIII and George VI were all waiting in line to wear the crown.

Charles was still waiting. At sixty-seven, he was already three years older than the oldest person ever to assume the throne—William IV, who succeeded George IV in 1830. On September 9, 2015, the Queen surpassed Victoria's reign of 63 years, 216 days, becoming the longest-reigning British monarch in history. The distinction, she said with a sly smile, was "not one to which I have ever aspired."

Yet there was a good chance she would reign longer still. Much, much longer. Her mother lived to be 101, and she was active and alert almost to the very last day of her life. At ninety, the Queen could live another decade or more. Were she to live as long as the Queen Mother, Charles would become king at seventy-eight, and Camilla his Queen at seventy-nine. If Charles, in turn, lived to be as old as Prince Philip, William and Kate would both be well past sixty by the time William assumed the throne.

For years the Queen privately brought up the notion of retiring, only to dismiss it out of hand. "Oh, that's something I can't do," she once told former Archbishop of Canterbury George Carey. "I am going to carry on to the end." Margaret Rhodes believed her cousin the Queen saw her duty to the British people as "something so deep and special" that she would fulfill it "until the day she dies."

Certainly the British people were overwhelmingly convinced that the Queen would never consider abdicating—although there were moments when they wavered in that belief. In December 2014, it was widely rumored that the Queen would announce her decision to retire during her annual Christmas broadcast, the contents of which were always kept secret. Speculation in the press ran rampant after Britain's betting industry suspending wagering on the Queen's abdication after a series of "highly specific" bets were placed indicating that someone with inside knowledge of the Queen's Christmas broadcast script might be seeking to cash in on her decision to step down.

She didn't make the announcement, of course. But the Queen did make it clear to members of her inner circle that she would voluntarily abdicate in the event of some debilitating event—like dementia, or a stroke. In the event she was no longer able to make that conscious decision, it would be made for her under the Regency Act of 1937. If any three of the following people agreed that the Queen could no longer do the job—the consort of the sovereign (Prince Philip), the Lord Chancellor, the Speaker of the House of Commons, the Lord Chief Justice of England and the Master of the Rolls—then Charles would become Regent. Given Elizabeth's advanced age, said one of her senior advisors, "we're definitely dusting off the Regency Act and taking a fresh look at it."

Were the Regency Act to be invoked, Charles would essentially become king in all but name. It had been two centuries since Britain's last regency, when George III's worsening mental illness made it impossible for him to fulfill his duties. His son, the future George IV, assumed his father's full duties and ruled as Regent from 1811 until 1820—England's Regency Period.

But even if the Queen remained in good health for years—and there was no indication that she wouldn't—there were currents of change that she could not ignore. Over an eighteen-month period in 2013 and 2014, there was a flurry of abdications across Europe: In April, 75-year-old Queen Beatrix of the Netherlands handed the crown to her son, Prince Willem-Alexander, 45. Three months later, 79-year-old Albert II of Belgium abdicated in favor of his son, Crown Prince Philippe, 53. The following year, after repeatedly insisting à la Queen Elizabeth that abdication for him was "not an option," Spain's 76-year-old King Juan Carlos shocked his countrymen by abruptly handing over the crown to his son Prince Felipe, 46. "A new generation must be at the forefront," Juan Carlos explained, "younger people with new energies."

Nothing so rattled the British monarch, however, as the events in Rome. "No, no," were the Queen's words when she was told that Pope Benedict XVI, who was one year younger than Elizabeth, had abdicated. "It cannot be! I don't understand." Neither did the world's 1.2 billion Roman Catholics. After all, there hadn't been a papal abdication in six hundred years.

The Queen did not have to look back quite so far. She was a girl of ten when an abdication thrust her own reluctant, stammering father onto the throne. Certainly there was something to be said for controlling her own destiny—for leaving on her own terms, rather than waiting for the Regency Act to be invoked by others. The idea of living out her nonagenarian years as Dowager Queen also had a certain appeal. Just as the Queen "always sought her mother's advice and approval," said a former lady-in-waiting to the Queen Mother, "Charles will always defer to his mother, whatever his title."

"Does he want the job? Yes, of course he wants it. It's what he's been training for all his life," a former advisor said. "Does it bother him that his mother has to die for him to get it? Of course, but she doesn't *have* to die for that to happen, does she?" In late 1998, Charles and Camilla both sensed that the furor over Diana's death had weakened the monarch and left an opening. He rashly allowed his press secretary, Mark Bolland, to leak the story that the Prince of Wales would be "privately delighted" if the Queen abdicated. Furious, Elizabeth summoned her son to Buckingham Palace, demanded that he explain, and then insisted on—and got—a profuse apology.

Charles sputtered when asked during a television interview if he thought about what it would mean for him when his mother died. "It is better not to have to think too much about it," he said. "I think about it a bit, but it's much better not. This is something that, you know, if it comes to it, and regrettably it comes as the result of the death of your parent, which is, you know, not so nice, to say the least."

Now both Charles and his mother were forced to think about it—a lot. "It is not quite true that the Queen has not entertained the thought," said the BBC's Andrew Marr. "She has discussed abdication privately with loyal and very senior figures." Three of those "loyal and very senior figures"—Baron Fellowes, Sir Robin Janvrin, and her current private secretary, Christopher Geidt—had already begun counseling the Queen on the very question of how and when to pass the torch.

Heir to his mother's particular brand of magic, husband to one of the most admired young women in the world, father of the world's two most famous and undeniably adorable toddlers, William was the overwhelming choice of the British people to become the next monarch. But Diana's devout wish of bypassing Charles altogether was impossible. No one could prevent the Prince of Wales from asserting his right to the crown.

In the halls of Buckingham Palace, it had long been accepted that Charles would be a place holder for the man who would carry the monarchy into the future. But even if he reigned as a transitional figure for a decade or perhaps a few years longer, that still gave King Charles III ample opportunity to make his mark on history.

One secret plan, first hatched in 2010, called for the Queen to retire (a far more palatable word than abdicate) so that her son might reign for a limited time before stepping down in favor of Prince William. There seemed little doubt that, if the Queen and Charles both agreed to her abdication, Parliament and the fifteen other nations that share the British sovereign would go along.

One nagging question remained. If Charles reigned for a specified time—say fifteen years—what would he become after he stepped down to make way for William? He could not revert to being the Prince of Wales or the Duke of Cornwall, since those titles are held by the eldest son of the monarch. He and Camilla would also lose their income from the Duchy of Cornwall—a staggering $45 million annually.

These details had yet to be worked out, but were far from insurmountable. "Titles can be revived, and rules changed," a longtime courtier said, "if the future of the monarchy is at stake. I can assure you Prince Charles, no matter what he ends up being called, is not about to starve."

In ways both subtle and surprisingly direct, the Queen was sending the message that her retirement was imminent—if not around the time of her ninetieth birthday celebration in 2016, then after the death of the Duke of Edinburgh. For sixty-four years, he had dutifully walked several paces behind his wife, arms folded behind his back as if he were pacing the deck of a ship—just as he had when he served with distinction in the navy during World War II. "My job first, second, and last," he once said, "is never to let the Queen down."

Perhaps. But Philip was known for his temper, his impatience, his often brusque demeanor—and his public gaffes. "Damn fool question!" Philip snapped when a BBC reporter politely asked the Queen if she was enjoying her stay in Paris. When he met Sir Michael Bishop, then chairman of Britain's Channel 4 television network, Philip said, "So you're responsible for the kind of crap Channel 4 produces!"

With the press looking on, he once asked a Scottish driving instructor, "How do you keep your natives off the booze long enough to get them through the test?" On a separate trip to Scotland, he drew the ire of the Indian community when he said a fuse box looked "as though it was put in by an Indian." Confronted about the comment, he stuttered, "I meant to say cowboys. I just got my cowboys and Indians mixed up."

"Aren't most of you descended from pirates?" he inquired when visiting the Cayman Islands. On a trip to Australia, he asked an aboriginal leader, "Do you still throw spears at each other?" To the president of Nigeria, who met the Prince wearing traditional dress: "You look like you're ready for bed."

While touring China, Prince Philip told a visiting British student, "If you stay here much longer you'll go home with slitty eyes." The Queen's spouse went on to declare Beijing "ghastly"—the same word he publicly used to describe any number of industrial cities and suburban towns he visited in England over the years. At a ceremony for his Duke of Edinburgh youth awards program, Philip told the audience that "young people are the same as they always were—just as ignorant." When a student parking attendant failed to recognize him during a tour of Cambridge University, Philip blurted out, "You bloody silly fool!"

The Duke of Edinburgh's lack of tact was never more in evidence than when the Queen asked a Northwest London Army cadet nearly blinded in an IRA bombing how much he could see. "Not a lot," Prince Philip interjected, pointing to the young man's chest, "judging by that tie." Similarly, when he met a group of children from the British Deaf Association who were standing near a Caribbean steel drum band, Philip declared, "If you're near that music it's no wonder you're deaf." The wheelchair-bound resident of a London nursing home scarcely knew how to react when Philip asked bluntly, "Do people trip over you?"

Not even his children were exempt. Of Princess Anne's love of horses, Philip commented, "If it doesn't fart or eat hay, she isn't interested."

Notwithstanding his famously prickly nature, the Queen still relied heavily on her husband's advice and support. "He has, quite simply, been my strength and stay all these years," she once tried to explain. "And I, his whole family, and this and many other countries, owe him a debt greater than he would ever claim or we shall ever know." According to her cousin Margaret Rhodes, Elizabeth and Philip remained very much in love. "She's always adored him," Rhodes said. "She never looked at anyone else. She was smitten from the start."

As he approached his ninety-fifth birthday in June 2016—within days of the Queen's ninetieth birthday Trooping the Colour ceremony—Prince Philip was described as being in "robust health" in spite of several recent scares. Mentally, the Duke of Edinburgh was, said his equerry, "as sharp as ever." By way of maintaining their mental agility and staying informed, both Philip and the Queen had become ardent Googlers. If either had a question about something, "they both go straight to their iPads."

The Queen, however, was nothing if not a realist. In late September 2015, she let it be known to her staff that, after the death of her husband, she intended to leave Buckingham Palace and make Balmoral her primary residence. At about the same time, the Queen's and Charles's communications departments were quietly merged under the control of one of the Prince's most senior courtiers—"another clear indication," said the *Times*, "that major changes are afoot."

The sovereign herself said as much when she bestowed a second knighthood on Sir Christopher Geidt, architect of both

Her Majesty's approaching "retirement" and the hand-off to the next generation. In words that went largely unnoticed at first, the Queen's citation explained that Geidt was being honored for forging "*a new approach to constitutional matters* . . . and the preparation for the *transition to a change of reign*."

"It was a surprising admission," declared the *Daily Mail*, which called the developments "hugely significant . . . the succession is rarely, if ever, talked about in official terms. But behind the Palace gates, preparations are being made." One royal confidante called it "the first step to bringing Charles to the throne."

To be sure, one had to look no farther than Clarence House for harbingers of things to come. There Camilla, who had hired noted interior designer Robert Kime to redo Clarence House, Highgrove, Ray Mill, and Birkhall, was already poring over plans to redecorate rooms in the private residence at Buckingham Palace—rooms that, for the most part, the Queen had left unchanged for decades.

There are those who persist in believing that the Queen will never abdicate, that the mere idea is anathema to her. Yet an awful lot of "nevers" have come to pass since Diana and Charles were wed thirty-five years ago. The Queen would never agree to pay income taxes. She did (and so did the rest of the Royal Family). The Queen would never give up the royal yacht *Britannia*. She did. The Queen would never open the doors of Buckingham Palace to the public. She has. The Queen would never allow her son and heir to divorce. She did. The Queen would never visit Ireland, and no Royal would ever shake hands with leaders of the Irish Republican Army. Elizabeth was the first British monarch to visit the Republic of Ireland, and Charles shook hands with Sinn Fein leader Gerry Adams thirty-six years after Adams gloated over the IRA's murder of his great-uncle Lord Mountbatten. There would never be an end to the thirteen-hundred-year-old law of primogeniture. There was. Would the monarch ever deign to ride in a taxicab, lift a pint at a pub, or eat at McDonald's? Her Majesty has done all of these things, and, determined not to be left out of the information age, she has also availed herself of Google, Facebook, and Twitter.

From the day she climbed down from a fig tree in Africa to assume the burdens of monarchy, Elizabeth II has been guided by a sense of duty to her subjects. Buffeted by the winds of change, the Queen also has shown a willingness to adapt to the times, if such was required to sustain the institutions and traditions she held dear.

To be sure, retirement would not be easy for history's longest-reigning, hardest-working sovereign. However, once convinced by Sir Christopher Geidt and others that it was needed to save the House of Windsor, it was just one last sacrifice she was willing to make.

....

THE QUEEN, SAID VETERAN ROYALS correspondent Robert Jobson, "is a traditionalist, dutiful to her core. But she knows that, for the monarchy to survive and be relevant . . . it must be in harmony with the people." That will only happen, she realizes, when the people have the king—and the queen—they want.

"The only thing against the Queen," agreed the *Telegraph*'s Tim Heald, "is her age, and although her son is obviously younger, time is not exactly on his side—particularly when one considers the popularity of his children."

Halfway through the twenty-first century, it seems all but certain that King William V and Queen Catherine will be waving at the multitudes with George, the Prince of Wales, and Princess Charlotte smiling beside them. It is even conceivable, given the Windsor genes, that a King George VII could extend the monarchy into the twenty-second century.

Elizabeth II has done more than just hope and dream this will happen. In the nineteen years since Diana's death threatened to sink the monarchy, she has deftly steered it away from the rocks and into open water. Even more treacherous seas lie ahead.

Before William can assume command, the House of Windsor will have to survive the reign of Charles III and Camilla—"The Rottweiler," "That Wicked, Wicked Woman," the next undoubted Queen of England.

ACKNOWLEDGMENTS

"I always knew," Diana said even though she was married to the next king, "that I would never be the next queen." Yet she was even more convinced that her husband's hugely unpopular mistress, then so resented by the rest of the Royal Family, would never wear the crown.

It is no small irony that, in life but even more in death, the doomed Princess of Wales made it possible for the monarchy to embrace change and ultimately reward her archrival with the most coveted title of all: Queen.

When I had my first up-close encounter with Elizabeth, Charles, Philip, and the rest of the Royal Family in 1977 during Silver Jubilee services at Westminster Abbey marking the Queen's twenty-fifth year on the throne, no one could have remotely imagined the tumult, scandal, triumph, and tragedy that lay in store for one of the world's most ancient and revered institutions. As the Queen celebrates her ninetieth birthday and her sixty-fourth year on the throne in 2016, she has—again, largely thanks to the rebel princess Diana—proven herself to be a modern sovereign, able to adapt to the times and do what is necessary for the monarchy, and, more important, for her people. It is a new side of the woman named Elizabeth that even close friends, still convinced that the Queen would never abdicate, are slow to recognize. Whether she steps aside upon the death of Prince Philip, as she strongly indicated in 2015, or at some later point, the fact remains that none of her successors is likely to reign as long or be as much a part of our collective psyches as Elizabeth II. Simply put, this iconic figure has been a central actor on the world scene longer than anyone in history. If we all take a moment to think of what the world will be like without her in it, then even the most cynical among us have to admit we shall miss the Queen.

Having covered the Royal Family for more than thirty-five years and written several *New York Times* best sellers about this complicated clan, I never cease to be amazed by the unexpected twists and turns taken in the continuing Windsor saga. As the Queen nears the inevitable end of her reign—now the longest in British history—the scramble for power behind the scenes has become even more riveting. In *Game of Crowns*, I sought to convey all the internecine drama, excitement, and intrigue going on behind palace walls.

Game of Crowns gave me yet another opportunity to work with the marvelous people at Gallery Books. Mitchell Ivers, with whom I share a love of theater, American popular music, and politics—yes, these things do go together—is as passionate about the work and as skilled an editor as any author could wish for. I'm also grateful to my many other friends who make up the Gallery/Simon & Schuster team, including Louise Burke, Carolyn Reidy, Jennifer Bergstrom, Jennifer Robinson, Felice Javit, Natasha Simons, Jean Anne Rose, Paul O'Halloran, Elizabeth Lotto, Lisa Rivlin, Jaime Putorti, Al Madocs, and Sean Devlin.

Ellen Levine—close friend and colleague for thirty-one (gulp) years—is the most talented literary agent in the publishing industry, bar none. As any of her legion of loyal clients will attest, Ellen has the amazing ability to make you feel as if you are simply the only writer in the cosmos. I also owe a debt of gratitude to the rest of the marvelous people at Trident Media Group, Ellen's associates Claire Roberts, Alexa Stark, Meredith Miller, and Alexander Slater.

For nearly a half-century (another, bigger gulp), my incredible wife, Valerie, has been both an inspiration and my partner in crime. Smart, funny, beautiful, unstoppable, and unafraid—perhaps the quality in her I most admire—Valerie has always had her own successful career and, as an active part of our community, made a difference in people's lives. Of course, she has also always been an indispensable part of my work and my life. Our elder daughter, Kate Andersen Brower, a respected Washington journalist whose first book reached number one on the *New York Times* Best Seller List in 2015, has now discovered just how indispensable her mother's input can be when crafting an important work of nonfiction. I realize it runs counter to the laws of nature, but I must confess I am extremely fond of my son-in-law, Brooke Brower. Not only is Brooke a highly-regarded, Washington-based network television news producer, but he and Kate are the parents of the inimitable Graham Andersen Brower and our Charlotte—Charlotte Beatrice Brower. We are also enormously proud of our younger daughter, Kelly, who has boldly chosen her own distinct path. Kelly is studying for her master's degree in contemporary art in London, and about to embark on her own promising career in the world of museums, auction houses, and galleries.

Additional thanks to Richard Kay, Peter Archer, Dr. Frederic Mailliez, Alan Hamilton, Jules Knight, Beatrice Hubert, Lord Mishcon, Mimi Massy-Birch, Lady Margaret Rhodes, Delissa Needham, Mark Shand, Lady Elsa Bowker, Philip Higgs, Hugh Massy-Birch, Lady Yolanda Joseph, Janet Jenkins, Guy Pelly, Hamish Barne, Andrew Gailey, Thierry Meresse, Elizabeth d'Erlanger, Andy Radford, Joan Rivers, Vivienne Parry, Jules de Rosee, Richard Greene, Adrian Munsey, Josy Duclos, Lynn Redgrave, Jeanne Lecorcher, the Countess of Romanones, Ezra Zilkha, Laura Watts, Harold Brooks-Baker, Mark Butt, John Kaufman, Geoffrey Bignell, Regina Feiler, Remi Gaston-Dreyfus, Natalie Symonds, Tom Freeman, Rachel Whitburn, Elizabeth Whiddett, Penny Russell-Smith, Kitty Carlisle Hart, Miriam Lefort, Pierre Trudeau, Penny Walker, Claude Garreck, Dee Ennifer, Patrick Demarchelier, Dudley Freeman, Peter Allen, Alfred Eisenstaedt, John Marion, Fred Hauptfuhrer, Jessica Hogan, Betty Kelly Sargent, James Whitaker, Alain-Phillipe Feutre, Ron Galella, Mary Robertson, Gered Mankowitz, Lord Olivier, Vivian Simon, Michelle Lapautre, Tom Corby, Cecile Zilkha, Kevin Lemarque, Pierre Suu, Hazel Southam, Norman Parkinson, Ray Whelan, Jr., Matthew Lutts, Tim Graham, Vincent Martin, Everett Raymond Kinstler, Sharman Douglas, Malcom Forbes, Tiffney Sanford, Amber Weitz, Andy Rouvalis, Yvette Reyes, Scott Burkhead, Bill Diehl, Tiffany Miller, Simone Dibley, Daniel Taylor, Ray Whelan, Sr., Paula Dranov, Mark Halpern, Rhoda Prelic, Liz Miller, Steve Stylandoudis, Julie Cammer, Marcel Turgot, Mary Beth Whelan, David McGough, Charles Furneaux, Connie Erickson, Mel Lyons, Lindsay Sutton, Andy Rouvalis, Francis Specker, Scott Burkhead, John Stillwell, James Price, Elizabeth Loth, Ian Walde, Wolfgang Rattay, Richard Grant, Mick Magsino, Lemma Salle, Tasha Hanna, Lawrence R. Mulligan, Jane Clucas, David Bergeron, Hilary Hard, Art Kaligos, Gary Gunderson, the Press Association, Buckingham Palace, St. James's Palace, Windsor Castle, Kensington Palace, Clarence House, Marlborough College, Downe House, St. Andrew's School, Eton, Ludgrove, St. Andrews University, Sandhurst, the BBC, Sky Television, Channel Four Television Ltd., the Times of London, the *Daily Mail*, the *Manchester Guardian*, the *Daily Telegraph*, the *Sunday Times*, the *Daily Express*, the New York Public Library, the Bancroft Library of the University of California at Berkeley, the Gunn Memorial Library, the Brookfield Library, the Silas Bronson Library, the Litchfield Library, the Reform Club, the Lotos Club, the Lansdowne Club, the *New York Times*, the Associated Press, Bloomberg, Reuters, Associated Press Images, Globe Photos, and Rex USA.

SOURCES AND CHAPTER NOTES

The following chapter notes have been compiled to give a general view of the sources drawn upon in preparing *Game of Crowns*, but by no means are they to be considered all-inclusive. Important sources at Buckingham Palace, Kensington Palace, Windsor Castle, Sandringham, St. James's Palace, Clarence House, Balmoral, Highgrove, Eton, Scotland Yard, and Sandhurst—as well as close friends, relatives, acquaintances, colleagues, and employees of the Royal Family—only agreed to cooperate once it was agreed that their names would not be mentioned. Many of these are the same highly reliable sources who have provided detailed and accurate information to me over the decades for my previous books on Princess Diana and the Windsors—allowing me, for example, to learn the date of William and Kate's wedding long before it became known to the public, and to time the publication of my book *William and Kate* to coincide with the big event in 2011. Therefore, the author continues his policy of respecting the wishes of many interviewed sources who wished to remain anonymous, and accordingly has not listed them, either here or elsewhere in the text. Obviously, the Queen, Camilla, Kate Middleton, and the rest of the Royal Family have generated untold thousands of articles and news reports. Having appeared on NBC News, CBS, ABC, CNN, Fox, and MSNBC, as well as programs such as *Entertainment Tonight/The Insider, Inside Edition, Extra, Access Hollywood,* and E! Entertainment to discuss the weddings of both Charles and Camilla and William and Kate as well as the Queen's Diamond Jubilee and the birth of both Prince George and Princess Charlotte, I can attest to the unprecedented amount of media coverage the Royal Family has received in recent years. Among those publications in which relevant articles appeared are the *New York Times*, the *Guardian*, the *Sunday Times* (London), the *Times* (London), the *Wall Street Journal*, the *Daily Mail*, the *Washington Post*, the *Boston Globe*, the *Los Angeles Times*, *Vanity Fair*, *Time*, *People*, *Newsweek*, the *New Yorker*, *Life*, *Le Monde*, *Paris Match*, and the

Economist, and carried over the Associated Press, Reuters, and Bloomberg wires.

CHAPTERS 1–2

Interview subjects included Alan Hamilton, Mark Shand, Dr. Frederic Mailliez, Margaret Rhodes, the late Lady Elsa Bowker, Lord Mishcon, Beatrice Humbert, Countess Mountbatten, Jeanne Lecorcher, Richard Kay, Thierry Meresse, Lady Yolanda Joseph, Richard Greene, Norman Parkinson, Peter Archer, Ezra Zilkha, Harold Brooks-Baker, Andy Radford, Mark Butt, Claude Garreck, Josy Duclos, Remi Gaston-Dreyfus, Peter Allen, Barry Schenck, Miriam Lefort, Janet Lizop, Ron Galella, Pierre Suu, Sharman Douglas, and Steve Stylandoudis. Published sources included Rob Price, "This Is What Happens When the Queen Dies: The Death of Queen Elizabeth Will Be the Most Disruptive Event in Britain in the Last 70 Years," *Business Insider*, May 6, 2015; Tom Sykes, "What Will Happen When the Queen Dies?," *Daily Beast*, June 2, 2015; "What Happens When the Queen Dies?," the *Week*, June 4, 2015; Matthew Weaver, "UK Republicans Debate How to React When the Queen Dies," the *Guardian*, July 12, 2015; Charles Moore, "An Act of National Communion—But What Will Happen at the Next Coronation?," the *Telegraph*, May 31, 2013; Robert Lacey, *Majesty* (New York: Harcourt Brace Jovanovich, 1977); Adrian Higgins, "How Britain Came to Revere Elizabeth II," the *Washington Post*, September 8, 2015; Robert Booth and Julian Borger, "Christopher Geidt: The Suave, Shrewd and Mysterious Royal Insider," the *Guardian*, May 31, 2013; "Queen Honors 'Big Paul' in Diamond Jubilee Honors List," the *Evening Standard*, September 13, 2012; "Sergeant at Arms Promotion for Queen's Faithful Servant," *Hello!*, January 9, 2008; "It Starts with Tea: A Day in the Life of Queen Elizabeth II," the *Mail* and *Guardian*, April 16, 2006; Emily Dugan, "Michael Fagan: Her Nightie Was One of Those Liberty Prints, Down to Her Knees," the *Independent*, February 18, 2012; "Text of Scotland Yard's Report on July 9 Intrusion into Buckingham Palace," the *New York Times*, July 13, 1982; Spencer Davidson, "God Save the Queen—Fast," *Time*, July 26, 1982; "You Look Like You Need a Drink," the *Mirror*, February 20, 2012; Pam Tobey, "Remember the Guy Who Got Into the Queen's Bedroom?," the *Washington Post*, September 24, 2014; Victoria Murphy, "Queen Camilla? How Once Sidelined Duchess Is Now Center-Stage . . . and Could Take Title When Charles Is King," the *Mirror*, June 6, 2012; Anna Pukas, "Revealed: Positive Impact of Camilla on Prince Charles After a Decade of Marriage," *Express*, April 8, 2015; Chris Pleasance, "All Eyes on Gorgeous George!," the *Daily Mail*, June 13, 2015; Angela Levin, "Will Prince Charles Risk Making Camilla, Duchess of Cornwall, His Queen?," *Yahoo News*, December 9, 2015; Duncan Hill, Alison Gauntlett, Sarah Rickayzen, Gareth Thomas, *The Royal Family: A Year By Year Chronicle of the House of Windsor* (New York: Parragon, 2013); Barbara Davies and Claudia Joseph, "The Extraordinary Story of How a Thrice-Married Crane Driver's Daughter Rose to Be the Queen's Right-Hand Woman," the *Daily Mail*, May 23, 2014; Richard Alleyne, "Royal Chef Reveals the Queen's Favorite Meals," the *Telegraph*, May 3, 2012; Rachel Cooke, "What the Royals Eat at Home," the *Guardian*, May 19, 2012; Sarah Karmali, "Angela Kelly on Dressing the Queen," *Vogue*, November 5, 2012; Andrew Alderson, "The Queen and I, By Her Majesty's PA," the *Telegraph*, December 9, 2007; "Key Aides Moves to Windsor Ahead of Queen's Retirement," the *Evening Standard*, November 18, 2006; Maria Puente, "Prince George Makes Palace Balcony Debut," *USA Today*, June 13, 2015; James Tapper, "Prince George Makes First Appearance on Buckingham Palace Balcony," the *Guardian*, June 13, 2015; Ben Pimlott, *The Queen: A Biography of Elizabeth II* (New York: John Wiley & Sons, Inc., 1996); Sally Bedell Smith, *Elizabeth the Queen* (New York: Random House, 2012); Sarah Lyall, "Peter Townsend Dies at 80; Princess Margaret's Love," the *New York Times*, June 21, 1995; Sarah Bradford, *The Reluctant King: The Life and Reign of George VI, 1895–1952* (New York: St. Martin's Press, 1990); "Princess Margaret and a Love Affair Denied," the *Daily Mail*, February 9, 2002; Theo Aronson, *Royal Family: Years of Transition* (London: Thistle Publishing, 2014); Noreen Taylor, "Saying What Everyone Thinks: Private Secretary Lord Charteris, Still With a Keen Finger on the Royal Pulse," the *Spectator*, January 7, 1995; Heather Timmons, "The Once and Future Camilla," the *New York Times*, April 3, 2005; Roxanne Roberts, "Fairy Tale for Grown-Ups: Charles and Camilla Once Upon a Time," the *Washington Post*, February 11, 2005; Penny Junor, "Camilla Has Won Us Over and Deserves to Become Queen," the *Telegraph*, April 8, 2015; Angela Levin, "Will Charles Risk Making Camilla, Duchess of Cornwall, His Queen?," *Newsweek*, December 9, 2015.

CHAPTERS 3–5

For these chapters, the author drew on conversations with Peter Archer, Jules Knight, Mimi Massy-Birch, Lady Yolanda Joseph, Emma Sayle,

Lord Bathurst, Lord Mishcon, Patricia Knatchbull, Lady Elsa Bowker, Hamish Barne, the Duchess of Alba, Hugh Massy-Birch, Charles Furneaux, Delissa Needham, Elizabeth d'Erlanger, Alice Tomlinson, Pat Charman, Richard Greene, Guy Pelly, Geoffrey Bignell, Lynn Redgrave, Penny Walker, Tess Rock, Jules de Rosee, Richard Kay, the Countess of Romanones, Farris Rookstool, Fred Hauptfuhrer, Cecile Thibaud, David McGough, Hazel Southam, Evelyn Phillips, Susan Crimp, Elizabeth Widdett, Janet Allison, and Mary Robertson.

Published sources included Matilda Battersby, "A Day That Shook The World: Windsor Castle Fire," the *Independent*, November 18, 2010; Richard W. Stevenson, "Big Fire in Windsor Castle Raises Fear About Artwork," the *New York Times*, November 21, 1992; "Text of the Queen's Annus Horribilis Speech, 24 November 1992," www.royal.gov.uk; Annick Cojean, "The Final Interview," *Le Monde*, August 27, 1997; Wendy Berry, *The Housekeeper's Diary* (New York: Barricade Books, Inc., 1995); Stephen Barry, *Royal Service: My Twelve Years as Valet to Prince Charles* (New York: Macmillan, 1983); "The Nation Unites Against Tradition," the *Observer*, September 7, 1997; Lord Stevens of Kirkwhelpington, The Operation Paget Inquiry Report Into the Allegation of Conspiracy to Murder Diana, Princess of Wales, and Emad El-Din Mohamed Abdel Moneim Fayed, December 14, 2006; Emily Nash, "Diana: The Verdict," the *Mirror*, December 11, 2006; "Farewell, Diana," *Newsweek*, September 15, 1997; "Charles Escorts Diana Back to a Grieving Britain," the *New York Times*, September 1, 1997; Anthony Holden, "Why Royals Must Express Remorse," the *Express*, September 3, 1997; Christopher Wilson, *A Greater Love: Prince Charles's Twenty-Year Affair with Camilla Parker Bowles* (New York: William Morrow, 1994); "The Princes' Final Farewell," the *Sunday Times of London*, September 7, 1997; Alan Hamilton, Andrew Pierce, and Philip Webster, "Royal Family Is 'Deeply Touched' by Public Support," the *Times*, September 4, 1997; "Diana, Princess of Wales 1961–1997," the *Week*, September 6, 1997; John Simpson, "Goodbye England's Rose: A Nation Says Farewell," the *Sunday Telegraph*, September 7, 1997; Robert Hardman, "Princes' Last Minutes with Mother," the *Daily Telegraph*, September 3, 1997; "Driver Was Drunk," *Le Monde*, September 3, 1997; Andrew Morton, *Diana: Her True Story* (New York: Simon & Schuster, 1997); Pascal Palmer, "I Gave Diana Last Rites," the *Mirror*, October 23, 1997; Robert Jobson and Greg Swift, "Look After William and Harry," the *Daily Express*, December 22, 1997; Marianne Macdonald, "A Rift Death Can't Heal," the *Observer*, September 14, 1997; Christopher Andersen,

The Day Diana Died (New York: William Morrow, 1998); Tess Rock and Natalie Symonds, "Our Diana Diaries," the *Sunday Mirror*, November 16, 1997; Simone Simmons, *Diana: The Last Word* (New York: St. Martin's Press, 2005); "Flashback to the Accident," *Liberation*, September 2, 1997; Howard Chua-Eoan, Steve Wulf, Jeffrey Kluger, Christopher Redman, and David Van Biema, "A Death in Paris: The Passing of Diana," *Time*, September 8, 1997; Rosa Monckton, "Time to End False Rumors," *Newsweek*, March 2, 1998; Jerome Dupuis, "Diana: The Unpublished Report of Witnesses at the Ritz," *L'Express*, March 12, 1998; Thomas Sancton and Scott MacLeod, *Death of a Princess: The Investigation* (New York: St. Martin's Press, 1998); James Hewitt, *Love and War* (London: Blake Publishing Ltd., 1999); Warren Hoge, "Queen Breaks the Ice: Camilla's Out of the Fridge," the *New York Times*, June 5, 2000; Sarah Ferguson, *Finding Sarah: A Duchess's Journey to Find Herself* (New York: Atria Books, 2011); Richard Kay and Geoffrey Levy, "Camilla and the Blonde Private Secretary Who's Paid the Price for Being Too Close to Prince Charles," the *Daily Mail*, June 13, 2008; Peter Foster, "Has the Puppet-Master of St. James's Palace Finally Pulled One String Too Many?" the *Daily Telegraph*, December l, 2001; P. D. Jephson, *Shadows of a Princess* (New York: HarperCollins, 2000); Robert Hardman, "Just (Call Me) William," the *Daily Telegraph*, June 9, 2000; David Leppard and Christopher Morgan, "Police Fears Over William's Friends," the *Sunday Times*, February 27, 2000; Claudia Joseph, *Kate* (New York: Avon, 2009); Michelle Tauber, "Speaking His Mind," *People*, October 16, 2000; Barbara Kantrowitz, "William: The Making of a Modern King," *Newsweek*, June 26, 2000; Andrew Pierce and Simon de Bruxelles, "Our Mother Was Betrayed," the *Times*, September 30, 2000; Alex O'Connell, "Prince Chases Adventure in Remotest Chile," the *Times*, September 30, 2000; Bob Colacello, "A Court of His Own," *Vanity Fair*, October 2001; Stephen Glove, "The Royals Must Change . . . or Die," the *Daily Mail*, November 11, 2003; Warren Hoge, "Charles's Response to Use of Drugs by Son is Praised," the *New York Times*, January 14, 2002; Paul Henderson, "I Was Raped by Charles's Servant," the *Mail on Sunday*, November 10, 2002; Christopher Andersen, "The Divided Prince," *Vanity Fair*, September 2003; Warren Hoge, "Palace Is Roiled Again by New Round of Revelations," the *New York Times*, November 11, 2002; Christopher Morgan and David Leppard, "Party Girl in William's Circle Snorted Cocaine," the *Sunday Times*, February 26, 2000; J. F. O. McAllister, "Once Upon a Time, There Was a Pot-Smoking Prince," *Time*, January 28, 2002; Ben Summerskill,

"The Trouble with Harry," the *Observer,* January 13, 2002; Antony Barnett, "Prince Taken to Drink and Drugs Rehab Clinic," the *Observer,* January 13, 2002; "The Queen Mother Dies Peacefully, Aged 101," the *Guardian,* March 30, 2002; Nicola Methven, "Hypno-Di-Sed: Hewitt Put in Trance," the *Mirror,* September 19, 2005; Robert Hardman, *Her Majesty: Queen Elizabeth II and Her Court* (New York: Pegasus Books, 2012; Deirdre Fernand, "The Girl Who Would Be Queen," the *Sunday Times,* December 31, 2006; Christopher Wilson, "Kate, the Coal Miner's Girl," the *Daily Mail,* December 22, 2006; Claudia Joseph, "The Making of the Middletons," the *Mail on Sunday,* December 30, 2007; Richard Kay, Geoffrey Levy, and Katie Glass, "Wild Side of Kate's Family," the *Daily Mail,* August 9, 2008; Mazher Mahmood and Amanda Evans, "I Called Wills a F***er," *News of the World,* July 19, 2009; John Elliott, "Charles Plans a Mansion Fit for Lovebirds," the *Sunday Times,* December 17, 2006; Susan Schindehette and Allison Adato, "Princes in Love," *People,* August 8, 2005; Michelle Green, "Is She the One?," *People,* October 17, 2005; Alex Tresniowski and Ashley Williams, "Will & Kate: The Perfect Match," *People,* December 11, 2006; Caroline Davies, "'Blackadder' Keeps Close Ties to Camilla," the *Telegraph,* January 6, 2003; *Dickie Arbiter, On Duty with the Queen: My Time as a Buckingham Palace Press Secretary* (London: Blink, 2014).

CHAPTERS 6–7

Information for these chapters was based in part on conversations with Richard Kay, Mark Shand, Philip Higgs, Ezra Zilkha, Mimi Massy-Birch, Peter Archer, Lord Mishcon, Alan Hamilton, Guy Pelly, Lady Elsa Bowker, Grigori Rassinier, Richard Greene, Emma Sayle, Geoffrey Bignell, Aileen Mehle, Joan Rivers, Muriel Hartwick, Alex Shirley-Smith, Sioned Compton, Gared Mankowitz, Cecile Zilkha, Natalie Symonds, Janet Lizop, and Hugh Massy-Birch. Among the published sources consulted: Josh Tyrangiel, "The Prince Proposes," *Time,* February 21, 2005; Patrick Jephson, "Everybody Loves a Royal Wedding . . . Usually," the *Sunday Telegraph,* March 27, 2005; Caroline Davies, "Duchess Gets a Glimpse of Life Behind the Veil in Saudi Arabia," *Daily Telegraph,* March 30, 2006; Tom Rawstorne, "William: In His Own Words," the *Daily Mail,* May 30, 2003; Matthew Bailey and Andrew Pierce, "'I'm Sorry for Wearing Nazi Swastika,' Says Prince Harry," the *Times,* January 13, 2005; Tom Morgan and Jonathan Reilly, "Their Royal Heilnesses," the

Sun, July 17, 2015; Michael White, "Queen's Nazi Salute a Sign of Ignorance Shared By Many in Scary Times," the *Guardian*, July 20, 2015; Max Hastings, "Should the Queen Be Judged By Her Decades-Old Nazi Salute?" *New York Post*, July 22, 2015; Richard Palmer and Lizzie Catt, "William and Kate on Ibiza 'Rave' Holiday," the *Daily Express*, September 2, 2006; Robert Jobson, *William's Princess* (London: Blake Publishing, Ltd., 2006); "Prince William Graduates as An Officer," the *Guardian*, December 15, 2006; Chris Hughes, "Salutes You, Sir," the *Mirror*, December 16, 2006; "The Battle to Protect Kate," the *Evening Standard*, January 9, 2007; "Lawyers Planning Test Case to Stop Paparazzi Hounding Kate Middleton," the *Times*, January 9, 2007; Kira Cochrane, "In Diana's Footsteps," the *Guardian*, January 9, 2007; "News of the World Journalist Jailed," Reuters, January 26, 2007; Don Van Natta, Jr., Jo Becker, and Graham Bowley, "Tabloid Hack Attack," the *New York Times Magazine*, September 5, 2010; Oliver Marre, "Girl, Interrupted," the *Observer*, March 18, 2007; Duncan Larcombe, "Wills & Kate Split," the *Sun*, April 14, 2007; Laura Collins, Katie Nicholl, and Ian Gallagher, "Kate Was Too Middle Class," the *Mail on Sunday*, April 15, 2007; David Smith, "Royal Relationships: The Breakup," the Guardian, April 15, 2007; Zoe Griffin and Grant Hodgson, "Wills & Kate 2002–2007: The Fairytale's Over," the *Sunday Mirror*, April 15, 2007; Rajeev Syal, "Tony Blair: Let Them Be, They Are Young," the *Times of London*, April 16, 2007; Victoria White and Stephen White, "Life After William," the *Mirror*, April 21, 2007; Laura Collins and Louise Hannah, "As Kate Re-Emerges More Tanned and Confident, a New Middleton Girl Takes a Bow," the *Daily Mail*, May 27, 2007; Karen Rockett, "It's Back On," the *Sunday Mirror*, June 24,2007; Eva Simpson and Sarah Tetteh, "Thrills & Kate: Exclusive," the *Mirror*, July 3, 2007; Sarah Knapton, "Prince Denounces 'Aggressive' Paparazzi Pursuit," the *Guardian*, October 6, 2007; Richard Woods, "Leave Us Alone," the *Sunday Times*, October 7, 2007; Andrew Alderson, "Prince Eyes Legal Action," *Sunday Telegraph*, October 7, 2007; Lisa Sewards, "The Day Prince William Pulled a Gun on Me," the *Daily Mail*, December 28, 2007; Robert Jobson and Keith Dovkants, "Kate, the 'New Royal,' Gets Her Own Bodyguards," the *Evening Standard*, January 9, 2008; Andrew Pierce, "Prince's Lawyers Warn Paparazzi Off Stalking Middleton," the *Daily Telegraph*, February 23, 2008; Rebecca English, "William Landed His Air Force Helicopter in Kate's Garden," the *Daily Mail*, April 21, 2008; Aislinn Simpson, "William Flies Into a Storm," *Daily Telegraph*, April 21, 2008; Ben Guy, "Will

Finds a Way to Get to Church on Time—in a Helicopter," the *Newcastle Journal*, April 23, 2008; BBC News, "William and RAF Sorry for Prince's FIVE Chinook Joyrides," April 23, 2008; Fred Redwood, "Helicopter Stunt That Put Kate's Home on the Map," the *Sunday Telegraph*, May 18, 2008; Lucy Cockcroft, "Prince William's Chinook Flight to Stag Party Costs 8,716 Pounds," the *Daily Telegraph*, June 30, 2008; Alan Hamilton, "A Feather in His Cap: Young Prince is New Recruit to the World's Oldest Order of Chivalry," the *Times of London*, June 17, 2008; Vicky Ward, "Will's Cup of Tea," *Vanity Fair*, November 2008; Christopher Wilson, "The Lonely Death of Charles's Other Mistress," the *Daily Mail*, October 10, 2008; Richard Eden, "Kate's 'Vulnerable' Mother Speaks Out for the First Time," the *Telegraph*, December 7, 2008; Geoffrey Levy and Richard Kay, "How Many MORE Skeletons in Kate's Closet?" the *Daily Mail*, July 22, 2009; James Whitaker and David Collins, "One's Been Frozen Out: Queen Tells Kate It's Family ONLY at Sandringham this Christmas," the *People*, December 20, 2009; Nicholas Watt, "How a Hung Parliament Would Put the Queen Center Stage," the *Guardian*, February 14, 2010; Liz Hoggard, "Let Them Eat Cake," the *Evening Standard*, February 18, 2010; Alex Tresniowski, "A Royal Love," *People*, May 3, 2010; ABC News, "Duchess of York Scandal," May 24, 2010; David Stringer, "Prince William Makes First Royal Rescue for RAF," Associated Press, October 5, 2010; George Pascoe-Watson, "Queen of the Spinners," *New Statesman*, May 30, 2012; Doug Saunders, "Britain's Crisis of Succession," *Globe and Mail*, August 23, 2012; Andrew Marr, *The Real Elizabeth* (New York: St. Martin's Press, 2012); Sarah Lyall, "A Traditional Royal Wedding, But for the 3 Billion Witnesses," the *New York Times*, April 29, 2011; Richard Palmer, "Hard-Working Kate Sets a Royal Standard," *Express*, January 2, 2013; Catherine Mayer, "The Queen's Era Is Drawing to an End as Prince Charles Assumes New Royal Duties," *Time*, May 7, 2013; "Prince George Makes Friends on Royal Tour of New Zealand," Reuters, April 9, 2014; Nicholas Witchell, "Royal Tour: Prince George Steals the Show as Support for Monarchy Rises," BBC News, April 25, 2014; Ingrid Seward, "Duchess of Dazzle: How Camilla Amassed a Treasure Trove of Jewels, Thanks to Charles and the Saudis," the *Daily Mail*, February 21, 2015; Catherine Mayer, *Charles: The Heart of a King* (London: W.H. Allen, 2015); Alice Philipson, "Queen and Prince Charles Using Power of Veto Over New Laws, Whitehall Documents Reveal," the *Telegraph*, January 15, 2013; Robert Booth, "Secret Papers Show Extent of Senior Royals Veto Over Bills," the *Guardian*, January 14, 2013; Emma Green, "Why It's

Now Easier for a Princess to Become Queen," the *Atlantic,* May 2, 2015; Tom Sykes, "William and Kate Should Stop Hiding Prince George and Princess Charlotte Away," *Daily Beast,* October 11, 2015; Vanessa Friedman, "The Duchess of Cambridge and Sartorial Diplomacy," the *New York Times,* October 21, 2015; Minyvonne Burke, "Prince William Reveals Christmas Plans for Prince George, Princess Charlotte," *International Business Times,* December 6, 2015.

BIBLIOGRAPHY

Allison, Ronald, and Sarah Riddell, editors, *The Royal Encyclopedia.* London: Macmillan, 1991.

Andersen, Christopher. *The Day Diana Died.* New York: William Morrow, 1998.

——*The Day John Died.* New York: William Morrow, 2000.

——*Diana's Boys.* New York: William Morrow, 2001.

——*After Diana: William, Harry, Charles and the Royal House of Windsor.* New York: Hyperion, 2007.

——*William and Kate: A Royal Love Story.* New York: Gallery Books, 2011.

——*William and Kate: Special Wedding Edition.* New York: Gallery Books, 2011.

——*William and Kate: Royal Baby Edition.* New York: Gallery Books, 2013

Arbiter, Dickie. *On Duty with the Queen: My Time as a Buckingham Palace Press Secretary.* London: Blink Publishing, 2014.

Aronson, Theo. *Royal Family: Years of Transition.* London: Thistle Publishing, 2014.

Barry, Stephen P. *Royal Service: My Twelve Years as Valet to Prince Charles.* New York: Macmillan, 1983.

Beaton, Cecil. *Beaton in the Sixties: More Unexpurgated Diaries.* London: Weidenfeld & Nicolson, 2003.

Berry, Wendy. *The Housekeeper's Diary.* New York: Barricade Books Inc., 1995.

Boca, Geoffrey. *Elizabeth and Philip.* New York: Henry Holt and Company, 1953.

Botham, Noel. *The Murder of Princess Diana.* New York: Pinnacle Books, 2004.

Bradford, Sarah. *Diana.* New York: Viking, 2006.

Brander, Michael. *The Making of the Highlands.* London: Constable and Company Ltd., 1980.

Bryan, J., III, and Charles J. V. Murphy. *The Windsor Story.* New York: William Morrow, 1979.

Burrell, Paul. *A Royal Duty.* New York: New American Library, 2004.

——*The Way We Were.* New York: William Morrow, 2006.

Campbell, Lady Colin. *Diana in Private.* London: Smith Gryphon, 1993.

Cannadine, David. *The Decline and Fall of the British Aristocracy.* New Haven: Yale University Press, 1990.

Cannon, John, and Ralph Griffiths. *The Oxford Illustrated History of the British Monarchy.* Oxford and New York: Oxford University Press, 1992.

Cathcart, Helen. *The Queen Herself.* London: W.H. Allen, 1983.

——*The Queen and Prince Philip: Forty Years of Happiness.* London: Hodder and Stoughton, 1987.

Clarke, Mary. *Diana Once Upon a Time.* London: Sidgwick & Jackson, 1994.

Clifford, Max, and Angela Levin. *Max Clifford: Read All About It.* London: Virgin, 2005.

Davies, Nicholas. Diana: *The Lonely Princess.* New York: Birch Lane, 1996.

——*Queen Elizabeth II.* New York: Carol Publishing Group, 1996.

——*William: The Inside Story of the Man Who Will Be King.* St. Martin's Press: 1998.

Delderfield, Eric R. *Kings and Queen of England and Great Britain.* London: David & Charles, 1990.

Delorm, Rene. *Diana and Dodi: A Love Story.* Los Angeles: Tallfellow Press, 1998.

Dempster, Nigel, and Peter Evans. *Behind Palace Doors.* New York: Putnam, 1993.

Dimbleby, Jonathan. *The Prince of Wales: A Biography.* New York: William Morrow, 1994.

Dolby, Karen. *The Wicked Wit of Queen Elizabeth II.* London: Michael O'Mara Books, 2015.

Edwards, Anne. *Diana and the Rise of the House of Spencer.* London: Hodder and Stoughton, 1999.

Ferguson, Ronald. *The Galloping Major: My Life and Singular Times.* London: Macmillan, 1994.

Fisher, Graham and Heather. *Elizabeth: Queen & Mother.* New York: Hawthorn Books, 1964.

Foreman, J. B., ed. *Scotland's Splendour.* Glasgow: William Collins Sons & Co. Ltd., 1961.

Fox, Mary Virginia. *Princess Diana.* Hillside, N.J.: Enslow, 1986.

Goldsmith, Lady Annabel. *Annabel: An Unconventional Life.* London: Phoenix, 2004.

Goodall, Sarah, and Nicholas Monson. *The Palace Diaries: A Story Inspired by Twelve Years of Life Behind Palace Gates.* London: Mainstream Publishing, 2006.

Graham, Caroline. *Camilla—The King's Mistress.* London: John Blake Publishing Ltd., 1994.

——*Camilla and Charles: The Love Story.* London: John Blake Publishing Ltd., 2005.

Graham, Tim. *Diana: HRH The Princess of Wales.* New York: Summit, 1988.

——*The Royal Year 1993.* London: Michael O'Mara, 1993.

Gregory, Martyn. *The Diana Conspiracy Exposed.* London: Virgin Publishing, 1999.

Hardman, Robert. *Her Majesty: Queen Elizabeth II and Her Court.* New York: Pegasus Books, 2012.

Hewitt, James. *Love and War.* London: John Blake Publishing Ltd., 1999.

Hill, Duncan, Alison Guantlett, Sarah Rickayzen, and Gareth Thomas. *The Royal Family: A Year by Year Chronicle of the House of Windsor.* London: Parragon, 2012.

Hoey, Brian. *All the King's Men.* London: HarperCollins.1992.

Holden, Anthony. *Charles.* London: Weidenfeld and Nicolson, 1988.

——*The Tarnished Crown.* New York: Random House, 1993.

Hough, Richard. *Born Royal: The Lives and Loves of the Young Windsors.* New York: Bantam, 1988.

Hutchins, Chris, and Peter Thompson. *Sarah's Story: The Duchess Who Defied the Royal House of Windsor.* London: Smith Gryphon, 1992.

Jephson, P. D. *Shadows of a Princess.* New York: HarperCollins Publishers, 2000.

Jobson, Robert. *William's Princess: The Love Story That Will Change the Royal Family Forever.* London: John Blake Publishing Ltd., 2006.

——*The New Royal Family: Prince George, William and Kate, The Next Generation.* London: John Blake Publishing Ltd., 2013.

——*Harry's War.* London: John Blake, 2008.

Joseph, Claudia. *Kate.* New York: Avon, 2009.

Junor, Penny. *Charles.* New York: St. Martin's Press, 1987.

——*The Firm.* New York: Thomas Dunne Books, 2005.

Lacey, Robert. *Majesty.* New York: Harcourt Brace Jovanovich, 1977.

——*Queen Mother.* Boston: Little, Brown, 1986.

Lathan, Caroline, and Jeannie Sakol. *The Royals.* New York: Congdon & Weed, 1987.

Lloyd, Ian. *William & Catherine's New Royal Family: Celebrating the Arrival of Princess Charlotte.* London: Carlton Books, 2015.

Maclean, Veronica. *Crowned Heads.* London: Hodder & Stoughton, 1993.

Marr, Andrew. *The Real Elizabeth: An Intimate Portrait of Queen Elizabeth II.* New York: St. Martin's Press, 2012.

Martin, Ralph G. *Charles & Diana.* New York: Putnam, 1985.

Mayer, Catherine. *Born to Be King: Prince Charles on Planet Windsor.* New York: Henry Holt, 2015.

Montgomery-Massingberd, Hugh. *Burke's Guide to the British Monarchy.* London: Burke's Peerage, 1977.

Morton, Andrew. *Diana: Her True Story.* New York: Simon & Schuster, 1997.

——*Inside Buckingham Palace.* London: Michael O'Mara, 1991.

——*Diana: In Pursuit of Love.* London: Michael O'Mara, 2004.

Pasternak, Anna. *Princess in Love.* London: Bloomsbury, 1994.

Pimlott, Ben. *The Queen: A Biography of Elizabeth II.* New York: John Wiley & Sons, Inc., 1996.

Reese-Jones, Trevor, with Moira Johnston. *The Bodyguard's Story.* New York: Warner Books, 2000.

Sancton, Thomas, and Scott Macleod. *Death of a Princess: The Investigation.* New York: St. Martin's Press, 1998.

Sarah, The Duchess of York, with Jeff Coplon. *My Story.* New York: Simon & Schuster, 1996.

Seward, Ingrid. *The Queen and Di.* New York: HarperCollins, 2000.

——*William & Harry: The People's Princes.* London: Carlton Books Ltd.

Simmons, Simone, with Susan Hill. *Diana: The Secret Years.* London: Michael O'Mara, 1998.

——*The Last Word.* New York: St. Martin's Press, 2005.

Smith, Sally Bedell. *Diana in Search of Herself.* New York: Times Books, 1999.

——*Elizabeth the Queen: The Life of a Modern Monarch.* New York: Random House, 2012.

Snell, Kate. *Diana: Her Last Love.* London: Granada Media, 2000.

Spencer, Charles. *The Spencers: A Personal History of an English Family.* New York: St. Martin's Press, 2000.

Spoto, Donald. *Diana: The Last Year.* New York: Harmony Books, 1997.

——*The Decline and Fall of the House of Windsor.* New York: Simon & Schuster, 1995.

Lord Stevens of Kirkwhelpington. The Operation Paget Inquiry Report into the Allegation of Conspiracy to Murder Diana, Princess of Wales, and Emad El-Din Mohamed Abdel Moneim Fayed. London, December 14, 2006.

Thornton, Michael. *Royal Feud.* London: Michael Joseph, 1985.

Wade, Judy. *The Truth: The Friends of Diana, Princess of Wales, Tell Their Stories.* London: John Blake Publishing Ltd., 2001.

Warwick, Christopher. *Princess Margaret: A Life of Contrasts.* London: Andre Deutsch, 2000.

Wharfe, Ken, with Robert Jobson, *Diana: Closely Guarded Secret.* London: Michael O'Mara Books, 2003.

Whitaker, James. *Diana v. Charles.* London: Signet, 1993.

Wilson, Christopher. *The Windsor Knot.* New York: Citadel Press, 2002.

——*A Greater Love: Prince Charles's Twenty-Year Affair with Camilla Parker Bowles.* New York: William Morrow, 1994.

Ziegler, Philip. *Queen Elizabeth II.* London: Thames & Hudson, 2010.

INDEX